THE
T. S. Eliot Studies
Annual

VOLUME 5

Advisory Board

Jewel Spears Brooker
Ronald Bush
David E. Chinitz
Robert Crawford
Anthony Cuda
John Haffenden
Benjamin Lockerd
Gabrielle McIntire
John D. Morgenstern
Jahan Ramazani
Christopher Ricks
Ronald Schuchard
Vincent Sherry
Jayme Stayer
John Whittier-Ferguson

THE
T. S. Eliot Studies
Annual

VOLUME 5

General Editors
Frances Dickey and Julia E. Daniel

© 2023 Clemson University
All rights reserved

First Edition, 2023

ISBN: 978-1-83764-051-5 (print)
eISBN: 978-1-80207-432-1 (e-book)

Published by Clemson University Press
in association with Liverpool University Press

Clemson University Press is located in Clemson, SC.
For more information, please visit our website at www.clemson.edu/press.

Typeset in Minion Pro by Carnegie Book Production.

Contents

Abbreviations of Works by T. S. Eliot   ix

Articles

The People of *The Waste Land*   1
     Douglas Mao

Through the Looking Glass: T. S. Eliot and Indian Philosophy   25
     Manju Jain

Exit Scenes: Towards an Anticolonial Eliot   57
     Ria Banerjee

Religion, Rites, and Emily Hale   79
     Sara Fitzgerald

Eliot among the Rag-Pickers: Waste, Hope, and the Ecocritical
    Imagination in *The Waste Land*   109
     Sarah Kennedy

The Unnatural Excesses of T. S. Eliot   137
     Leonard Diepeveen

Special Forum: Teaching *The Waste Land*

Introduction   157
    Megan Quigley and John Whittier-Ferguson

Students-as-Pound: Creative Assignment on *The Waste Land*   163
    Brian Kennedy

Duets and Deadness   167
    Josh Epstein

Teaching Difficulty   173
    Johanna Winant

Teaching *The Waste Land*, Teaching Composition   179
    Joshua Logan Wall

What Have We Given? Notes on *The Waste Land* from India   185
    K. Narayana Chandran

Teaching *The Waste Land* to Japanese Students   191
    Junichi Saito

Teaching Past *The Waste Land*'s Annotation Problem   195
    Martin Lockerd

Teaching *The Waste Land* with the Hale Archive   201
    Frances Dickey

The Wrong Way to Teach *The Waste Land*   207
    Anthony Cuda

Research Notes

Reading Eliot Aloud   215
    Isabelle Stuart

What the Thunder Said: Environmental Agency in *The Waste Land*   229
    Caylin Capra-Thomas

Towards a Reparative Reading of "Portrait of a Lady"   239
    Huiming Liu

Book Reviews

A "Companionable Guide" to T. S. Eliot: Review of Robert
    Crawford's *Eliot After* The Waste Land   247
        Timothy Materer

Eliot among the Women: Review of Lyndall Gordon's *The
    Hyacinth Girl* and Ann Pasternak Slater's *The Fall of a Sparrow*   255
        Frances Dickey

From Tom Eliot to T. S. Eliot: Finding Voice and Audience in
    Jayme Stayer's *Becoming T. S. Eliot*   271
        Edward Upton

Giving Eliot a Seat at the Table: Review of Derek Gladwin's
    Gastro-modernism   279
        Christina J. Lambert

Review of Rick de Villiers' *Eliot and Beckett's Low Modernism*   285
        Peter Lang

Bibliography

T. S. Eliot Bibliography 2021   291
        Joshua Richards

Notes on Contributors and Editors   299

Abbreviations of Works by T. S. Eliot

Complete Prose 1 — *The Complete Prose of T. S. Eliot: The Critical Edition, Vol. 1: The Apprentice Years, 1905–1918*, ed. Jewel Spears Brooker and Ronald Schuchard. Johns Hopkins University Press and Faber & Faber, 2014.
Complete Prose 2 — *Vol. 2: The Perfect Critic, 1919–1926*, ed. Anthony Cuda and Ronald Schuchard. 2014.
Complete Prose 3 — *Vol. 3: Literature, Politics, Belief: 1927–1929*, ed. Frances Dickey, Jennifer Formichelli, and Ronald Schuchard. 2015.
Complete Prose 4 — *Vol. 4: English Lion, 1930–1933*, ed. Jason Harding and Ronald Schuchard. 2015.
Complete Prose 5 — *Vol. 5: Tradition and Orthodoxy, 1934–1939*, ed. Iman Javadi, Ronald Schuchard, and Jayme Stayer. 2017.
Complete Prose 6 — *Vol. 6: The War Years, 1940–1946*, ed. David E. Chinitz and Ronald Schuchard. 2017.
Complete Prose 7 — *Vol. 7: A European Society, 1947–1953*, ed. Iman Javadi and Ronald Schuchard. 2018.
Complete Prose 8 — *Vol. 8: Still and Still Moving, 1954–1965*, ed. Jewel Spears Brooker and Ronald Schuchard. 2019.

Complete Poems and Plays — *The Complete Poems and Plays of T. S. Eliot*. Faber & Faber, 1969.

Criterion — *The Criterion*. Collected edition, 18 vols., ed. T. S. Eliot. Faber & Faber, 1967.

Inventions — *Inventions of the March Hare: Poems 1909–1917*, ed. Christopher Ricks. Faber & Faber, 1996.

Letters 1	*The Letters of T. S. Eliot, Vol. 1: 1898–1922*, revised, ed. Valerie Eliot and Hugh Haughton. Faber & Faber, 2009.
Letters 2	*Vol. 2: 1923–1925*, ed. V. Eliot and H. Haughton. 2009.
Letters 3	*Vol. 3: 1926–1927*, ed. V. Eliot and John Haffenden. 2012.
Letters 4	*Vol. 4: 1928–1929*, ed. V. Eliot and J. Haffenden. 2013.
Letters 5	*Vol. 5: 1930–1931*, ed. V. Eliot and J. Haffenden. 2014.
Letters 6	*Vol. 6: 1932–1933*, ed. V. Eliot and J. Haffenden. 2016.
Letters 7	*Vol. 7: 1934–1935*, ed. V. Eliot and J. Haffenden. 2017.
Letters 8	*Vol. 8: 1936–1938*, ed. V. Eliot and J. Haffenden. 2019.
Letters 9	*Vol. 9: 1939–1941*, ed. V. Eliot and J. Haffenden. 2021.
Poems 1	*T. S. Eliot: The Poems, Vol. 1*, ed. Christopher Ricks and Jim McCue. Faber & Faber, 2015.
Poems 2	*Vol. 2*, ed. Christopher Ricks and Jim McCue. 2015.
Waste Land Facsimile	*The Waste Land: A Facsimile and Transcript of the Original Drafts*, ed. Valerie Eliot. Faber & Faber, 1971; Harcourt, Brace, Jovanovich, 1971.

The People of *The Waste Land*
43rd Annual T. S. Eliot Memorial Lecture

Douglas Mao

2022, the centenary of *The Waste Land*. What might one say, what might one even begin to say, about Eliot's momentous poem in its hundredth anniversary year? As I thought about this question in reference to the present lecture, it occurred to me that however arbitrary the century mark may be in some respects, it holds a particular significance for the relation between a work of art and the people, real or fictional, associated with it. For that mark is very close to the outer reaches of the span of a human life. Few of the people alive in the years when *The Waste Land* was written and published are still with us; and the same holds true, *mutatis mutandis*, for the poem's fictional characters. If the people mentioned therein were inhabitants of our own world in 1921 or 1922, none of them, except possibly "young George," could be alive today, except by exceeding in longevity all but a handful of human beings in recorded history.[1] The world of 1922 may still, in many senses, be our world. But it's fast becoming *not* our world if a shared world means an overlap of breathing generations. They who were living are now dead, with a few exceptions.

In the spirit of commemorating this transition, I begin with a question about the people of *The Waste Land*. That is, with a question principally about the fictional or quasi-fictional beings who appear as individual characters (Marie, Madame Sosostris, and so on) but also, by extension, about those who appear en masse (the crowd flowing over London Bridge, the hordes swarming over endless plains, indeed anyone in the London of the poem, or even perhaps in the world adumbrated by the poem, circa 1921 or 1922). And that question—which, like the matter of passing generations, has to do with the distance between the people of *The Waste Land* and ourselves—is this: On the evidence of the poem, do we, or should we, find these people sympathetic?

By this, I mean to ask not so much whether we do or should find them *sympatico* (people we might like because we share common values or interests) as whether we find them capable of being sympathized with. And this is not perhaps the easiest of questions to answer. Some readers may find it impossible or misguided to bestow sympathy on any of these desiccated souls; others may feel that all of them must be sympathized with on the basis of their shared plight—some version of "spiritual dryness," as that handy term from early Eliot criticism encapsulates matters. (*Half* a century ago, in a piece entitled "*The Waste Land* Fifty Years After," A. Walton Litz asserted against prior readings that the poem "is not *about* spiritual dryness; it is about the ways in which that dryness can be perceived and expressed.")[2]

I imagine that most readers will feel more sympathetic toward some of the inhabitants of *The Waste Land* than toward others. And surely how sympathetic one feels to each, or to all together, will depend to a large degree on how heartily one *blames* them for their condition. Are they victims of a spiritual drought, or does their own iniquity constitute that drought? Did they lay the land waste, metaphorically speaking, by living inadequately or reproachably? Or are they powerless inhabitants of a place they would live in more commendably were it more capable of sustaining life?

The more one thinks about it, the harder it is either to blame the people of *The Waste Land* wholly for their state or wholly to refrain from blaming them. This is so in part, of course, because such a difficulty presents itself even when we think about people in the real world. When we look back, and further back, and further back still to the conditions that make a person who that person is, the very idea of responsibility can start to seem strange, illusory. Even the idea of a core self that *should* be thoroughly blamable can come to seem a sort of shorthand, a too-convenient escape hatch when ethical thinking takes us to uncomfortable places.

On the other hand, the idea that no one is blamable for anything would seem tough to entertain abstractly and almost impossible to advocate for pragmatically.

Yet the people of *The Waste Land* may be particularly difficult to blame or not blame, for a number of reasons. There is, to start with, the poem's title. *The Waste Land*: this is about a place that's also a condition. Everyone in it may harbor some responsibility, some guilt, for its wrongness. And yet it's where they are, and in a sense who they are. How could these souls possibly get up and leave? Enhancing the title's effect, in this regard, is that we learn little of the characters' backstories. Our glimpse of Marie sledding as a child only heightens our awareness that we don't know much, at least not from the poem, about her history or what she has thought or how she has treated people. The words of the speaker in the pub scene imply a good deal about her personality and her social class, but they tell us next to nothing about how she came to be the specific person she is. We know still less about the hyacinth girl, Stetson, the woman who drew out her hair, and so on. Further, many of the characters seem, even in the snapshots we get of them, at once culpable for something and victims of injury—sinned against as well as sinning. The woman in the chair and her companion, who set the tone in this regard, seem to hurt each other and to be hurt by each other.

I use the phrase "sinned against and sinning" with intention. For if we frame the dual condition of being both culprit and victim in these terms, we may be led to consider the situation of the people of *The Waste Land* not just in a personal or psychological register but also in a quasi-religious one. And when I think in these terms, what strikes me about this situation is that, within it, sin and punishment are surprisingly difficult to distinguish from each other, or are unnervingly fused. Again, the ways in which the people of *The Waste Land* live seem their responsibility at some level, but those ways also seem something to which they're condemned. Their waste land is not an afterlife, not the Dantean Inferno or Purgatory as such, and yet, with Eliot's Dantean allusions ever hovering over the scene, it's difficult not to feel that some sort of inexact *contrapasso* obtains here.

But if sin and punishment can seem strangely at one for the people of *The Waste Land*, what lesson is the reader to draw from this fusion? Or, to put this another way: how might Eliot defend as ethical a representation, or indeed a created world, in which sin and the wages thereof are one? We cannot know what Eliot would say. But one way he *might* help us make sense of the oneness of sin and punishment for *The Waste Land*'s inhabitants would be by invoking the concept of *Original* Sin. Original Sin in Judeo-Christian doctrine is something to which human beings are condemned, but it's also something they partake of or perform. Sins are things for which each person can be held responsible in the sense of being held to account; yet as doctrine does not admit the possibility of sinless human beings (apart from Mary, and Jesus in his human incarnation), sin is also a universal condition. It seems to me that the question of whether the people of *The Waste Land* are responsible for their state, as well as the question of how we can make sense of a condition of sin that's also punishment, might find something of a resolution with Original Sin, which is not exactly or only existential; which is not exactly or only volitional; which is indubitably present and indeed ubiquitous.

I should be clear, here, that I'm not claiming that Eliot consciously thought of Original Sin as the premise or the truth of *The Waste Land*'s condition. But I'm not the first critic to see Original Sin woven through this poem, and I do think Eliot had to have the concept somewhere in his mind as he wrote it.[3] It bears noting, in this regard, how well Original Sin comports with the state of the waste land as it was rendered in that potent source text, Jessie Weston's *From Ritual to Romance*. Surveying various versions of the Grail legend, Weston presents some accounts in which the parching of the land follows upon bad behavior, but she presents many more in which the drought is either not explained at all or the consequence of something other than what we would regard as a moral fault.[4] The condition of Original Sin, unearned yet somehow cosmically condign, seems to fit not only with the world of Eliot's poem but also with the waste land in Weston, as yet unsaved by the questing knight.

That Eliot would have had Original Sin in his intellectual toolkit when he wrote *The Waste Land* is beyond question. At the time of writing, he had not yet come around fully to the Anglican faith, institutions, and doctrine that would be the ground of his life from 1927 on, but he *had* come around to great admiration for the ideas of the poet, critic, and philosopher T. E. Hulme, among them that there was much to be said for the notion of Original Sin. Hulme found Original Sin useful principally as a riposte to the liberal progressivism that he felt ruled the day in Western European intellectual circles, and which he associated with Jean-Jacques Rousseau's bare contention that human beings are naturally good. Hulme also associated a care for Original Sin with the "classical" point of view, which he favored, as against the Romantic, which he abhorred. "The 'classical' point of view," he wrote in 1912, "I take to be this. Man is by his very nature essentially limited and incapable of anything extraordinary. He is incapable of attaining any kind of perfection, because, either by nature, as the result of original sin, or the result of evolution, he encloses within him certain antinomies."[5] Hulme would elsewhere "define Romantics [...] as all who do not believe in the Fall of Man" and argue that a great turning point in European life came with the abandonment of the centrality of Original Sin, in moral thinking, around "the Renascence."[6]

Hulme was not only interested in Original Sin as a dogma that might be wielded against the claim of human beings' innate goodness, however. In his view, Romanticism compounded the mistake of believing humans to be good with the mistake of regarding humans as the sole center of value in the universe. Modern confusion about religion, Hulme averred, arose from a "failure to recognise the *gap* between the regions of vital and human things, and that of the *absolute* values of ethics and religion. We introduce into human things the *Perfection* that properly belongs only to the divine. [...] We place *Perfection* where it should not be—on the human plane."[7] Hulme surely draws, here, on the point that sin, Original and otherwise, undoes human claims to be "the measure of all things" (in the Protagorean phrasing) by dint of its very structure. For sin implies a moral relation to something that is not human. We can speak informally about people sinning against each other, as I did earlier. But sin in a rigorous sense implies a wrong against divinity or some other extra-human power or scheme. If sin—really *sin*—exists, something external to the human must matter in moral life. If sin is real and active, the people of *The Waste Land* are not the only loci of value in their world.

In this, the dogma of Original Sin—especially as associated, by Hulme, with a conviction that perfection can be an attribute only of the divine, never of the human—seems diametrically opposed to a key argument of one of the great sociologists with whom Eliot engaged in his early prose writings, Émile Durkheim. At the heart of *The Elementary Forms of*

Religious Life, Durkheim's influential study of 1912, are two claims: first, that the totem is the defining feature of "primitive" religious practice; and second, that the totem is the product of a kind of hypostatization in which believers project the attributes of their society, as they intuit them, onto an animal or object. For Durkheim, grasping these two points leads to a fundamental insight about religious belief in general: that "the believer is not deceived when he believes in the existence of a moral power upon which he depends and from which he receives all that is best in himself: this power exists, it is society."[8]

Eliot refers to Durkheim in "The Interpretation of Primitive Ritual," a paper that he submitted for a course taught by Josiah Royce at Harvard in 1913; he mentions Durkheim also in some of the book reviews he wrote in the years leading up to *The Waste Land*. In these pieces, Eliot has positive things to say about Durkheim but is clearly skeptical about anything like a theory of social projection. In a review of Clement C. J. Webb's *Group Theories of Religion* from 1916, he writes, "M. Durkheim talks far too much about 'society'; everything is ascribed to its influence."[9] And in a review of *The Elementary Forms of Religious Life* itself, also from 1916, Eliot writes that Durkheim "does not convince us that his social psychology is anything but an admission of the inexplicable, that the 'group-consciousness' and the 'collective representation' are more than a definition of the limits of individual psychology."[10]

Part of the reason Eliot demurs from Durkheim's theory is because it seems purely speculative, an unproveable interpretation rather than a demonstrable fact. In the paper for Royce's course, Eliot asks, "what is the fact of" religious behavior?" And he answers, "It is the actual ritual in a complex which includes [the] previous stage's interpretation of the ritual of the preceding stage, and so on back indefinitely." But "the only part of the fact which can be handled scientifically, historically is the ritual" itself.[11] Inferences about what individuals believe are scarcely to be countenanced, and still less so are inferences about what believers are really up to when they think they believe something.

Taking up Eliot's preference for fact as against interpretation, Jewel Spears Brooker has noted how the paratactic style of *The Waste Land* accords with precisely this disposition: "Transitions, especially subordinating conjunctions," Brooker observers, "are interpretive by definition, for they point to temporal or logical relations."[12] And while modernist parataxis may have many genealogies, in Eliot's case,

> the genealogy is unambiguous. His contrast of fact and interpretation was a direct result of his analysis of Durkheim's assumptions about the scientific method, and his preference for constructing poems out of disconnected survivals and objectified feelings was a conscious adaptation of the comparative methodology of the later volumes of *The Golden Bough*.[13]

What we might notice here is that among the elements excluded by the parataxis of *The Waste Land*—among the interpretations it does not admit—are inferences about *why* the people of *The Waste Land* are the way they are. (Thus do we return to the question of blame and responsibility that I raised earlier.) Eliot offers little personal history for the individual characters, as we've noted, and for the most part he relies on the reader to supply larger historical frames for what happens in the poem. More to the point for us in the present context, he gives scant indication of how the ways of being of *The Waste Land*'s people might have been shaped by what we would call social forces. For Durkheim, society is always the answer to the riddle; in Eliot's early prose and poetry, it's rarely the answer, at least not explicitly. No one's behavior is explained with reference to larger social systems.

Of course, there's no reason why Eliot qua poet should make the role of social forces explicit—a point to which I'll return—nor does his parataxis on this front preclude us from bringing such explanations to bear if we choose to. We're certainly free to say that the typist's predicament is rooted in the way in which careers open to "the New Woman" both challenged and extended patriarchal exploitation. We can certainly say that if Mr. Eugenides's weekend invitation is a gay one, its discretion as well as its unsavoriness, as painted by Eliot, is attributable to the cultural and legal persecution of homosexuality. And we can regard those people crossing London Bridge in Part I as undone by finance capital, ideologies of social mobility, and the imperial centrality of the City of London.

But if the poem doesn't close off such analysis, it certainly doesn't offer much encouragement thereto. Part III of *The Waste Land* is overtly interested in the New Woman's attitudes toward sex and musical recordings but not (at least not overtly) in the economic changes that gave rise to armies of women typists. Similarly, the combination of experienced desire and legal circumscription that might meet in Mr. Eugenides is not mentioned, "The Fire Sermon" seeming concerned, rather, with unholy loves and a more general debasement of love in the modern world. The crowds flowing over London Bridge are deadened by their work, but they're also compared to those in *Inferno* III who did neither good nor evil—thralls to the financial system, perhaps, but also vaguely complicit in their acedia (and in this a fine synecdoche for the blameworthy but hard-to-blame denizens of *The Waste Land* in general).

To get a still sharper sense, should we need it, of the poem's distance from sociological explanation, we can speculate on how its author might have responded to the suggestion that the predicaments of the people in *The Waste Land* could be resolved by progressive or revolutionary social policies. For the typist, a path to a better life via a transformation of gender relations benefiting from the insights of feminism? For Mr. Eugenides, the legalization of gay sex, and a concomitant cultural embrace of gay people, as a way of making overtures such as his less inevitably sleazy and degrading? For the clerks and others flowing over London Bridge, a restructuring of professional work life, or even of the world economic order, under which those who perform such work are not entombed in lives of grim emptiness or under which such work is not even done? As someone who was willing to think about anything, no matter how antithetical to his own point of view, Eliot would surely have been interested in these suggestions. But it's difficult to imagine the poet of *The Waste Land* ultimately embracing them, and perhaps even more difficult to imagine him not recoiling in horror on being presented with them initially. Surely for Eliot, so much taken by the formulations of Hulme and other self-described reactionaries, such solutions could only reshuffle a tainted deck. They couldn't imaginably be the path by which the desiccated land would be restored to vitality.

Again, *The Waste Land* is a poem, not a work of sociological analysis, and it can hardly be faulted for not offering solutions to the problems it apprehends. Simply in surveying present conditions, one might say, it does a great deal. Nonetheless, it's worth thinking about Eliot's published writing up to 1922, not only *The Waste Land* but also his prose, against the background of some of his close associates' strong interest in how the modern world was being shaped by social forces that could be named. Eliot certainly didn't doubt that politics could matter—that the actions of human beings in positions of power, and the ideas motivating them, could decisively affect people's lives; indeed, by 1927, he was ready to insist that "[p]olitics has become too serious a matter to be left to the politicians."[14] But where around this time Ezra Pound, Wyndham Lewis, Rebecca West, and to an extent Virginia Woolf were exploring the shaping power of the press, of educational systems, of capitalism, of imperial authority, of constructions of gender and race, Eliot omits these more or less entirely from his published writing up to 1922. To be sure, it might be pointed out that in the assignment of that work, he was most often tasked with assessments of books on culture and religion rather than politics and economics; and it can be added that in those writings he showed, if often by implication, a sophisticated understanding of the society of his time. But it remains the case that the power of human beings to change their world, and the specific means they might use to do so, are not topics to which he devotes much explicit attention.

Viewed from this angle, *The Waste Land* comports almost too perfectly with György Lukács's famous denunciation of modernism, in "The Ideology of Modernism," as a mode in which obsession with psychopathology leads to a rejection of the possibility that the world can be changed through human doing. Having just quoted from "The Hollow Men" in that essay of 1955, the Marxist Lukács argues that in modernism the "disintegration of personality is matched by a disintegration of the outer world," and that the "protest expressed by this flight into psychopathology is an abstract gesture; its rejection of reality [...] wholesale and summary, containing no concrete criticism."[15] He adds further on: "As the ideology of most modernist writers asserts the unalterability of outward reality (even if this is reduced to a mere state of consciousness), human activity is, *a priori*, rendered impotent and robbed of meaning."[16]

There's certainly not much of a sense, in *The Waste Land*, that human agency has the capacity to make things better. And this absence holds at the level of the individual as well as that of society. Characters weep, sit, and muse, and the prophetic voice (apart from that of Ezekiel, to whom we'll return) reports observations or cries out in helpless pain. The Sibyl is imprisoned and wishes to die; Tiresias "can see" and "foresuffer[s] all" but exhibits no capacity to intervene.[17] The character most affiliated with direct action is perhaps Madame Sosostris, whose fortune-telling undoubtedly promises her clients a path to improvement in life. But it's instructive that the "famous clairvoyante," like Tiresias, is at base not a doer but a see-er, and a limited one at that: capable of discerning "crowds of people, walking round in a ring," she's nonetheless "forbidden to see" what the "one-eyed merchant" carries on his back.[18] Moreover, the single piece of advice she dispenses is an instruction not on what to do but on what to worry about: "Fear death by water."[19] The implied counsel may be to avoid the aqueous, but it's only implied, and in any case the recommended action is really a form of refraining, a not-doing rather than a doing. What the people of *The Waste Land* do seem to be doing, on the whole, is "dying/With a little patience," where "patience" evokes not just a state of mind but a form of solitaire using playing cards.[20] Read with "patience" in that acceptation, life in *The Waste Land* is about a dying slightly enlivened by card games for one or the occasional tarot reading, if not a game of chess.

Other forms of human activity appearing in the poem are, like the avoiding of death by water, as fitly described in terms of non-action as of action. Eliot's last footnote to "The Fire Sermon" does point to a possibly valid form of life practice: "The collocation of these two representatives of eastern and western asceticism," he writes, referring to the Buddha and Augustine, "as the culmination of this part of the poem, is not an accident."[21] There's no question but that asceticism involves a strong exercise of will; and yet it's equally well described as a negative kind of action, a withholding or avoidance. The greatest boldness adumbrated in the poem is meanwhile the "awful daring of a moment's surrender," by which only "we have existed," in Part V.[22] But surrender again partakes of the negativity of not doing as much as of the positivity of doing. It's a cessation of resistance, a form of acceding.

To be sure, the allusive backdrop of the poem gives us figures who decisively act, including Procne and Philomela. Yet the characters from antique legend evoked in the poem read as foils to *The Waste Land*'s denizens, not inhabitants; and, in any case, as other critics have noted, most of the figures of myth and legend are notable for acts of *violence*.

Procne and Philomela themselves parallel the woman in the chair and her companion in being both agents of violence and its victims, even if their violence is fleshly where the modern is verbal and psychological. Meanwhile, that most active of figures in the constellation of legends Weston aggregates, the Grail Knight, may be shadowily desired or dreaded in Eliot's *Waste Land* but does not explicitly appear. At least, not on the evidence of the poem's ending—where, the Chapel Perilous having been described in its emptiness, the Fisher King is still wondering, with the yet "arid plain" behind him, whether he shall "at least set [his] lands in order."[23]

Of course, it's possible to regard the Grail Knight, Eliot's footnote about Tiresias notwithstanding, as the true unifying beholder of *The Waste Land* and to regard the poem, in turn, as the story of that figure's journey—a point supported, at least to a degree, by the footnote in which Eliot marks "the *approach* to the Chapel Perilous" as one of the three themes employed in "the first part of Part V" [emphasis added].[24] If we take that footnote seriously, we'll surely find it impossible to argue that the questing-and-redemption trajectory many readers have found in the poem is purely chimerical. I'll come back to this further on. For now, however, we must note that, as described in Weston, the questing knight isn't exactly *of* the people of *The Waste Land*. His origins are in many legends obscure, and more crucially he doesn't enlist, let alone lead, *The Waste Land*'s inhabitants in the achievement of their redemption. In this sense, he brings salvation from without. And what I want to linger over, for a bit, is precisely the point that in *The Waste Land* sharp limits on human agency are repeatedly set in opposition to the more credible, if by no means certain, prospect of external intervention.

In the poem's opening lines, dull roots awaken. But they don't awaken all by themselves; they're stirred by April's spring rain. The rest of the poem then reiterates this scenario, by and large: if there's stirring at all, it's initiated not by the stirred but by other powers. And I would argue, in this vein, that it matters profoundly that when the voice of the prophet first appears in the poem proper—as the next voice after Marie's in Part I—the prophet in question is Ezekiel. This is significant because Ezekiel is, among the Old Testament prophets, one of the two (with Jeremiah) most strongly associated with the saving of a sinful people by a transformative action of

God rather than human-initiated repentance. As the biblical scholar Mark Boda notes in *A Severe Mercy: Sin and Its Remedy in the Old Testament*,

> Pessimism over humanity's ability to respond penitentially explains the regular appearance of the theme of divine transformation throughout the Old Testament. [...] Isaiah speaks of a new day of grace that will prompt a response from the people, and Hosea speaks of a time when God will pursue his people (Hosea 2–3) and heal them (Hosea 14), but Jeremiah and Ezekiel are the ones who develop this the most with their visions of transformation. In their future expectation, God will forgive and transform his people from within through a new covenant with a new spirit and a new heart, on which the law will be written (Jer 24:6–7, 31:33–34, 32:37–44; Ezek 11:19, 36:26–27, 37:14, 39: 26).[25]

And indeed this is what we find at Ezekiel 36:26–28 in the King James Version:

> A new heart also will I give you, and a new spirit will I put within you: and I will take away the stony heart out of your flesh, and I will give you an heart of flesh. And I will put my spirit within you, and cause you to walk in my statutes, and ye shall keep my judgments, and do them. And ye shall dwell in the land that I gave to your fathers; and ye shall be my people, and I will be your God.[26]

"What are the roots that clutch, what branches grow/Out of this stony rubbish? Son of man,/You cannot say, or guess," writes Eliot in *The Waste Land* Part I.[27] The King James Version of Ezekiel features the word "stony" only twice. And in both cases—the passage quoted here and also one at 11:20—"stony" modifies "heart." Read within the framework of the book of Ezekiel, then, *The Waste Land*'s "stony rubbish" would appear to be the heart untransformed.

We can then see near the poem's close, in the *Damyata* passage, a possible realization of God's promise to replace the heart of stone with a heart of flesh. As M. E. Grenander and K. S. Narayana Rao noted in an essay published just shy of the fiftieth anniversary of *The Waste Land*, "[i]n the original Sanskrit, there is no object for the verb *damyata*; to the Hindu, however, this command would normally mean 'self-control.'"[28] But, as many readers have observed, self-control is not what we actually find in *The Waste Land* Part V:

> *Damyata*: The boat responded
> Gaily, to the hand expert with sail and oar
> The sea was calm, your heart would have responded
> Gaily, when invited, beating obedient
> To controlling hands[29]

Not self-control here, but the heart under other hands' control, its very "beating" now sonically contained within "o-*bed*-ien[ce]." Grenander and Rao go on to locate within Hindu philosophy itself a rationale for Eliot's displacement of self-control with control by another power. But I think we can also, or alternatively, see here something like the arrival (if only in the subjunctive: "would have responded") of the new heart promised by God in Ezekiel—a scenario in which change from within follows upon, rather than precedes, external intervention.

With these points before us, we might take note of another passage from Ezekiel. For that book of the Bible might have been attractive to Eliot for a reason in addition to the one just mentioned. As David Ward and Luke J. Rapa point out in readings from 1973 and 2010 respectively, Ezekiel contains a reference—the only direct one in the Christian or the Hebrew Bible, we might add—to Tammuz, whom Weston describes as the "earliest known representative of [the] Dying God."[30] In Ezekiel 8, God directs the prophet's attention to the abominations practiced by Israel in exile; and at verses 13–14 in that chapter, "He said also unto me, Turn thee yet again, and thou shalt see greater abominations that they do. Then he brought me to the door of the gate of the LORD's house which was toward the north; and, behold, there sat women weeping for Tammuz."[31] Weeping for Tammuz at the gate of the Lord's house is an obvious affront to the god of Israel. But lamentation for Tammuz is also, in Weston's construing, a form of supplication. The "fragmentary cuneiform texts" of Sumer and Babylon pertaining to Tammuz, writes Weston, are of a uniform character; they are all "Lamentations," or "Wailings," having for their exciting cause the disappearance of Tammuz from this upper earth, and the disastrous effects produced upon animal and vegetable life by his absence. The woes of the land and the folk are set forth in poignant detail, and Tammuz is passionately invoked to have pity upon his worshippers, and to end their sufferings by a speedy return.[32]

To weep for Tammuz is thus to engage in a form of practical activity, as Tammuz may perhaps come when called. This contrasts sharply with God's replacement of stony hearts with fleshly ones in Ezekiel, which occurs not in response to supplication but in spite of a people that turns away and revels in its sins. (This replacement of the stony heart with the fleshly one finds a further echo in Ezekiel 37's vision of the valley of dry bones: "Thus saith the Lord GOD unto these bones; Behold, I will cause breath to enter into you, and ye shall live"; "Son of man, these bones are the whole house of Israel.")[33] We might say, in fact, that the extremity of Ezekiel highlights a basic tension between supplication (or repentance), on the one hand, and grace, on the other. As callings upon God, supplication and repentance are human-authored, whereas grace is God's alone to give.[34] And thus grace that seems to respond to supplication can seem a little less purely grace (just as in Derrida, hospitality delivered with anything less than total openness to the other may seem a little less purely hospitality).[35]

The book of Ezekiel is not, however, the only text in which humans turn away from the divine that Eliot calls up in this section of *The Waste Land*. "Only/There is shadow under this red rock": the evocation is of the desert landscape, of course.[36] But there's an evocation too of a 1913 poem that, much to his embarrassment, won William Butler Yeats a cash prize from *Poetry* magazine.[37] This poem was "The Grey Rock," whose intertextual presence is surely confirmed by what seems the earliest version of the lines in question, from "The Death of Saint Narcissus": "Come under the shadow of this gray rock—/Come in under the shadow of this gray rock, . . ."[38]

In Yeats's poem, the divine Aoife tells her fellow gods the story of how, at the Battle of Clontarf in 1014, she offered the gift of two hundred years' life to the mortal man she loved, Dubhlaing. But Dubhlaing refused the gift, choosing instead to die in battle in support of his friend Murrough, "the King of Ireland's son."[39] The climactic lines of Yeats's poem are those of Aoife's heartrending summary cry: "Why must the lasting love what passes,/Why are the gods by men betrayed?"[40] The gift of life beyond the human span is, in this case, two centuries, but it's of course not the only such bestowal at play in *The Waste Land*. Eliot's epigraph launches the poem with a gift of lengthened life accepted, with disastrous consequences, by the Sibyl; and the gift hovers too over the legend of Tiresias, who in some tellings lived for seven or nine generations. In alluding to "The Grey Rock," Eliot incorporates in yet another way the threat and promise of divine offers of prolonged life, even though in Yeats's poem the offer is spurned. But if "The Grey Rock" attaches on one side to Tiresias and the Sibyl, it attaches on another to Ezekiel, since in Yeats's poem as in the biblical book, what's represented is a god seeking out human beings and being rebuffed. Aoife is a very human god who fails to retain Dubhlaing's faith—very unlike, on the whole, the god of Israel who asserts his power to implant new hearts in his people. But no more than Aoife does the god of Israel seem able to prevent people from spurning him, at least given the hearts they have. They give their hearts, so to speak, elsewhere. And indeed the Old Testament as a whole is, like "The Grey Rock," a story of people turning away, again and again, from the God who seeks them.

Of course, just before *The Waste Land* closes (just under the wire, as it were), the reader is treated, in citation, to a scene in which a person does turn toward God—sort of: "*Poi s'ascose nel foco che gli affina.*"[41] In the *Purgatorio* XXVI, Arnaut Daniel follows his final words to Dante the pilgrim by concealing himself in the fire that refines sinners guilty of lust. Here, seven lines before the close, we do see a person performing a worthy action, indeed one that contributes to the saving of his soul. And we can say that by the end of *The Waste Land* we've perhaps encountered two figures who point toward a redemptive path, both of them notably associated with resistance to sexual indulgence: the Grail Knight and Arnaut. But Arnaut is not, any more than the Grail Knight, an inhabitant of *The Waste Land* per se; it's possible that he too appears as a foil to those inhabitants. And, more to the point, his return to the fire occurs within the structure of an afterlife that the divinity has determined. His penance isn't a call upon God but something dispensed by God; his return to the flames is not an initiating but an acceding—just as the Grail Knight fulfills a design that is, in the true way of folk tales, anything but his own creation.

Taking into consideration the many ways *The Waste Land* casts doubt on the efficacy of human action, it becomes difficult—or at least it has become difficult for me—not to think of the poem as centered on the possibility that people can do little to help themselves, and that any changes in human fortunes must originate with forces outside them. I've come to think of *The Waste Land*, in other words, as something of an experiment in applied T. E. Hulme. Of course, even first-time readers may observe that the people of *The Waste Land* aren't poised to transform their world of their own accord, which is to say that if my sense of the poem is correct, something close to a naive reading may be the truest reading. Yet I also want to highlight a less straightforward point that seems to follow from the relentlessness with which, and the particular modes in which, *The Waste Land* subordinates human beings' capacity to help themselves to the prospect of impulsion by some power beyond them. And this is that *The Waste Land* doesn't so much pose complex ethical questions as flirt with the possibility of abandoning the ethical, at least as we ordinarily understand it, altogether.

Eliot does, certainly, seem to endorse some forms of conduct, particularly asceticism and sexual restraint. But *The Waste Land* is not a text about moral choices as a realist novel is (say one by its author's namesake George Eliot); indeed, it could in some ways not be farther from that prose form. It's arguably much closer to those fairy tales and grail legends where magical powers preside and the consequences of deeds seem out of proportion, or in arbitrary relation, to those deeds' goodness or badness, largeness or smallness.[42] There *is* a moral atmosphere to *The Waste Land*, unquestionably. But it's one that decenters the human, that admits and indeed demands a place for something else that may not be subject, quite, to human standards of probity, of justice, of proportion between sin and punishment, of difference between sin and punishment. To read *The Waste Land* as if this something larger doesn't, at least potentially, upset all our other schemes of value is, I think, to read it from a position that's not its own.

Certainly, it remains possible to see in the poem's progress a sort of movement toward eventual redemption, where the subject of that movement is the possessor of the lyric voice that appears overtly in key sections—recalling coffee with Marie, recalling the scene with the hyacinth girl—and who observes, with Tiresias, what happens in *The Waste Land*. But if the poem does have such a "protagonist," the trick of Part V is to insist that this protagonist is *not* to be identified with the Grail Knight. "Shall I at least set my lands in order?"[43] Here, the protagonist's "I," if there is one, merges with the voice of the Fisher King—not a figure of decisive action on a heroic quest, only another inhabitant of *The Waste Land*, waiting.

Thus it seems to me that another of the oldest of old saws about *The Waste Land* is, in its way, quite on the money: this *is* fundamentally a poem about waiting. But where I used to conceive of this waiting in terms that would also fit Yeats's "Second Coming," I've now come to a slightly different sense of the poem's character. Yes, *The Waste Land* is animated by a hope for dramatic renewal that's at one with a dread of apocalyptic destruction. Yes, the same rain that might make the waste land green again might prove a deluge that drowns the land and its people. And yes, this is a poem whose grim alternatives may be immiserating stasis, on the one hand, and excruciating transformation, on the other. But where before I had thought of the poem as about waiting mostly in the adventitious sense that the people of *The Waste Land* might be wondering what will happen and when, I now think it's about waiting in the stronger sense that waiting is—profoundly and crucially—the only game in town. And there's a further turn of the screw to this waiting game, of course. The multiply ramifying figure of Ezekiel notwithstanding, the force or power that might finally intervene is not yet certainly God, as it would be for the later Eliot. And the fact that it's not yet certainly God gives *The Waste Land* a peculiar ambience, one almost of a waiting for proper waiting—of a meta-waiting in which what's awaited is knowing what to wait for and, in a sense, how to wait.

If we see *The Waste Land* in these terms, however, a final question may suggest itself. Does this poem stage a massive disappointment with people in general? Or, to put this slightly differently: Is *The Waste Land*, or its author, misanthropic? And if so, what would this misanthropy portend?

Over the years, Eliot has been deemed a misanthrope by more than one reader, and it's clear that his admiration for the greatest of misanthropes among English-language writers, Jonathan Swift, has substantive bearing on *The Waste Land*. The original drafts, after all, contain the notorious heroic couplets on Fresca in which misanthropy, as in Swift and Alexander Pope too, is distilled into (or displaced by) misogyny.[44] It might be argued that the deleted Fresca section harbors the foundational attitude of the poem as a whole or, contrarily, that in excising this section in accord with Pound's instructions, Eliot sought to prevent *The Waste Land* from reading as a pure judgment of disdain upon his fellow mortals. I'd like to conclude, however, by examining *The Waste Land* in the light cast by a text of misanthropy less directly implicated in the poem than works by Pope and Swift—but also a text that returns us, if only glancingly, to the year 1922.

For, as it happens, that year itself marked a literary anniversary, in this case a tricentenary, of which Eliot could scarcely have been unaware. The fifteenth of January 1622 had witnessed the birth, or rather the christening (the birth date being unknown), of Jean-Baptiste Poquelin, remembered to history as Molière. Accordingly, 1922 saw a variety of celebrations of Molière in performance and in print, in France and in the world of English letters.[45] Eliot doesn't comment on these events, so far as I know; but in his early prose criticism, the name of Molière does occasionally appear. In those pieces, Eliot suggests that he holds that playwright in high regard but also disfavors him in comparison to Marivaux, who was in essence more civilized, free of Molière's tendency to bad punning and worse buffoonery. In making this judgment, however, Eliot does appear to exempt—to a degree—*The Misanthrope*, which premiered on 4 June 1666, and which Eliot read as a student at the Smith Academy in St. Louis.[46] In the essay "Marivaux," from 1919, Eliot remarks, "even *Le Misanthrope*, isolated as it is, has a farcical touch."[47]

How might the Eliot of the early 1920s have felt about Alceste, the misanthrope of Molière's title, whose high standards of conduct set him at odds with humanity? How to take Alceste will be a vexed question for any reader or viewer given that the play itself seems at some junctures to laud that character's rectitude while at others reproving his rigidity. And the question might have been complicated, for Eliot, by the fact that Hulme's bogey, Rousseau, praised the play as Molière's best comedy but also criticized it for mocking Alceste's fidelity to his ideals.[48] Would Eliot have aligned himself with those ideals even if this meant allying himself with Rousseau? Or would he have rejected Alceste's Timon-like denunciations in favor of some more charitable view of humanity that would leave him, alas, in too-close proximity to Rousseau's assertion of humans' natural goodness? However Eliot might have negotiated this conundrum, it's hard not to think that he would have identified with Alceste, at least to a point. Or, to put this in terms of *The Waste Land*: it's hard not to see the poem's perspective as that of an Alceste-like figure who, on the basis of what he has observed, generally doubts humans' capacity to do good. That said, two important differences between Alceste's perspective and that of *The Waste Land* are worth noting. First, *The Waste Land* doubts not only humans' capacity to do good but also their capacity to do much. And second, the poet of *The Waste Land* might have to follow a path somewhat different from Alceste's, in the end.

In Act 1 of *The Misanthrope*, Alceste imagines exiling himself—taking himself away from his fellow human beings in all their corruption and horror:

> Sometimes I'm seized upon by sudden longings
> To flee from all mankind, and live in deserts.
>
> [De fuir dans un désert l'approche des humains.][49]

And then, at the play's climax, he tells his adored Célimène that he'll pardon her betrayals if she agrees to join him in his exile:

> I'll find it in my heart to pardon all,
> And tell myself that they are weaknesses
> To which the vices of the time misled you,
> If only you'll consent to that design
> Which I have formed, to flee from all mankind,
> And be resolved at once to follow me
> Into my desert, where I've vowed to live.
>
> [Et que dans mon désert, où j'ai fait vœu de vivre,
> Vous soyez, sans tarder, résolue à me suivre.][50]

Célimène declines, upon which Alceste vows to go into exile—a fuller exile, companionless—anyway:

> I'll leave this den of thieves vice reigns among,
> And find some lonely corner [un endroit écarté]
> Where one is free to be an honest man.[51]

In these passages from *The Misanthrope*, the desert is where one goes in order to avoid people. And to whatever degree he actually found people unbearable, Eliot might have been tempted by the idea of heading off to a desert, that terrain so hospitable to prophets and eremites. Yet the human scene of *The Waste Land* is already a desert; and in thinking of Alceste at the beginning of the 1920s, Eliot would surely have considered how he was already removed from his natal society—if not truly in a state of exile, still in a condition often described that way by expatriate writers. Of course, one might still flee: one might leave the populated desert for one free of other people. But it seems to me that one of the things said by Eliot's poem (that most influential of all twentieth-century poems in English, that miracle of 1922) is that you don't have to choose exile, and perhaps you can't, however you may feel about your fellow human beings. Rather, you might have to stay among the people of the waste land—and wait, with them, for grace.

Notes

1 *Poems* 1:60.
2 A. Walton Litz, "*The Waste Land* Fifty Years After," *Journal of Modern Literature* 2, no. 4 (1972): 459.
3 On Hulme and Original Sin in relation to Eliot, see, above all, Ronald Schuchard, *Eliot's Dark Angel: Intersections of Life and Art* (Oxford University Press, 1999), especially 52–86, and Ronald Schuchard, "Did Eliot Know Hulme? Final Answer," *Journal of Modern Literature* 27, nos. 1–2 (2003): 63–69. See also, among other contributions on Eliot and Original Sin of recent decades, Jewel Spears Brooker, *Mastery and Escape: T. S. Eliot and the Dialectic of Modernism* (University of Massachusetts Press, 1994); G. Douglas Atkins, *T. S. Eliot, Lancelot Andrewes, and the Word: Intersections of Literature and Christianity* (Palgrave Macmillan, 2013); Scott Freer, *Modernist Mythopoeia: The Twilight of the Gods* (Palgrave Macmillan, 2015); David Soud, *Divine Cartographies: God,*

History, and Poiesis in W. B. Yeats, David Jones, and T. S. Eliot (Oxford University Press, 2016); Anthony Domestico, *Poetry and Theology in the Modernist Period* (Johns Hopkins University Press, 2017); and Vincent Pecora, *Land and Literature in a Cosmopolitan Age* (Oxford University Press, 2020).

4 Jessie L. Weston, *From Ritual to Romance* (Doubleday Anchor, 1957), 12–17, 20, 22–23, 116.
5 T. E. Hulme, *The Collected Writings* (Clarendon Press, 1994), 234.
6 Hulme, *Collected Writings*, 250, 445.
7 Hulme, *Collected Writings*, 437.
8 Émile Durkheim, *The Elementary Forms of Religious Life*, translated by Joseph Ward Swain (George Allen, 1976), 225.
9 *Complete Prose* 1:431.
10 *Complete Prose* 1:671.
11 *Complete Prose* 1:113.
12 Jewel Spears Brooker, *T. S. Eliot's Dialectical Imagination* (Johns Hopkins University Press, 2018), 71.
13 Brooker, *Dialectical Imagination*, 71.
14 *Complete Prose* 3:287.
15 György Lukács, *The Meaning of Contemporary Realism* (Merlin, 1963), 25, 29.
16 Lukács, *Meaning of Contemporary Realism*, 36.
17 *Poems* 1:63, 64.
18 *Poems* 1:56.
19 *Poems* 1:56.
20 *Poems* 1:68.
21 *Poems* 1:75.
22 *Poems* 1:70.
23 *Poems* 1:71.
24 *Poems* 1:76.
25 Mark Boda, *A Severe Mercy: Sin and Its Remedy in the Old Testament* (Eisenbrauns, 2009), 522. My thanks to Elliott Rosen for calling my attention to Ezekiel just as my work on this lecture commenced in earnest.
26 Ezekiel 36:26–28 KJV.
27 *Poems* 1:55.
28 M. E. Grenander and K. S. Narayana Rao, "*The Waste Land* and the Upanishads: What Does the Thunder Say?," *Indian Literature* 14, no. 1 (1971): 92.
29 *Poems* 1:71.
30 Luke J. Rapa, "Out of This Stony Rubbish: Echoes of Ezekiel in T. S. Eliot's *The Waste Land*," Master's thesis, Grand Valley State University, 2010, 30; David Ward, *T. S. Eliot between Two Worlds* (Routledge, 1973), 78, cited in Rapa, "Out of This Stony Rubbish," 30; Weston, *From Ritual to Romance*, xii (also cited by Rapa).

31 Ezekiel 8:13–14 KJV.
32 Weston, *From Ritual to Romance*, 37.
33 Ezekiel 37:5 KJV; Ezekiel 37:11 KJV.
34 For an important discussion of Karl Barth on grace in relation to later Eliot, see Domestico, *Poetry and Theology*, especially 41–64.
35 Jacques Derrida and Anne Dufourmantelle, *Of Hospitality*, translated by Rachel Bowlby (Stanford University Press, 2000).
36 *Poems* 1:55.
37 Russell K. Alspach, "Yeats's 'The Grey Rock,'" *Journal of American Folklore* 63, no. 247 (1950): 57–58.
38 *Poems* 1:270.
39 W. B. Yeats, *The Collected Poems* (Collier, 1989), 105.
40 Yeats, *Collected Poems*, 106.
41 *Poems* 1:71.
42 For a Romantic note on the amorality of old tales featuring offended supernatural beings, see Samuel Taylor Coleridge recalling a discussion of his "Rime of the Ancient Mariner": "Mrs. Barbauld once told me that she admired the Ancient Mariner very much, but that there were two faults in it,—it was improbable, and had no moral. As for the probability, I owned that that might admit some question; but as to the want of a moral, I told her that in my own judgment the poem had too much; and that the only, or chief fault, if I might say so, was the obtrusion of the moral sentiment so openly on the reader as a principle or cause of action in a work of such pure imagination. It ought to have had no more moral than the Arabian Nights' tale of the merchant's sitting down to eat dates by the side of a well, and throwing the shells aside, and lo! a genie starts up, and says he must kill the aforesaid merchant, because one of the date shells had, it seems, put out the eye of the genie's son." *The Collected Works of Samuel Taylor Coleridge, Volume 14: Table Talk, Part II* (Princeton University Press, 2019), 100.
43 *Poems* 1:71.
44 *Waste Land Facsimile*, 22–23, 26–29, 38–41.
45 See, for example, Paul Van Dyke, "Molière's Tercentenary," *New York Times*, February 12, 1922, S89; "A Molière Exhibition: Features of the Public Library's Tercentenary Display," *New York Times*, April 30, 1922, E35; and H. Carrington Lancaster, "The Tercentenary of Molière: Its Contribution to Scholarship," *Modern Language Journal* 8, no. 2 (1923): 65–72.
46 Martin Scofield, *T. S. Eliot: The Poems* (Cambridge University Press, 1988), 14.
47 *Complete Prose* 2:3.
48 Jean-Jacques Rousseau, *Politics and the Arts: Letter to M. D'Alembert on the Theatre*, translated by Allan Bloom (Cornell University Press, 1960),

36–45. Alceste is explicitly invoked, as it happens, in another of the literary masterworks of 1922, Virginia Woolf's *Jacob's Room*. In the novel's penultimate chapter, Jacob's inamorata Sandra Wentworth Williams thinks of him, "He is . . . like that man in Molière," at which the narrator explains, "She meant Alceste. She meant that he was severe. She meant that she could deceive him." Virginia Woolf, *Jacob's Room* (Harvest, 2008), 179.

49 Molière, *Le Misanthrope* (*The Misanthrope*), translated by Curtis Hidden Page (G. P. Putnam's Sons, 1913), 13; Molière, *Le Misanthrope* (Fernand Sorlot, 1942), 25.

50 Molière, *Le Misanthrope*, translated by Page, 99; Molière, *Le Misanthrope*, 94.

51 Molière, *Le Misanthrope*, translated by Page, 101; Molière, *Le Misanthrope*, 95.

Through the Looking Glass
T. S. Eliot and Indian Philosophy

Manju Jain

The publication of Eliot's collected and uncollected poems, his complete prose, and nine volumes of his letters have revealed a wealth of information on Eliot's lifelong fascination with and ambivalence towards Indian philosophy. As late as 1946, Eliot testified to the influence of Indian thought and sensibility on his poetry.[1] In 1947, he recalled that long before he was a Christian, he was "a student of Indian philosophy, and of the Buddhist scriptures in Pali: both from study of some original texts, under teachers of Indic philology and philosophy at Harvard, and from an early interest in Schopenhauer and Deussen also in connexion with Sanskrit."[2] In "An Autobiographical Sketch" of 1945, Eliot reminisced that when he returned to Harvard from Paris to study philosophy with the intention of making it his career, he also "took up the study of Sanskrit and Pali," "as Indian thought had always had a strong attraction" for him, and he had then thought of "proceeding to the study of comparative religion."[3] In a revealing letter of 1936 to his brother, Henry Ware Eliot Jr., Eliot explained that the consequence of his conversion to Anglicanism "was indicated by my previous interests—my interest in Sanskrit and Pali literature [...] and in the philosophy of Bergson; and that my abortive attempt to make myself into a professor of philosophy was due to a religious preoccupation."[4] Eliot was responding to Henry's long diatribe of September 12, 1935, fiercely denouncing his conversion.[5] And yet it seemed to him, after two years of struggling with "Indian

25

metaphysics in Sanskrit," that it was "impossible to be on both sides of the looking glass at once."[6] Though it is difficult to do justice to this complex subject in the space of an article, drawing on the new editions of Eliot's writing, I propose to trace the trajectory of his lifelong engagement with Indian philosophy and to highlight the tensions and ambivalences that he experienced in attempting to understand and to integrate it into his philosophical and creative vision.[7] I shall also explore some of the reasons why Eliot gave up the study of Indian philosophy after "two years spent in the study of Sanskrit under Charles Lanman, and a year in the mazes of Patanjali's metaphysics under the guidance of James Woods," which left him in a state of "enlightened mystification."[8]

I have discussed elsewhere Eliot's courses in Indic studies as well as his indebtedness to and differences with his mentors at Harvard.[9] I shall focus here on the struggles with the problem of the duality or the identity of subject and object, and the fear of the loss of the self, with which Eliot, as well as the Harvard philosophers with whom he studied, were preoccupied in their interpretations of the Upanishads and Buddhism.[10] I shall go on to discuss the ways in which Eliot consequently perceived the differences between Christianity and the Vedanta and Buddhism.

Eliot took five courses in Indic studies as a graduate student at Harvard from 1911 to 1913, two in Elementary Sanskrit and two in Pali with Charles Rockwell Lanman, and one in Philosophical Sanskrit with James Haughton Woods.[11] Looking back upon his study of Sanskrit and Pali towards the end of his life, Eliot recalled that he had "worked on the elements of Sanskrit and Pali for two years with Professor C. R. Lanman, and on Sankhya philosophy with Professor J. H. Woods." Since that period, he went on to reminisce,

> I have never had the leisure to pursue these studies seriously, and have, indeed, lost all my slight proficiency in the languages. It was during this period that I read with Professor Lanman, the *Bhagavad-Gita*, some selected Upanishads in Sanskrit, as well as some of the Nikayas in Pali. I also read the *Sankhya-Bhasya-Karika* and commentary in Palanjali [sic] with Professor Woods. I have never written anything specifically about these studies.[12]

Although Eliot acknowledged here that he did not continue seriously with his study of Sanskrit and Pali after his Harvard years, what he learned then seemed to have been deeply embedded in his consciousness and continued to provide a point of departure for his reflections as well as a challenge to his beliefs. I should like to emphasize that Eliot's interest in Indian philosophy ought to be considered not in isolation but in relation to the several other philosophical systems with which he was engaged. Also, it was primarily limited to some texts in the Brahmanical and Buddhist canons in Sanskrit and Pali which he had studied at Harvard.

The philosophical giants at Harvard who influenced Eliot—William James, Charles Rockwell Lanman, and Josiah Royce—interpreted the Upanishads in terms of an extreme monistic idealism, of an absolute identity of subject and object. Such interpretations were then prevalent through the work of German Orientalists such as Arthur Schopenhauer and Paul Deussen, whom Eliot later criticized for their "romantic misunderstanding" of Indian philosophy.[13] It is my contention that these Harvard philosophers, as well as Eliot himself, with their deeply ingrained American individualism, could not accept the loss of individuality which they saw inherent in this monistic idealism.

James and Lanman used Emerson's poem "Brahma" (1857) as a *locus classicus* for their discussions of this problematic of the duality or the identity of subject and object. The main sources of the poem are Horace Hayman Wilson's translations of the *Rig Veda Sanhita* and of the *Vishnu Purana: A System of Hindu Mythology*, Charles Wilkins's translation of *The Bhagavat-Geeta: or Dialogues of Kreeshna and Arjoon*, which Emerson had acquired in 1845, and E. Röer's translation of the *Katha Upanishad*. The relevant passage from the *Gita*, which Emerson read in 1845, is "the man who believeth that it is the soul which killeth, and he who thinketh that the soul may be destroyed, are both alike deceived; for it neither killeth, nor is it killed" (II.19). Emerson must have been struck by the similarity with the following passage from the *Vishnu Purana*, which he copied in his journal the same year: "What living creature slays or is slain? What living creature preserves or is preserved? Each is his own destroyer, as he follows evil or good." In 1856, eleven years later, Emerson came across the following passage from the *Katha Upanishad*: "If the slayer thinks that I slay, or if the slain thinks that I am slain, then both of them do not know well. It (the soul) does not slay, nor is it slain" (I.2.19).[14] This is the reply that Yama, the Lord of Death, gives to the nine-year-old boy Nachiketas, who goes to Yama's abode and insists on being told whether the soul exists after death. Emerson dramatized this concept in "Brahma":

> If the red slayer think he slays,
>   Or if the slain think he is slain,
> They know not well the subtle ways
>   I keep, and pass, and turn again.
> […]
> They reckon ill who leave me out;
>   When me they fly, I am the wings;
> I am the doubter and the doubt,
>   And I the hymn the Brahmin sings.[15]

Emerson's notion of "Brahma" as the supreme force of the universe is a development of his conception of the "Oversoul," in which, as he explicates, "the seer and the spectacle, the subject and object are one."[16] I argue, however, that Emerson could not accept the absolute identity of subject and object that he found in his interpretation of the *Gita* and the *Katha Upanishad*; the problem of the duality of subject and object remained unresolved for him. The paradoxes and the antitheses evident in the use of the pronouns "I" and "They" in "Brahma" remain unreconciled. In his journal entry of May 26, 1837, he had lamented, "A believer in Unity, a seer of Unity, I yet behold two."[17] There is in the poem, in fact, a deep anxiety and fear of the loss of individuality implicit in the notion of the absolute identity of subject and object.

    James and Lanman shared this anxiety about the loss of the individual self which they found implicit in the philosophy of nonduality in the Upanishads. Ironically, however, Emerson's poem, which was a dramatizing of this anxiety and fear, was for them an illustration and a confirmation of the concept of nonduality. They failed to perceive the tensions and antitheses that Emerson had struggled to articulate in the poem.[18]

    William James's awareness of Indian philosophy goes back at least as far as 1870, when he read several books on Buddhism and Hinduism.[19] James's engagement with Indian philosophy was perhaps deepened by his encounter with Swami Vivekananda, whom he met in 1894 and then again in 1896 when Vivekananda lectured at Harvard on the religions of India and on comparative religions.[20] James was drawn to the meditation practices of Vivekananda's *Raja-Yoga*, which included the aphorisms of Patanjali, with Vivekananda's introductory chapters. Apparently, he himself did try to practice some of the breathing exercises recommended by Vivekananda but found that he was too critical and docile to benefit from them.[21] James included several quotations from Vivekananda and Indian philosophy in his *Varieties of Religious Experience* (many of which Eliot copied in his note cards on mysticism).[22] He used them mainly to establish the validity of mystical and religious experience from his pragmatist and pluralist standpoint.

Despite his admiration for Vivekananda, however, James rejected his Vedantic monism, which was opposed to his own pragmatist and pluralist philosophy. In *Pragmatism*, James ridicules Vivekananda and the absolute monism of the Vedanta where separation is not simply overcome by the One, but it is denied to exist: "*An Absolute One, and I that One*, surely we have here a religion which, emotionally considered, has a high pragmatic value; it imparts a perfect sumptuosity of security."[23] In fact, James was skeptical of both the monism of the Vedanta and the Nirvana of Buddhism for being afraid of experience and of life: "The peace and rest, the security desiderated at such moments is security against the bewildering accidents of so much finite experience. Nirvana means safety from this everlasting round of adventures of which the world of sense consists. The hindoo and the buddhist [...] are simply afraid, afraid of more experience, afraid of life.[24] In *The Will to Believe*, James uses "Brahma" to reject not only the "Hegelism" implicit in it, but also the monistic philosophy of the Vedanta to which "Brahma" was indebted:

> The sense of a universal mirage, of a ghostly unreality, steals over us, which is the very moonlit atmosphere of Hegelism itself. [...] Just as Romanists are sure to inform us that our reasons against Papal Christianity unconsciously breathe the pure spirit of Catholicism, so Hegelism benignantly smiles at our exertions, and murmurs, "If the red slayer thinks he slays;" "When me they fly, I am the wings," etc.[25]

Josiah Royce, Eliot's supervisor for his doctoral dissertation on F. H. Bradley, devoted several pages to the Upanishads in his critique of mysticism in *The World and the Individual*. He expounded passages translated for him by Lanman and based his discussion on Deussen's interpretation to criticize the notion of the absolute identity of subject and object in the Upanishads. For Royce, "There is the murderer no longer murderer, nor the slave a slave, nor the traitor a traitor. Differences are illusory." Royce, like James, criticized the conception of the Absolute in the Upanishads as the absence of error, sin, finitude, and individuality. It was therefore indistinguishable from mere nothing, "an apparent zero."[26] Royce also opposed the quietism of Buddhism to "the creative attitude which Christianity requires the will to take." He criticized Buddhism for its objective of the extinction of the individual self in contrast to the infinite worth given to an individual in Christianity, and for not teaching the transformation of the self through loyalty to a community.[27]

Lanman, too, like James and Royce, critiqued the monism of the Upanishads, and, like James, he used Emerson's "Brahma" to reject it. The Upanishads, Lanman asserts in his lecture on *The Beginnings of Hindu Pantheism*, "teach the absolute identity of man and God, of the individual soul and the 'Supreme Spirit.'" "The doctrine of the absolute unity," Lanman goes on to say, "finds perhaps its most striking expression in Sanskrit in the *Katha Upanishad*; but nowhere, neither in Sanskrit nor in English, has it been presented with more vigor, truthfulness, and beauty of form than by Emerson in his famous lines paraphrasing the Sanskrit passage." For Lanman, however, such a vision is "a prospect, dark and void, this Supreme Spirit, before whom all human endeavor, all noble ambition, all hope, all love, is blighted," and he turns with relief to "the teachings of the gentle Nazarene."[28]

It was Lanman who drew Eliot's attention to the connection between "Brahma" and the passage from the *Katha Upanishad* to which it was indebted. On 6 May 1912, Lanman presented Eliot a copy of Vasudeva Laxman Shastri Panshikar's edition of *The Twenty-Eight Upanishads*. Attached inside is a handwritten note from Lanman, dated 22 May, listing twelve passages for Eliot's attention. Among the passages listed is the one from the *Katha Upanishad*, which Emerson had used, with Lanman's annotation from the first line of "Brahma": "If the red slayer thinks he slays."²⁹

Eliot also encountered "Brahma" through F. H. Bradley, the subject of his doctoral dissertation. In *Appearance and Reality*, Bradley suggested a connection between Emerson's poem and Charles Baudelaire's "L'Héautontimorouménos" ("The Executioner of the Self"), also published in 1857, to illustrate his position on the contradictions inherent in the notion of the absolute identity of subject and object in the religious consciousness:

> Je suis la plaie et le couteau!
> Je suis le soufflet et la joue!
> Je suis les membres et la roue,
> Et la victime et la bourreau !

[I am the wound and the knife/I am the blow and the cheek/I am the limbs and the wheel/And the victim and the executioner].³⁰

For Bradley, religion implies a relation between man and God, and a relation, in his metaphysics, is always inconsistent and self-contradictory. Bradley's position is that all such contradictions and antitheses between subject and object, the human and the divine, the finite and the infinite, are absorbed in the Absolute, which is not the God of religion. As far as Bradley is concerned, then, the duality of subject and object remains unreconciled in "Brahma" as well as in Baudelaire's poem.³¹

As I have argued elsewhere, for Eliot, this undifferentiated Absolute, in which there would be a complete identity of subject and object and a loss of the distinct identity of the individual self, represented the void of which he was terrified, an extinction of consciousness, "annihilation and utter night."³² And Eliot, like Emerson, felt a desperate need to preserve and to hold on to this unique identity. In rejecting Bradley's Absolute, in which there is no differentiation between subject and object, Eliot was perhaps also rejecting his teachers' interpretations of the monistic idealism of the Vedanta, as well as any system of absolute authority in which there is a loss of the individual self.³³

Eliot interwove "Brahma," the *Gita*, the *Katha Upanishad*, Baudelaire, as well as Christ's words from the Gospel of St. John (11:25) in his short poem, "I am the Resurrection and the Life," to explore the relationship of subject and object, the human and the divine, within a Christian framework:

> I am the Resurrection and the Life
> I am the things that stay, and those that flow.
> I am the husband and the wife
> And the victim and the sacrificial knife
> I am the fire, and the butter also.[34]

A decade after writing "I am the Resurrection and the Life," Eliot brought the Upanishads, "Brahma," and Baudelaire together when he found in Paul Valéry's *Le Serpent* "a theme as old as the Upanishads and perpetually new: the Red Slayer and *la plaie et le couteau*." And he quoted the uniqueness and "magnificence of the ending" to illustrate his point: "... éternellement,/Éternellement le bout mordre."[35] (... eternally, Eternally the tip bites). The violence in these lines, as well as in "I am the Resurrection" and in Baudelaire's poem, emphasizes conflict, division, and duality, rather than integration, reconciliation, unity, and oneness.

These passages from the *Katha Upanishad*, the *Gita*, and the *Vishnu Purana*, first used by Emerson, represent one of the most interesting intertextualities in poetry and philosophy which continued to exercise a fascination across centuries and cultures, perhaps because of their power to resist appropriation and to challenge existing beliefs.

Besides the passage from the *Katha Upanishad*, Lanman had also listed for Eliot's attention the verse from the *Brihadarnyaka Upanishad* on the triple injunction of Prajapati to his three orders of offspring: gods, men, and demons. Lanman's reference to this passage, with the page number of Panshikar's edition, reads: "Brihadaranyaka, 220 (v. 1, 2, 3), Da-da-da = dāmyata datta dayadhvam."[36] Eliot, in his note to this passage in *The Waste Land*, refers the reader to "*Brihadaranyaka—Upanishad*, 5, 1" and to Deussen's translation in German.[37] However, it is probably Lanman's translation that he may have had in mind. Since Eliot's use of Sanskrit sources has been the subject of so much debate, it is important here to emphasize and to recapitulate the differences and divergences between Lanman's contemptuous Orientalist interpretation and Eliot's more positive and tentative appropriation.[38] For Lanman, "the Great-Forest-Upanishad gives to some of the cardinal virtues the sanction of supernatural revelation," a sanction which Lanman considers to be "as needless as it is quaint." The Brahmans, he adds, are "never weary of inculcating the duty of free-handedness, and deem it more blessed (at least for others) to give than to receive." Lanman concludes scoffingly, "old as it is, there is in it an amusing touch of modernity, and the thunder is still rolling."[39] Lanman thereby glosses over the other two imperatives, compassion and self-control. He also ignores the conclusion of the passage: "This very thing the heavenly voice of thunder repeats *da, da, da,* that is, control yourselves, give, be compassionate. One should practise this same triad, self-control, giving and compassion."[40] Eliot alters the sequence to *Datta, Dayadhvam, Damyata* (give, sympathize, control), perhaps to suggest that to give and sympathize are necessary prerequisites to the attainment of self-control. (Elsewhere Eliot had added the word *hridayam* to the triad from the section that follows, V.3.1.)[41] *Hridayam* is "heart, that is the seat of intelligence."[42]

In the original passage, the triple injunction is itself an interpretation by the threefold offspring of Prajapati—gods, men, and demons—of the thunder's utterance, the root syllable, "da," being an etymological replication of the sound of the thunder. Their interpretation in turn, as well as its validation by Prajapati, is also an interpretation by the author of the text, who summarizes the moral of the tale. Eliot, too, gives the triad his own interpretations and contexts.[43] If, for Lanman, the fable of the thunder has "an amusing touch of modernity," Eliot uses it to suggest the inadequacies and failures of Western modernity. The all-encompassing generosity of "give" in the thunder's admonition is in contradistinction to a momentary surrender, long forgotten memories, and the material benefits left behind us in our wills with "seals broken by lean solicitors." "Sympathize," or "be compassionate," is opposed to the monadic isolation of the self; and control is not the self-control advocated by the thunder but the control of others. In Eliot's ecological landscape of aridity and barrenness, the lifegiving rains do not come, perhaps because of the failure to follow the injunctions of the Thunder, and Ganga remains sunken.[44] In Indian mythological and literary traditions, however, as Harish Trivedi cogently points out, it is inconceivable for the Ganga ever to be sunken, and for it "to flow in any barren or waste land without being able to irrigate, suffuse, and revive it."[45]

The significance that Eliot attaches to "Shantih" is also more affirmative than Lanman's dismissive interpretation. According to Lanman, "even of things which we regard as intrinsically good the Hindu sees too plainly the vanity; and he longs for the peace which the world cannot give, the peace that passeth all understanding. His word for this peace is *shānti*, and its literal meaning is 'a quieting down,' 'a coming to rest.'"[46] Lanman's interpretation, "a quieting down," "a coming to rest," probably held a resonance for the final invocation in *The Waste Land*, but Lanman condescendingly implies that the Hindu was wrong to have seen the vanity of what is intrinsically good. Eliot's use of "shantih," on the contrary, suggests that he had to look beyond Christianity to find an appropriate word. This implication was more evident in his note to the early editions of *The Waste Land*, where he wrote that the "'Peace which passeth understanding' is a feeble translation of the content of this word."[47] Eliot probably also had in mind the positive comparison of the Buddhist Nirvana with the Christian peace made by Irving Babbitt, Lanman's student and Eliot's teacher: "One should grant the Buddhist his Nirvana if one is willing to grant the Christian his peace that passeth understanding. Peace, as Buddha conceives it, is an active and even ecstatic thing, the reward not of passiveness, but of utmost effort."[48] Eliot is also careful to use the spelling "shantih" to try and reproduce accurately the pronunciation of the word in Sanskrit.[49] The invocation in the poem, however, is a tenuous solace invoked against the fear of madness—"Hieronymo's mad againe"—one of the fragments that the poet narrator shores against his ruins, suggesting his failure to exercise the will and effort required to attain a resting place. For the quotation, "shantih shantih shantih" is itself a fragment. The complete line is "Om shantih shantih shantih."[50] Ezra Pound thought that there wouldn't be anything missing if the last three words were omitted.[51] Eliot, however, chose to retain them.

Eliot, in his Notes, casually directs the reader to Paul Deussen's German translation, "*Sechzig Upanishads des Veda*, p. 489," for "the fable of the meaning of the Thunder."[52] He assumes that readers who do not know Sanskrit will know German, further mystifying them when they are already lost in a maze of allusions and quotations. Eliot does not himself give a translation of either the fable or of its meaning. However, in this polyglot poem, Eliot does not translate quotations from the European languages either, so that readers would have to labor to track their sources, meanings, and contexts as well. In this bricolage of multilingual quotations and allusions, the inclusion of Sanskrit is a challenge to and a disruption of the hegemony of European languages.

In early 1913, Woods invited Rabindranath Tagore to give a series of lectures at Harvard (later published as *Sadhana: The Realisation of Life*). Tagore spoke at the Harvard Philosophy Club on February 18, 1913 about "Brahma." Eliot attended one of Tagore's lectures but any comments that he may have made on it do not survive.[53] Ten years later he wrote to Stanley Rice, who had cited the "cult of Tagore" as an example of Oriental influences on Europe: "As for Tagore, I cannot read at all, but his work in translation seems to me a miserable attenuation of the robust philosophy of early India."[54] In fact, Eliot condescendingly mocked Tagore's stature as well as his own popularity among Bengali readers in a spoof to Hayward after the closing of the *Criterion* in 1939. This was a supposed letter, presumably to Faber, from "some of us Eastern students" who sought Faber's "benison" to establish in Bengal "THE CRITERION OF INDIA," which had "the support of Rabindranath Tagore himself." They hoped that "your Mr Eliot" whose "celebrated *Wasteland* has been a call of inspiration to all of us in Bengal" could be persuaded to contribute a poem to the first issue.[55] For his part, Tagore was critical of Eliot's modernist focus on squalor and aridity, and he cautioned poets against losing "the organic touch in trying to imitate Eliot, Pound, and Auden."[56] Valerie Eliot told Andrew Robinson, who was working on Tagore, that she had never heard Eliot mention Tagore, nor had she found any correspondence in connection with Tagore's translation of *Journey of the Magi*.[57] Faber, though, did publish two anthologies by Tagore's son-in-law, Nagendranath Gangulee, *The Testament of Immortality* (1941) and *Thoughts for Meditation* (1951), with prefaces by Eliot.

While at Harvard, the teacher who influenced Eliot most deeply was Irving Babbitt, to whom he paid homage in 1964, almost at the end of his life, as "the man who had the greatest influence on me."[58] It was primarily Babbitt who inspired Eliot to study Sanskrit and Indian philosophy, especially Buddhism.[59] Babbitt had studied Sanskrit and Indian philosophy with Sylvain Lévi in Paris.[60] While in Paris, he had also studied Pali and Buddhism. He continued his study of Indian philosophy with Lanman after returning to Harvard, and he later went on to translate the *Dhammapada* from Pali.

Babbitt's sympathetic, discriminating understanding of Buddhism must have countered for Eliot the prevalent "Romantic Orientalism," which Babbitt dismissed as a kind of "subrational spontaneity,"[61] as well as the Schopenhauerian nihilistic interpretations of the concept of Nirvana as understood by James and Royce, and perhaps by Eliot himself, during the period when he was influenced by Jules Laforgue. For Eliot recalled that his literary hero Laforgue was fascinated by "the Kantian pseudo-Buddhism of Schopenhauer."[62] In Schopenhauer, Babbitt explains, "the Buddha is converted into a 'heavy-eyed, pessimistic dreamer' whereas he was 'one of the most alert and vigorous figures of whom we have historical record.'"[63] Babbitt discriminatingly points out that the teachings of Buddhism appear strange to the Westerner because they cut across "certain oppositions that have been established in Western thought since the Greeks, and have come to seem almost inevitable"—such as the One and the Many, idea and flux, thought and feeling. In a passage that reverberates in "The Fire Sermon" of *The Waste Land*, Babbitt explains that Nirvana must be understood with reference to "the special quality of will put forth in meditation," a will to renounce and to extinguish the expressive desires—especially "the three fires of lust, ill-will and delusion." The craving for extinction in the sense of annihilation or non-existence, Babbitt emphasizes, "is indeed expressly reprobated in the Buddhist writings." Babbitt also explains that there is a doctrinal divergence between this quality of will, with its spiritual autonomy, its emphasis on meditation, and its stress upon the principle of control, and the Christian reliance upon divine grace.[64]

Eliot's interest in Buddhism drew him to attend Masaharu Anesaki's 1913–14 course on "Schools of the Religious and Philosophical Thought of Japan, and their Connexions with those of India and China." Anesaki, a leading authority on Buddhism, was a visiting professor at Harvard on Woods's invitation. Eliot took copious notes from the course on some key issues with which he was preoccupied then and later, such as the view that life is pain, the importance of mental training and moral discipline, the concepts of the "turning of the wheel," or *samsara*—the incessant cycle of birth, death, and rebirth—and *shunyata*, or "the ultimate emptiness of the world of things." Anesaki's emphasis on the importance of the community in Buddhism, on the idea of the salvation of the self through saving others, would have counteracted, for Eliot, Royce's criticism of Buddhism for not teaching the transformation of the self through loyalty to a community. Anesaki's comments on the lotus perhaps reverberated later in *Burnt Norton* in the lines "And the lotos rose, quietly, quietly,/The surface glittered out of heart of light."[65] The lotus alone is perfect, Eliot noted, "because it has many flowers and fruits at once. The flowers and fruit are simultaneous." The real entity is represented in the fruit, its manifestation in the flower, so that there is a mutual relation of the final reality and its manifestation.[66]

Eliot's interest in Buddhism continued after he left Harvard. He attended meetings of the Buddhist Society in London in 1915.[67] Stephen Spender believed that Buddhism was a lifelong influence in his work. Spender recounts Eliot's comment to the Chilean poet, Gabriel Mistral, who was herself a Buddhist, that at the time when he was writing *The Waste Land*, "he almost became a Buddhist."[68] Eliot, in fact, had at one time even thought of learning Tibetan "in order to be able to read certain Buddhist texts which are not otherwise available."[69]

As Eliot remarked, he brought the Buddha and Saint Augustine, the two representatives of eastern and western asceticism, into a collocation in "The Fire Sermon" of *The Waste Land*.[70] However, he later took issue with Babbitt on the question of grace from his Christian standpoint in his essay of 1927 on Bradley, emphasizing the need for a doctrine of grace and distinguishing between "man's mere will" and "the will of the divine."[71] Eliot severely reprimanded Paul Elmer More for More's assertion that God did not make Hell, and he opposed the Christian concept of Hell with the Buddhist elimination of it: "The Buddhist eliminates Hell . . . only by eliminating everything positive about Heaven (*uttama paranibbana* being obviously not heaven)."[72]

The deep impact of Buddhist concepts as well as their subsumption within a Christian framework, with its need for grace, is poetically rendered in *Burnt Norton*:

> The inner freedom from the practical desire,
> The release from action and suffering, release from the inner
> And the outer compulsion, yet surrounded
> By a grace of sense, a white light still and moving[.][73]

Besides the Vedanta and Buddhism, Eliot also studied the metaphysics of Patanjali and the dualistic philosophy of the *Sankhya* system in Woods's course in "Philosophical Sanskrit." Woods had studied Sanskrit with Lanman, and Indian philosophy with Deussen and Hermann Jacobi, who specialized in the *Sankhya*. He later translated Deussen's *Outline of the Vedanta System of Philosophy According to Shankara* (1906). Woods travelled to India twice, in 1902–4 to study in Banaras, Poona, and Kashmir, and again in 1907.[74] It was Woods who, encouraged by James, took the initiative in introducing courses in Indian philosophy at Harvard around 1890. His *Yoga System of Patanjali*, which was published in the Harvard Oriental Series in 1914, is "one the first systematic scholarly works in America on Indian philosophy."[75] It includes an introduction, an analytical summary, and a translation of Patanjali's *Yoga-Sutras*, a translation of the four books of the *Yoga-Bhashya* (which are a commentary on the *Yoga-Sutras* attributed to the sage Veda Vyasa), and a translation of Vachaspati Mishra's explanation of the *Yoga-Sutras*. The meditation practices requiring deep concentration and withdrawal of the senses for an attainment of the stillness and the equilibrium of the mind elaborated in Patanjali, and the scholastic classifications of the *Sankhya* system, would have counteracted for Eliot the superficial, romantic interpretations of Indian philosophy propagated by Schopenhauer and Deussen, as well their appropriations by James, Lanman, and Royce.[76] During this period, Eliot was also deeply engaged with mystical, visionary, pathological, and hallucinatory states of consciousness that lay beyond the frontiers of ordinary experience, and with the role played by the intellect and intuition in mystical phenomena, in his note cards on mysticism and in his poems on pathological mysticism such as "The Burnt Dancer," "The Love Song of St. Sebastian," and "The Love Song of St. Narcissus."[77] The study of Patanjali would have emphasized for Eliot the importance of the intellect and of discipline in the spiritual life in Indian philosophical systems.[78]

Eliot remained in touch with Woods for several years after he left Harvard. Woods recommended Eliot for a Sheldon Fellowship in 1914, writing to Dean Briggs that Eliot had "read philosophical Sanskrit effectively."[79] It was Woods, in fact, who was keen to get Eliot an appointment in the Harvard Philosophy Department in 1915 and then again in 1919.[80] Eliot wrote to Woods on July 10, 1915, informing him of his marriage to Vivien and telling him how much he had "enjoyed the Sânkya [sic] and Patañjali course."[81] On December 28, 1915, Eliot requested Woods to send "the Patañjali" as it would "revive very pleasant memories."[82] He wrote again on September 7, 1916, that he was "still clamouring for the Patanjali"; on November 20, 1918, he complained, "You never sent me Patañjali, but I am not in a position to reproach you!"[83] And on April 10, 1930, he wrote to Woods, paying tribute to him and claiming to be his "old pupil in the mysteries of Patanjali and Vachaspati Michra and Vijnana Bikshu [sic]." Eliot concluded by hailing Woods as "Bo Brahmana" ("Salutation to a Brahman or priest") [84] It is evident from this correspondence that Patanjali exercised a strong influence on Eliot, though he later confessed to being lost in the mazes of his metaphysics.[85] For instance, writing of his concern with time, and of the temporal and the timeless in *Burnt Norton*, Eliot acknowledged his debt to Indian philosophy, "such as the commentary of Patanjali," though with the caveat that this was so insofar as the influence was not Christian.[86]

Eliot referred to the *Sankhya* school that he had studied in Woods's course in a couple of little-known reviews that he wrote after he left Harvard, emphasizing its distinctiveness from the Vedas and the Upanishads. An introduction to Indian philosophy, Eliot clarifies, "ought to make quite clear to the Occidental mind the difference between the Vedas and the Upanishads, which are properly religious texts, and the earliest philosophical texts of the primitive Sankhya." He goes on to argue that though "native writers are apt to obscure the fact," there is "as certainly a History of Indian philosophy as of European; a history which can be traced in the dualistic Sankhya, for instance, from the cryptic early couplets through the commentary of Patanjali to the extraordinarily ingenious and elaborate thought of Vachaspati Misra and Vijnana Bhikshu." Moreover, Eliot continues, there is "extremely subtle and patient psychology in the later writers; and it should be the task of the interpreter to make this psychology plausible, to exhibit it as something more than an arbitrary and fatiguing system of classifications."[87] Eliot here assumes a position of superiority both to the "Occidental mind" and to the "native writer." In a review of a book on Jainism, Eliot praises it for not being "an interpretation into terms of Western philosophy." He does not discern any fundamental difference from the three cardinal principles of Jainism, "karma, relativism, and *ahimsa* or non-injury of living beings," and "some forms of Buddhism." He also points out that Jainism is dualistic and wishes to know what relation it bears to "the dualism of early Sankhya."[88]

It has been suggested that Eliot's interest in Indian philosophy was reawakened at the time of the composition of *Four Quartets* by his encounter with Purohit Swami, after a narrowing of his interests following his conversion to Christianity in 1927.[89] Eliot claimed to "have had some business acquaintance" with the Swami in May 1934.[90] On August 2, he wrote to Yeats praising the Swami's translation of the *Kena Upanishad* as being excellent, though he had been unable to compare it with the only good translation he knew, which was in German.[91] Eliot wrote to the Swami on October 31, expressing his great interest in the Swami's translation of the Upanishads, which Eliot thought had "a better chance of success than the *Bhagavad-Geeta*" because, "to the ordinary occidental reader who has no first hand experience of Indian thought, and no real perception of the seriousness of the subject, the *Bhagavad-Geeta* is likely to seem at first sight repetitious and prolix." It might have seemed so to him as well, Eliot clarified, if he had not "many years ago read it in the original," once again recalling his own study of the text at Harvard.[92] Eliot had written a reader's report for Faber on September 26, lightheartedly calling it "Murder of my Swami," on the Swami's translation of the *Gita*, lauding it as "a good translation, though not so good as the original." He praised the translation of the *Kena Upanishad*, too, as "a good translation," though he had not had the opportunity of comparing it with the original or with Müller or Deussen.[93] In November 1934, Faber published the Swami's translation of Bhagwan Shri Hamsa's *The Holy Mountain: The Story of a Pilgrimage to Lake Manas and of Initiation on Mount Kailas in Tibet*, for which Yeats wrote an introduction and Eliot a blurb.[94]

Faber published the Swami's translation of the *Gita* in May 1935, from which Eliot quotes in *The Dry Salvages*.[95] In the same year, Eliot published a translation of the *Mandukya Upanishad* by the Swami in the *Criterion*. In early 1937, Faber published *The Ten Principal Upanishads* translated jointly by the Swami and Yeats.[96] In his blurb for the book, Eliot praised "the magnificence of the poetry of the original" and "the beauty and simplicity of the Sanskrit," which the translations of Max Müller had failed to convey.[97] Here again, Eliot's views on Sanskrit and on the Upanishads are opposed to those of his old teacher Lanman who, for all his pioneering efforts in promoting the study of Sanskrit and his renowned *Sanskrit Reader*, denounced the Upanishads as being "repellent to the Occidental mind" because of the "grotesque and fantastic form in which much of their lofty thought is clothed"; and the "Hindu poets" for originating a "style of writing which is so artificial, so elaborate, so unnatural," as to be seldom paralleled in the history of world literature.[98] The next year Faber published the Swami's translation of Patanjali's *Aphorisms of Yoga* with an introduction by Yeats.

The *Bhagavad Gita* influenced Eliot from the time of his course with Lanman in 1911–12.[99] "My own scholarship is very slender," Eliot modestly said in a statement that reveals his own deep reflection on the text, "but I learnt to distrust people who talk about the *Bhagavad Gita* without mentioning that it is a syncretism of half a dozen philosophical systems."[100] In 1929, after his conversion, Eliot referred to the *Gita* as the "next greatest philosophical poem to the *Divine Comedy* within my experience."[101] Of course, from his Christian standpoint, he placed it below the *Divine Comedy*. Many years later, towards the end of his life, Eliot reminisced, "the present writer is very thankful for having had the opportunity to study the *Bhagavad Gita* and the religious and philosophical beliefs, so different from his own, with which the *Bhagavad Gita* is informed."[102] Here again, it is difference that Eliot emphasizes. But then influence can be strongest when there is an acute awareness of difference.

Eliot's differences from the beliefs of the *Gita* as well as his fascination with the text find their deepest poetic expression in *Four Quartets*. Numerous critics, including Helen Gardner, have commented on Eliot's use of the *Gita* in *The Dry Salvages* (1941) and *Little Gidding* (1942) for its relevance during the Second World War.[103] The contemporary situation in Europe must have inspired Eliot to turn to the colloquy between Krishna and Arjuna on the battlefield when kinsmen were ranged opposite each other. Eliot refers directly to Krishna in section III of *The Dry Salvages*: "I sometimes wonder if that is what Krishna meant—/Among other things—or one way of putting the same thing[.]"[104] As in his use of the Fable of the Thunder, Eliot is careful to emphasize that this is his interpretation, tentative and not authoritative. He thereby disclaims any authoritative knowledge and preempts the criticism that he is taking liberties with the original text.

Eliot appears to reflect upon what Krishna may have meant when he quotes "a voice descanting [...] not in any language": "consider the future/And the past with an equal mind./At the moment which is not of action or inaction/You can receive this:" He then quotes Krishna from Purohit Swami's translation: "'on whatever sphere of being/The mind of a man may be intent/At the time of death[.]'"[105] The quotation from the *Gita* (a quote within a quote) is left incomplete, for the complete quotation is: "On whatever sphere of being the mind of a man may be intent at the time of death, thither will he go./Therefore meditate always on Me, and fight; if thy mind and thy reason be fixed on Me, to Me shalt thou surely come."[106] From his Christian standpoint, Eliot does not accept the notion of the reincarnation of the individual soul in Krishna's admonition. He interprets Krishna's injunction of disinterested action in order to extend the repercussions of the actions of an individual to the lives of others: "that is the one action/(And the time of death is every moment)/Which shall fructify in the lives of others:/And do not think of the fruit of action."[107] In emphasizing the consequences of an individual's action on "the lives of others," Eliot was perhaps harkening back to the importance that his old teacher Josiah Royce had given to loyalty to the community. Eliot, however, also invokes Heraclitus and St. John of the Cross: "And the way up is the way down, the way forward is the way back." Krishna's views on time are therefore integrated with the Heraclitean, Bergsonian, and Buddhist notions of flux and change: "Fare forward, you who think that you are voyaging;/You are not those who saw the harbour/Receding, or those who will disembark."[108] In *The Dry Salvages*, then, Eliot integrates Krishna's philosophy of *karma*, or disinterested action, St. John of the Cross, Heraclitus, Bergson, Royce, and Buddhism.

Eliot continues his reflection on action and detachment in section III of *Little Gidding* with reference to the *Gita*. In chapters 3 and 18 of the *Gita*, Krishna explains the difference between Karma Yoga, the Path of Right Action, when the mind controls the senses, and inaction: "No man can attain freedom from activity by refraining from action; nor can he reach perfection by merely refusing to act."[109] In chapter 18, in response to Arjuna's query, Krishna explains the difference between the three states of attachment, indifference, and non-attachment, specifically in the context of the ongoing battle: "It is not right to give up actions which are obligatory; and if they are misunderstood and ignored, it is the result of sheer ignorance. [...] He who has no pride, and whose intellect is unalloyed by attachment, even though he kill these people, yet he does not kill them, and his act does not bind him." And he further elaborates: "He whose mind is entirely detached, who has conquered himself, whose desires have vanished, by his renunciation reaches that stage of perfect freedom where action completes itself and leaves no seed."[110]

Eliot speculates upon these three conditions of attachment, detachment, and indifference in the opening lines of section III of *Little Gidding*:

> There are three conditions which often look alike
> Yet differ completely, flourish in the same hedgerow:
> Attachment to self and to things and to persons, detachment
> From self and from things and from persons; and, growing
>   between them, indifference
> Which resembles the others as death resembles life, [...][111]

Eliot invokes Krishna's injunctions to explore his recurrent theme of a death-in-life existence. Moreover, he gives them a Christian interpretation. Whereas Krishna had emphasized renunciation and the vanquishing of desire, for Eliot, liberation lies in the "expanding/Of love beyond desire,"[112] in the apprehension of "the point of intersection of the timeless/ With time," which is "Incarnation."[113]

I have analyzed Eliot's engagement with the *Gita* at such length to demonstrate that Eliot uses his interpretation of it to reflect upon his own meditations on time and eternity, flux and stability, action and inaction, attachment and detachment. The *Gita* provides an important point of departure for his reflections, but its teachings are either contrasted with or subsumed within his Christian beliefs. Nevertheless, *Four Quartets* are a complex meditation on Indian and Western philosophical and spiritual traditions—the Upanishads, the *Gita*, Patanjali, and Buddhism, together with Heraclitus, St. Augustine, Dante, St. John of the Cross, Julian of Norwich, Richard of St. Victor, *The Cloud of Unknowing*, Bergson, Royce, and Bradley. As Eliot himself acknowledged in 1947, "I have little learning; but I do think that some of my poetry is peculiar in a kind of poetic fusion of Eastern and Western currents of feeling."[114]

Eliot turned again to Indian philosophy towards the end of his creative career in his plays. Harcourt-Reilly's quoting of the Buddha's injunction in *The Cocktail Party*, "Work out your salvation with diligence," is of course well known. Even more significantly, Eliot turns to the Upanishads in his last play, *The Elder Statesman*, to dramatize the concept of the witnessing or impersonal self, and the active or personal self. The *Mundaka Upanishad* elaborates the concept of two selves in a human being, in the parable of two birds on a fruit tree: the personal self that wanders hither and thither and so falls into dejection, and the higher, impersonal, witnessing self that looks on and is detached. In the translation by Purohit Swami and Yeats, which Faber had published in 1937 on Eliot's recommendation:

> Two birds, bound one to another in friendship, have made their homes on the same tree. One stares about him, one pecks at the sweet fruit.
> The personal self, weary of pecking here and there, sinks into dejection; but when he understands through meditation that the other—the impersonal Self—is indeed Spirit, dejection disappears.[115]

Lord Claverton, in *The Elder Statesman*, wonders:

> What is this self inside us, this silent observer,
> Severe and speechless critic, who can terrorise us
> And urge us on to futile activity,
> And in the end, judge us still more severely
> For the errors into which his own reproaches drove us?[116]

Characteristically, Eliot gives his own interpretation to this philosophical concept of the detached, higher, impersonal self. For "this silent observer" is not a detached witness, but a critic with agency who terrorizes, judges, and impels to activity and is in fact responsible for "the errors into which his own reproaches drove us."

Despite his lifelong interest in Indian philosophy, Eliot was more aware of its differences from his own beliefs and of its intractability. His views are most comprehensively expressed in a letter of August 9, 1930 to I. A. Richards where he highlights the hermeneutical problems of translating and understanding belief systems that are different from one's own. Recalling his struggle for two years with "Indian metaphysics in Sanskrit," Eliot wrote that the conclusion he came to then "was that it seemed impossible to be on both sides of the looking-glass at once." It seemed to him that all he was trying to do, "and all that any of the pundits had succeeded in doing, was to attempt to translate one terminology with a long tradition into another; and that however cleverly one did it, one would never produce anything better than an ingenious difformation." Just as Deussen, who Eliot supposed to be "the very best interpreter of the Upanishads," had "merely transformed Indian thought into Schopenhauerian." And "the orientalism of Schopenhauer, for Eliot, was "as superficial as superficial can be." The only way he could ever come to understand Indian thought, Eliot concluded, would be to erase not only his education in European philosophy, "but the traditions and mental habits of Europe for two thousand years." Nonetheless, he believed "that some such study [...] is profitable, as getting outside of one's own skin, or jumping down one's throat."[117]

The tension and conflict that Eliot must have experienced in his engagement with Indian philosophy are vividly evoked in the images of "being on both sides of the looking-glass at once," of "getting outside of one's own skin," and of "jumping down one's throat." Eliot's articulation here of his own inadequacy in understanding the complexities of Indian philosophy as well as of its intractability is a mark of his respect for Indian philosophy as well as an acknowledgment of the challenge that it posed to his own Western identity and beliefs.

Eliot believed in a hierarchy of religions, however, with Christianity as the most superior, as in the Choruses from *The Rock*. He acknowledged "the need for a Christian examination and understanding of Eastern thought, which the Christian philosophy of the future cannot afford to neglect." But he also believed that "wisdom that is not Christian" turned to folly.[118] And yet, despite his belief in the superiority of Christianity, Indian philosophy posed a threat to his Christian orthodoxy. "I have been sometimes told," Eliot confided to A. Frank-Duchesne in a letter of November 5, 1945, "that the influence of Indian thought and sensibility in my poetry has sometimes led me at least very near the edge of heterodoxy."[119] Indian thought continued to hold an irresistible fascination for him until the end of his career, even though, or perhaps because, he was discriminatingly aware of the differences between Indian and Western philosophy, and of the hermeneutical problem of translating and interpreting one culture, one tradition of thought, into the terms of another. As he told an audience in 1946, "But generally, poets are not oriental scholars—I was never a scholar myself; and the influence of oriental literature upon poets is usually through translations."[120] And, for Eliot, "any translation must be a personal interpretation."[121]

Eliot was highly critical of superficial, facile, "romantic interpretations" of Indian philosophy, especially those of the German Orientalists such as Schopenhauer and Deussen, and of their appropriations by his Harvard mentors, James, Lanman, and Royce. He valued the logical, scholastic schools of Indian thought. Eliot told an audience in 1949 that he had always

> cherished the belief that we have much to learn from India; and that the fault of the European admirers of Indian thought in the nineteenth century, has been that in their admiration for Indian philosophy and mysticism, they have sought to substitute the Eastern vision for the Western vision, the Brahmanic philosophy for the Christian, instead of trying to integrate, slowly and patiently, the one with the other.[122]

There may have been errors and misinterpretations in Eliot's understanding of Indian philosophy but, as he suggested, "there may be an essential part of error in all interpretation, without which it would not be interpretation at all," and interpretation, in his view, is inescapable.[123] The influence of Indian philosophy may have been difficult to appropriate, but it was this very awareness of difficulty, of attempting to be "on both sides of the looking glass at once" that, to use Eliot's own word, "fructified" his poetry and his thought.

Notes

1. "Die Einheit der europäischen Kultur" (1946), *Complete Prose* 6:712; appended to *Notes towards the Definition of Culture* (1948) as "The Unity of European Culture," *Complete Prose* 7:270.
2. Letter of February 23, 1947, to Egon Vietta, quoted in *Poems* 1:976.
3. *Poems* 2:xi.
4. January 1, 1936, *Letters* 8:11.
5. *Letters* 7:748-763.
6. Letter of August 9, 1930, to I. A. Richards, *Letters* 5:284.
7. For a detailed discussion of the influence of Indian philosophy on Eliot, see P. S. Sri, *T. S. Eliot, Vedanta and Buddhism* (University of Columbia Press, 1985) and Cleo McNelly Kearns, *T. S. Eliot and Indic Traditions* (Cambridge University Press, 1987). Sri explores the correspondences between some themes and symbols of the Vedanta and Buddhism and Christian doctrine, to demonstrate an "East–West ideosynthesis" in Eliot's poetry and plays. He does not, however, discuss Eliot's differences with the Vedanta and Buddhism. Moreover, Eliot's works that have been published since Sri wrote his book were not available to him. Kearns's exhaustive, though abstruse, study discusses Eliot's use of Indian philosophical traditions as a catalyst for his creative vision, his identification with and detachment from them, and their resistance to superficial Western appropriations, their radical assertions compelling him to reevaluate "his entire relationship with his own culture and beliefs" (190). She also consults some of Eliot's early papers and essays on philosophy which were then unpublished as well as archival material available at Harvard University and King's College Library, Cambridge. I place greater emphasis on Eliot's ambivalences, tensions, and sense of difference than on his identification.
8. "After Strange Gods" (1934), *Complete Prose* 5:32.
9. Manju Jain, *T. S. Eliot and American Philosophy: The Harvard Years* (Cambridge University Press, 1991), 102-11.
10. See Jewel Spears Brooker, *T. S. Eliot's Dialectical Imagination* (Johns Hopkins University Press, 2018) for Eliot's lifelong preoccupation with the duality of mind and body, flesh and spirit, the human and the divine, and his quest for transcending these dualities. She does not, however, discuss these issues in relation to Eliot's study of and engagement with Indian philosophy.

11 For a list of the courses taken by Eliot while at Harvard, see Jain, *T. S. Eliot and American Philosophy*, 252–56.
12 Eliot's letter of March 6, 1952, to M. S. S. Iyengar, *Letters* 5:138. See also Eliot's letter of September 5, 1963, to Bandana Lahiri, acknowledging that there were "obviously certain Indian influences" on his writing, at least on some of his poetry. He recalled that during his two years in the Graduate School at Harvard studying Sanskrit and one year studying Pali, he had read in Sanskrit the "Maha Bharata" and several of the Upanishads, especially "the Katha and the Isha." He had also read, "and was thoroughly confused by, the commentary of Patanjali on the Sankhya Bashya Kharika [sic]," as well as "several of the Buddhist scriptures, but only in the transliteration into the Latin alphabet." *Letters* 5:139. By the "Maha Bharata," Eliot probably meant the episode of the *Bhagavad Gita* in the Mahabharata. The Houghton Library at Harvard has Eliot's copy of the *Bhagavad Gita*, translated by Lionel D. Barnett (Dent, 1905). It is autographed: "T. S. Eliot, Cambridge, 1912." See Jain, *T. S. Eliot and American Philosophy*, 278n176 and *Poems* 1:1159–60.
13 "After Strange Gods" (1934), *Complete Prose* 5:32.
14 Arthur E. Christy, *The Orient in American Transcendentalism* (1932; Octagon Books, 1963), 166–68 and Shanta Acharya, *The Influence of Indian Thought on Ralph Waldo Emerson* (Edwin Mellen Press, 2001), 60.
15 "Brahma," in *The Complete Essays and Other Writings of Ralph Waldo Emerson*, edited, with an introduction, by Brooks Atkinson (Modern Library, 1950), 809.
16 Acharya, *Influence of Indian Thought*, 184–85.
17 Quoted in Stephen Whicher, *Freedom and Fate: An Inner Life of Ralph Waldo Emerson* (University of Pennsylvania Press, 1957), 31.
18 Eliot later thought that Emerson had stimulated "an interest, of a more or less undesirable kind, in Oriental religion and philosophy," and that he was "'a Representative Man,' of a deplorable variety, representative of much modern American 'spirituality.'" *Letters* 3:810.
19 Norris Frederick, "William James and Swami Vivekananda: Religious Experience and Vedanta/Yoga in America," *William James Studies* 9 (2012): 42.
20 Frederick, "William James and Swami Vivekananda," 38.
21 Frederick, "William James and Swami Vivekananda," 49. James had also read Vivekananda's *Yoga Philosophy* (1896), besides the *Raja-Yoga*.
22 Eliot's note cards, "Notes on Philosophy," are in the Eliot Collection, Houghton Library, Harvard. See Jain, *T. S. Eliot and American Philosophy*, 161–62.
23 William James, *Pragmatism* (1907; Harvard University Press, 1975), 74–75; italics in the original.
24 James, *Pragmatism*, 140.

25 William James, *The Will to Believe and Other Essays in Popular Philosophy* (1897; Harvard University Press, 1979), 216.
26 Josiah Royce, *The World and the Individual* (Macmillan, 1901), 156, 167, 168, 181.
27 Josiah Royce, *The Problem of Christianity* (1913; Chicago University Press, 1968), 190–93.
28 Charles Rockwell Lanman, *The Beginnings of Hindu Pantheism* (Charles W. Sever, 1890), 23–24. Lanman's interest in Sanskrit was ignited when, at the age of 10, he read a translation of a textbook of Hindu astronomy in the *Journal of the American Oriental Society*. He went on to study Sanskrit under W. D. Whitney at Yale. He later went to Germany to study Sanskrit with Albrecht Weber and Rudolf von Roth, and philology under Georg Curtius and August Leskien. Lanman traveled to India in 1889 and brought back around 500 manuscripts in Sanskrit and Prakrit. These formed the basis of the *Harvard Oriental Series*, which he edited. "Charles Rockwell Lanman," http://en.wikipedia.org; Dale Riepe, *The Philosophy of India and its Impact on American Thought* (Thomas, 1970), 81.
29 Vasudeva Laxman Shastri Panshikar, *The Twenty-Eight Upanishads* (Tukaram Javaji, 1906). Eliot's copy is in the Hayward Bequest, Cambridge University. Eliot annotated in the text only the passages listed by Lanman. These are also the passages that Lanman had listed in the record of his course for 1911–12. C. R. Lanman Papers, "Records of My Courses in Harvard College, 1892–1926," Harvard University Archives; Jain, *T. S. Eliot and American Philosophy*, 103, 278n178. See also Robert Crawford, *Young Eliot: From St. Louis to "The Waste Land"* (Jonathan Cape, 2015), 168–71 and *Poems* 1:699.
30 *Baudelaire*, edited and introduced by Francis Scarfe (Penguin Books, 1964), 160. See also *Poems* 1:1159–60.
31 F. H. Bradley, *Appearance and Reality: A Metaphysical Essay*, 2nd ed. (Oxford University Press, 1930), 395–96.
32 Jain, *T. S. Eliot and American Philosophy*, 207; *Knowledge and Experience in the Philosophy of F. H. Bradley* (1916), *Complete Prose* 1:256.
33 See Eliot's letter of January 6, 1915, to Norbert Wiener: "it is all one if one call the Absolute, Reality or Value. It does not exist for me." *Letters* 1:88. See also his letter of January 6, 1930, to Frederick Pollard: "The ultimate identity of the True, the Good and the Beautiful is only in the Absolute, where all cows are of the same colour." *Letters* 5:18.
34 *Waste Land Facsimile*, 130. The poem is dated 1914 or even earlier by Valerie Eliot. She notes that it was influenced by the *Bhagavad Gita* (with perhaps a nod to Emerson's "Brahma").
35 "A Brief Introduction to the Method of Paul Valéry" (1924), *Complete Prose* 2:562.
36 See above, n29. Underlining in the original.

37 *Waste Land Facsimile*, 148.
38 For a discussion of Eliot's divergences from Lanman in his interpretation of the "Fable of the Thunder" and of "Shantih" in *The Waste Land*, see Jain, *T. S. Eliot and American Philosophy*, 105–6, 278n178 and Manju Jain, *A Critical Reading of the "Selected Poems" of T. S. Eliot* (1991; Oxford University Press, 2001), 189–90, 194.
39 Charles Rockwell Lanman, *Hindu Law and Custom as to Gifts* in *Anniversary Papers by Colleagues and Pupils of Lyman Kittredge* (Ginn & Co., 1913), 1–2. Lanman's translation was first pointed out by David Daiches, *English Literature* (Prentice-Hall, 1964), 80; *Poems* 1:699. See also Jain, *T. S. Eliot and American Philosophy*, 105–6.
40 S. Radhakrishnan, *The Principal Upanishads* (HarperCollins, 1994), 290.
41 *Poems* 1:708: "On the rear pastedown of Frank Morley's copy of *Poems* 1920 (once apparently TSE's own), TSE wrote '"damyata/datta/dayadhvam/hridayam."'
42 Radhakrishnan, *The Principal Upanishads*, 292.
43 For a discussion of the dialectics of relativism and interpretation in "What the Thunder Said," see Brooker, *T. S. Eliot's Dialectical Imagination*, 99–101. Brooker, however, uses E. B. Tylor's 1871 concept of "survivals" to interpret the Sanskrit commands as being "remote in time and place, primitive in culture, objective facts." This would be unacceptable to Hindus, for whom the Upanishads are profoundly complex philosophical texts, as indeed they were for Eliot himself.
44 For Eliot's "ecological orientalism," and an ecocritical reading of Eliot's poetry, especially *The Waste Land* and *Four Quartets*, as well as his "poetic reinvention of Buddhism and its affirmative environmental importance for his poetry," see Etienne Terblanche, *T. S. Eliot, Poetry, and Earth: The Name of the Lotos Rose* (Lexington Press, 2016), 22, 25.
45 Harish Trivedi, "'Ganga was sunken . . .': T. S. Eliot's Use of India," in *The Fire and the Rose: New Essays on T. S. Eliot*, ed. Vinod Sena and Rajiva Verma (Oxford University Press, 1992), 61. Trivedi discusses Eliot's alterations, misinterpretations, and misrepresentations of his Sanskrit sources for his thematic usage in order to emphasize the superiority of Christianity over Indian spiritual traditions (44–62). Jahan Ramazani, however, argues that the discordance between the ethical injunctions of the Upanishad and the English responses "shows up not the East's but the West's spiritual inefficacy, its helplessness to redress its crisis," and that it would be erroneous "to read back into the poem the logic of the salvific Christianity which Eliot later embraced." Jahan Ramazani, *A Transnational Poetics* (University of Chicago Press, 2009), 109–10.
46 Charles Lanman, the Turnbull Lectures on "The Poetry of India" (1898); C. R. Lanman Papers, Harvard University Archives.

47 *Waste Land Facsimile*, 149; Jain, *T. S. Eliot and American Philosophy*, 105–6. See also Eloise Hay's comment on this note: Eliot's words "undercut any reading of an affirmatively Christian kind." Eloise Hay, *T. S. Eliot's Negative Way* (Harvard University Press, 1982), 67. Hay also makes the significant point that Eliot did not delete the word "feeble" until after his conversion to Christianity in 1927 (196n25). "The peace which passeth understanding" was a phrase that was often used negatively for the Versailles Treaty. *Poems* 1:709. See Eliot's letter of December 18, 1919, to his mother, criticizing the Versailles Treaty: "The destitution, especially the starvation in Vienna, appears to be unspeakable. I suppose Americans realise now what a fiasco the reorganisation of nationalities has been: The 'Balkanisation of Europe.'" *Letters* 1:425.
48 Quoted in Hay, *Eliot's Negative Way*, 67. The quotation is from Irving Babbitt, "Interpreting India to the West," which originally appeared in the *Nation* in 1917. Hay, *Eliot's Negative Way*, 196n26.
49 For Eliot's pronunciation of Shantih, Ganga, and Dayadhvam, see *Poems* 1:708, 698, 702: "In TSE's 1933 recording he clips and lifts the second syllable of each 'shantih,' whereas in those of 1948 and 1950 each trails away." Ganga is "pronounced with two hard *g*'s in Eliot's recordings." Dayadhvam is pronounced "*Dye-it-vahm*."
50 See Jain, *Critical Reading of the "Selected Poems*," 194–95.
51 Pound's letter to Eliot [January 24, 1922], *Letters* 1:625.
52 Eliot had bought a copy of the book in September 1913, along with Deussen's *Die Sutras des Vedanta*. Crawford, *Young Eliot*, 170.
53 Crawford, *Young Eliot*, 181; Krishna Dutta and Andrew Robinson, *Rabindranath Tagore: The Myriad-Minded Man* (Bloomsbury,1995), 173; *Letters* 9:58–59n1.
54 October 1, 1923, *Letters* 2:230.
55 To John Hayward [January 18, 1939], *Letters* 9:58–59. See also Eliot's rather exasperated comment on "my most recent Bengali, doing the usual thesis on 'The Mystical Element in Modern English Literature' . . ." *Poems* 1:709.
56 Swapan Chakravorty, "Tagore as Literary Critic," in *The Cambridge Companion to Rabindranath Tagore*, ed. Sukanta Chaudhury (Cambridge University Press, 2020), 362. Tagore, though, did admit to R. F. Rattray, Eliot's classmate at Harvard who had looked after Tagore in 1913, that some of Eliot's poetry had moved him by its "evocative power and consummate craftsmanship." Krishna Dutta and Andrew Robinson, *Rabindranath Tagore: The Myriad-Minded Man*, 173; *Letters* 9:58–59n1.
57 *Letters* 9:58–59n1.
58 *Letters* 3:866.
59 Hay, *Eliot's Negative Way*, 70. Eliot's interest in Buddhism was probably inspired initially by his reading, as a boy, of Edwin Arnold's *The Light of*

Asia in his family's library, for which, Eliot recollected much later, he had "preserved a warm affection." "What is Minor Poetry?" (1944), *Complete Prose* 6:569.

60 Eliot believed that Sylvain Lévi was the greatest authority on Buddhism, but that Babbitt was also very good. Letter of April 17, 1930, to Charles Harris, *Letters* 5:152–53.
61 Quoted in Riepe, *The Philosophy of India*, 101.
62 Clark Lecture VIII (1926), *Complete Prose* 2:746. For a discussion of the implications of Laforgue's interpretation of the Absolute for Eliot, see Jain, *T. S. Eliot and American Philosophy*, 202–3.
63 Quoted in Riepe, *The Philosophy of India*, 101–2.
64 Irving Babbitt, "Buddha and the Occident" (1927), in *The Dhammapada* (New Directions, 1965), pp. 77, 88, 96.
65 *Poems* 1:180.
66 Eliot's notes from the lectures are in the Eliot Collection, Houghton Library, Harvard. (Underlining in the original). See Jain, *T. S. Eliot and American Philosophy*, 198–99. See also Crawford, *Young Eliot*, 175–76. For a detailed discussion of Eliot's notes from Anesaki's course, see Jeffrey M. Perl and Andrew P. Tuck, "The Hidden Advantages of Tradition: On the Significance of T. S. Eliot's Indic Studies," *Philosophy East and West* 35, no. 2 (1985): 115–31. Thomas Michael LeCarner reads *The Waste Land* through the lens of Eliot's graduate studies, especially Masaharu's lectures, to show that it is a didactic, artistic representation of the Buddhist doctrines of "*shunyata*" and "*samsara*." Thomas Michael LeCarner, "T. S. Eliot, Dharma Bum: Buddhist Lessons in *The Waste Land*," *Philosophy and Literature* 33, no. 2 (2009): 402–16. Anita Patterson discusses Anesaki's influence on Eliot, especially on his preoccupation with moral action and impersonality. Anita Patterson, "T. S. Eliot and Transpacific Modernism," *American Literary History* 27, no. 4 (2015): 665–82.
67 Letter to Isabella Stewart Gardner, April 4, [1915], *Letters* 1:100.
68 Stephen Spender, *Eliot* (Fontana/Collins, 1975), 26.
69 Letter of November 28, 1939, to Marco Pallis, *Poems* 1:699.
70 *Waste Land Facsimile*, 149. One of the books recommended for his course by Lanman was Henry Clarke Warren's *Buddhism in Translations*, to which Eliot refers in *The Waste Land*. Eliot had read the Buddha's "Fire Sermon" in Dines Andersen's *Pali Reader* in Lanman's course. Crawford, *Young Eliot*, 170. Eliot later commented: "The method—the analogy, and the repetition—is the same as that once used by a greater master of the sermon than either Donne or Andrewes or Latimer: it is the method of the Fire-Sermon preached by the Buddha." "The Preacher as Artist" (1919), *Complete Prose* 2:167.

71 "Francis Herbert Bradley" (1927), *Complete Prose* 3:310. Eliot later remarked in 1937 that "Babbitt sometimes appears to be unaware of differences as well as of resemblances between Buddhism and Christianity." "Introduction to *Revelation*," *Complete Prose* 5:481.
72 *Letters* 5:210.
73 *Poems* 1:181.
74 "James Haughton Woods," Department of East Asian Languages and Civilizations, https://ealc.fas.harvard.edu/james-haughton-woods; James Haughton Woods, *The Yoga-System of Patanjali* (Harvard University Press, 1914), xii.
75 Riepe, *The Philosophy of India*, 91–93.
76 The *Sankhya* school believes in the "distinction between the subject and the object," consciousness and matter. S. Radhakrishnan, *Indian Philosophy*, Vol. 2 (Oxford University Press, 1999), 248.
77 See Jain, *T. S. Eliot and American Philosophy*, 159ff.
78 In his Clark Lectures of 1926 on Metaphysical Poetry, Eliot drew attention to the similarities between some Indian mystical treatises and the analytical and dialectical abilities of Scottish mystics such as Richard of St. Victor. *Complete Prose* 2:652.
79 *Poems* 1:540.
80 See Jain, *T. S. Eliot and American Philosophy*, 30–35.
81 *Letters* 1:117.
82 *Letters* 1:136.
83 *Letters* 1:168, 302.
84 *Letters* 5:138. Vachaspati Mishra was a philosopher in the ninth or the tenth century, renowned for his commentaries on various schools of Indian philosophy. Vijnana Bhiksu was a sixteenth-century philosopher who wrote commentaries on the *Yoga Sutras* of Patanjali. See Eliot's paper on "The Relativity of the Moral Judgment," which he read at a meeting of the Moral Sciences Club held on March 12, 1915, in Bertrand Russell's rooms at Cambridge. Eliot here evokes the scene of the ancient Chinese philosopher, Ye Bo the wise, as he lay on his deathbed and gave instructions to his disciples. This essay also anticipates Eliot's use of the dictum "work out your salvation with diligence," given by Ye Bo to his disciples, in *The Cocktail Party* by Sir Harcourt Reilly. See Jain, *T. S. Eliot and American Philosophy*, 198; *Complete Prose* 1:212.
85 "After Strange Gods" (1934), *Complete Prose* 5:32.
86 *Poems* 1:907.
87 A review of *Brahmadarsanam, or Intuition of the Absolute: Being an Introduction to the Study of Hindu Philosophy*, by Śrî Ānanda Āchārya," *International Journal of Ethics* (1918), *Complete Prose* 1:704–5.
88 A review of *Outlines of Jainism*, by Jagmanderlal Jaini (1918), *Complete Prose* 1:708–9.

89 Vinod Sena, "The Lotos and the Rose: *The Bhagavad Gita* and T. S. Eliot's *Four Quartets*," in Sena and Verma, *New Essays on T. S. Eliot*, 188–89.
90 Letter of May 18, 1934, to Olivia Shakespear, *Letters* 7:192.
91 *Letters* 7:292. Eliot is here referring to Deussen's *Sechzig Upanishads des Veda*.
92 *Letters* 7:365.
93 *Letters* 7:364.
94 *Letters* 7:59, 160, 333. In a letter of April 20, 1934, to Stephen Spender, Eliot had mockingly contrasted "the delightfully matter of fact style of the Holy Man and the occultism effect of Yeats." *Letters* 7:160.
95 Eliot wrote in a letter of November 17, 1955: "While it is true that I knew the *Bhagavad-Gita* long before Purohit Swami made his translation, and did indeed, at one time read it in the original (I have long since even forgotten the alphabet) [...] when I came to quote from the *Bhagavad-Gita* in *The Dry Salvages*, I quoted from the Swami's translation." *Poems* 1:977.
96 Sena, "The Lotos and the Rose," 188–89. Robert Crawford suggests that the "lotos" in *Burnt Norton* may have come from mentions of the "lotus" within the heart and the "white lotus" of God in the Yeats/Purohit Swami translation of the Upanishads. Robert Crawford, *Eliot After The Waste Land* (Vintage, 2022), 243.
97 *Letters* 8:274. See also Eliot's comment on Simone Weil: "I do not know whether she could read the Upanishads in Sanskrit; or, if so, how great was her mastery of what is not only a very highly developed language but a way of thought the difficulties of which only become more formidable to a European student the more diligently he applies himself to it." Preface to Simone Weil, *The Need for Roots* (1952), *Complete Prose* 7:665.
98 Charles Lanman, the Lowell Lectures on "The Beginnings of Hindu Pantheism" and the Turnbull Lectures on "The Poetry of India" (1898), C. R. Lanman Papers, Harvard University Archives. See Jain, *T. S. Eliot and American Philosophy*, 104–5.
99 See above, discussion on "I am the Resurrection and the Life." For Eliot's allusion to the *Gita* in the image of "a black moth" in "The Burnt Dancer" (June 1914), see *Poems* 1:1133–34.
100 Eliot's reader's report, "The Poems of Dadu" (1926), *Poems* 1:976. Eliot also admitted, in a reader's report in 1940, to being "always prejudiced by books about Brahmanism, Buddhism etc. by people who are presumably quite ignorant of the original languages..." *Poems* 1:699–700.
101 "Dante" (1929), *Complete Prose* 3:718.
102 Eliot, *George Herbert* (1962), *Complete Prose* 8:513.
103 Helen Gardner, *The Composition of* Four Quartets (Faber & Faber, 1978), 56.
104 *Poems* 1:197.

105 *The Dry Salvages*, Poems 1:198.
106 *The Geeta*, translated by Shri Purohit Swami (1935; Rupa & Co., 1992), 39.
107 *The Dry Salvages*, Poems 1:198.
108 *The Dry Salvages*, Poems 1:197–98.
109 *The Geeta*, 20.
110 *The Geeta*, 74–75, 78.
111 *Little Gidding*, Poems 1:205–6. See Gardner, *The Composition of* Four Quartets, 56–57 and Sena, "The Lotos and the Rose," 183–88. See also Eliot's comments on Arjuna in defending his own position of neutrality during the Spanish Civil War: "That balance of mind which a few highly-civilized individuals, such as Arjuna, the hero of the Bhagavad Gita, can maintain in action, is difficult for most of us even as observers . . ." "A Commentary," *Criterion*, January 1937, *Letters* 8:784.
112 *Little Gidding*, Poems 1:206.
113 *The Dry Salvages*, Poems 1:199–200.
114 Letter to Egon Vitta, February 23, 1947, Poems 1:976–77. See also Kearns: "The *Four Quartets* gain their strength in part from a subtle and sustained coordination of different and indeed at times opposed philosophical traditions." *T. S. Eliot and Indic Traditions*, 230.
115 *The Ten Principal Upanishads*, translated by Shree Purohit Swami and W. B. Yeats (1937; Rupa & Co., 1992), 54–55.
116 *Complete Poems and Plays*, 545. The connection between this parable and Eliot's play was suggested by Damayanti Ghosh, *Indian Thought in T. S. Eliot: An Analysis of the Works of T. S. Eliot in Relation to the Major Hindu-Buddhist Religious and Philosophical Texts* (Sanskrit Pustak Bhandar, 1978), 111ff.
117 *Letters* 5:284–85; emphasis in the original. See also Jain, *T. S. Eliot and American Philosophy*, 109–10.
118 "The Christian Conception of Education" (1941), *Complete Prose* 6:250, 255n6*.
119 Poems 1:976. Eliot had been criticized because *The Dry Salvages* were "too deeply influenced by Indian thought." Poems 1:899.
120 "Die Einheit der europäischen Kultur," *Complete Prose* 6:712.
121 Letter to Hermann Peschmann, September 12, 1945, Poems 1:906.
122 "The Idea of a European Society" (1949), *Complete Prose* 7: 411–12. (Underlining in the original). See also letter to Egon Vitta, February 23, 1947, on Eliot's hope for the reconciliation and incorporation of "Eastern religious thought into that of Christianity," just as "the scholastics, notably St. Thomas, incorporated Aristotelianism into Christian thought." Poems 1:976.
123 Introduction to *The Wheel of Fire* by G. Wilson Knight (1930), *Complete Prose* 4:151.

Exit Scenes
Towards an Anticolonial Eliot

Ria Banerjee[1]

Eliot was fascinated by the tension between staying and leaving, though the valences of movements *out of* and *away from* vary considerably throughout his career. Eliot's use of place-based imagery is part of a career-long interest in drafty houses, windy corridors and galleries, and, in the drawing room dramas, in airless closed up rooms that provide physical and symbolic locations into and out of which his characters move. His prose from the 1920s and 30s also reflects an essentially spatial understanding of the interactions between religion, culture, and modern life. He campaigned against the destruction of certain disused churches in central London as a physical emblem of Anglicanism, for example, and celebrated a place-based "Idea of Europe" where diverse cultures flourished within stable national borders. Subsequently, in his drawing room dramas, characters abruptly exit for unseen foreign, colonial places, leaving behind familiar English domestic spaces after a spiritual epiphany. I am particularly interested in reading these "exit scenes" for their anticolonial possibilities, placing the stage experiments of the poetic drama on a continuum with Eliot's spatial politics and his prose. The plays show him contorting history and politics to express spiritual prescriptions that he formulated in the prose. The poetic drama thus concentrates the struggles we find in Eliot's interwar era prose, to reconcile paradoxical beliefs in dogmatic religious doctrine and antiauthoritarianism for modern audiences.

In what follows, I do not spend a lot of time on particulars from each play because of the repetitive regularity of the exit scene trope. All the plays have crucial scenes in which characters make drastic decisions to leave, go away, and discard the familiar for the unfamiliar after a circuitous encounter with well-known domestic interiors.[2] As if suddenly possessed by an uncanny double-vision that turns familiar and safe rooms into unhomely and spiritually dangerous spaces, Eliotic protagonists reencounter the domestic and reject previously unquestioned loyalties to king and country. Julia Daniel has recently shown the embedded ecocritical logic of Eliot's rejection of the English country house in *The Family Reunion* (1939), while Patrick Query uncovers the importance of ritual as spiritual discipline in religious spaces contra fascist politics in his writing about the "Idea of Europe."[3] Daniel and Query help clarify what the characters depart *from*; but where do they go? Eliot provides scant few details about the locations and pursuits that his characters take up after they leave England, but his repeated use of the trope of the exit and the information in the plays and prose writings present a tantalizing critical opportunity. Here I take up that invitation to speculate on the meanings of the obverse of the English drawing room, those foreign colonial spaces that form the spiritual ballast of the Eliotic epiphany in the plays.

I. Exits Past the Fringe of Feeling

To leave a scene, to exit the stage space, is also to become unseen, unheard, and easy to dismiss and forget. Since places like Kinkanja or San Marco remain unrepresented by Eliot onstage in their full complexity, it is risky to argue that they are equally as meaningful as the London drawing rooms or English country houses represented on stage. For instance, reviews of the plays show that it is devastatingly easy for audiences to miss Eliot's spatial politics and their central message – that in spiritual terms those elsewheres are far more important than the closed up, familiar spaces of British domesticity. A reviewer writes about *The Family Reunion*, "No one should miss reading this play, if it happens, as may well be, to prove a failure on the stage," even though encountering it on paper flattens Eliot's experiments with actors' bodily movements within and outside stage space.[4] Critical grouchiness about Eliot's poetic drama and the implied or overt sentiment that they would have been better as poems can be found throughout the contemporaneous reviews. One critic deflates audience and play, writing about *The Confidential Clerk* (1954): "The consciousness that all around them lie immensities of experience—surely Mr. Eliot is meaning more than that!—gives a crossword puzzle fever to intellectual playgoers, who snap up clues with hungry solemnity all through this crypto-farce."[5] If the plays mean "more than that," it is in their experiments with speech and movement in stage spaces seen and unseen. Against their ostensible investment in Englishness and use of troubling primitivist tropes in genre set pieces, their evocation of immanent spaces within the diegesis of the play presents a subtle critique of imperialism.

The trope of dramatizing an exit from English domesticity as a shorthand for an exit from national politics allows us to understand more broadly the role that modernist interiors play in reimagining the nation-state in light of the twentieth century's anticolonial and freedom movements. A fuller integration of Eliotic drama into contemporary critical discourse makes possible what Aarthi Vadde calls "a postnational approach to literary study," since in their idiosyncratic way, the plays insistently "multipl[y] the geographies through which [they] can and should be read."[6] We need not excuse away Celia Coplestone's death after torture in *The Cocktail* Party (1949) or that in *The Elder Statesman* (1958), Michael Claverton goes off to get rich from mines in Central America that will destroy the ecology and economy of those places through extractive practices. Rather, an audience's stray thoughts about such details reinsert twentieth-century realities into the space of the theater and explain the peculiar emphasis that Eliot placed on these spiritual-cum-physical exits. In "Poetry and Drama" (1951), Eliot writes: "It seems to me that beyond the nameable, classifiable emotions and motives of our conscious life [...] there is a fringe of indefinite extent, of feeling which we can only detect, so to speak, out of the corner of the eye and can never completely focus."[7] The exits that pepper his drawing room dramas draw attention to this "fringe of feeling," of sensation made visible as absence from the scene. Eliot repeats the idea of this liminal fringe space several times in his writings about poetic drama, adding that, "It is a function of such plays to suggest ideas to those who hear and read them [...] the great play will affect different people differently; it will be capable of innumerable interpretations; and it will have a fresh meaning for every generation."[8] In such a view, the plays function as aesthetic monuments for their audiences akin to a well-frequented church for parishioners; the edifice of the play is intended to accommodate different audiences over time.

Eliot's *Criterion* Commentaries register the keen interest he took in global politics and economics and the interjection of non-English twentieth-century elsewheres into the seemingly insulated English drawing room in the plays breaks from his poetic method. In *The Waste Land* and "The Dry Salvages," for instance, an imagined idea of "the East" stands in for actual places and people who might recite shlokas or crave the monsoons. Critics since Edward Said on have derided the habit in European literature to posit colonized spaces as somehow mystically distant from shared political, social, and economic realities of a globe crisscrossed by trade and other kinds of exchange for centuries, and we can fault Eliot for continuing to prefer an ahistorical Indian religion to real people or their concerns in his poetry. In contrast, the people of Eliot's imaginary Kinkanja occupy the same twentieth century as the Chamberlaynes in London. They understand Celia as a representative of colonial rule – which she is, even if she disavows that position – and treat her as a political enemy. Even in the scant report about her in Act 3 of *The Cocktail Party*, audiences are made aware of a teeming planet full of conflicting violences, including Britain's ambitions to retain global power.

Eliot has been labeled a reactionary apologist for British imperialism based on scenes like the one in *The Cocktail Party*, but scanning the few lines about Kinkanja reveals how incommensurate the perspective of a London drawing room is to understand the political situation there with any depth, and how much more complex human motivations can be when one discards the impulse to remain safe. Celia goes through an intense spiritual crisis and decides that familiar urban places no longer fit her, but her decision to leave London does not land her in some expat British club where she can reiterate the platitudes of the Raj. Rather, she goes as a nurse and her fate is simply ghastly: a character reports that she was taken captive by rioting natives and "must have been crucified/Very near an ant-hill."[9] Within the spatial logic of the London apartment, her death seems purposeless and cruel, especially as it takes place offstage and away from characters and the audience. In the play, the British who rule Kinkanja can offer no solace or consolation to give her death meaning, only an official report that will appear many months later and predictably come to no conclusions. Audiences have been befuddled by this offstage treatment of Celia since the play was first staged. In his *New York Times* review from January 1950, Brooks Atkinson asks, "If the frame of reference is still a London drawing room, why is Celia's crucifixion at the hands of the savages a triumphant destiny rather than a harrowing disaster?"[10] Atkinson inadvertently strikes at the heart of Eliot's method: by the end of the play, its frame of reference is no longer the London drawing room, although its visual vocabulary remains restricted there. Celia moves outside London spaces and their lexicon of comfort and value. The ordered logics and self-preservative imperative of such places no longer apply to her. Oddly but exquisitely, stage space remains anchored to London while the play locates purpose and peace beyond the stage wings. The characters who stay in London, choosing conventional marriages instead of spiritual rebellion, are subject to "stale food mouldering in the larder" and "stale thoughts mouldering in their minds."[11] Their acquiescence to the everyday is both normal and presented by Eliot as a mark of moral failure.

Eliot does not dramatize the end of Empire, giving the plays an air of conservatism belied by careful readings of their commentaries on politics and governance. For instance, one may seriously question Eliot's decision to imagine Saharan North Africa in *The Family Reunion* as deserted open spaces of oases and sand in 1939, as if Harry were entering a touristic postcard of the wadis instead of an important theater of war where people with conflicting political affiliations disputed the global balance of power. Despite such frustrating features, the exit scenes prize apart stage space that is visually restricted to English domesticity. They invite into the diegesis of the play other places that do not usually fit within the parameters of a drawing room drama, thereby bringing in political consciousnesses other than Eliot's own. At the fringes of feeling where he leads us, we may give these glimpsed non-English spaces as much importance as the characters do. If our sense of the world impels us to pay as much attention to a fictional Central American republic as to a London apartment, then we multiply the geographies of Eliot's stage spaces and access an altogether more radical imaginative angle for understanding his plays.

Since Eliot was himself resolutely centrist in his politics, his prose and plays are unexpected places to find anti-authoritarian or anticolonial arguments. He habitually located totalitarianism in movements from the political left and right, and equated Russian Bolshevism, Italian Fascism, and Western liberalism any time he felt individual rights to be in peril. He called himself "no warm friend of the imperialist government," but his Anglican-influenced anticolonialism was mild at best.[12] In *The Cocktail Party*, Harry explicitly refuses the term "missionary" as his future goal, even though the character is modeled on a French missionary whom the poet admired, Brother Charles de Foucauld (discussed below). Eliot makes no sustained effort in his voluminous prose to address the grotesque history of religious missions or colonial invasions throughout early modern European expansion. In 1940, he wrote with mild irony about Churchill and Britain's Imperial policies, just three years before those same policies culminated in the deaths of two to three million people by preventable starvation and disease in the Bengal Famine that swept through eastern India.[13] And yet, Eliot considered his role of public intellectual as deeply antithetical to those of politicians and economists, and any consideration of his late career must acknowledge that pacifism, anti-racism, and anticolonialism are foundational to his Anglicanism.[14] Neither a protester nor a picketer, he struggled to reconcile the growing imperatives of his religious doctrine with the self-imposed limits of his public-facing work. For instance, in the mid-1930s, he joined the Moot Society enthusiastically but became an infrequent attendee at meetings once the group began discussing ways to directly influence churchgoers; a decade later, he refused to join UNESCO when invited and conducted a public letter-writing campaign against them. In both cases, he was unwilling to articulate pragmatic alternatives to the political and economic philosophies they espoused, even though he set himself against what he saw as their entrenched desire to dictate to their publics.

In contrast, on stage, the possibilities held out by Eliotic exits are expansive and multiple. An anticolonial Eliot—such a figure is not intuitively recognizable, and yet the plays ascribe an excessive wrongness to contemporary politics, including British management of its colonies. Westernized urban modernity is characterized as so straitjacketed that any right-thinking person ought to question why they have not had a hysterical breakdown like Celia's from it. An anti-authoritarian Eliot sounds almost unreal, and yet in *Murder in the Cathedral* (1935), Thomas Becket's fierceness to defy royal authority in the cause of justice reverberates in the determination shown by his secular saints. Eliot's decision to de-emphasize Christian doctrine in the drawing room dramas allows us to understand their spirituality more broadly and apply their criticisms widely. The trope of the exit scene onstage preempts that other exit which everyone experiences once the curtain falls and the house lights come on. The stage is strongly imbricated with modern well-to-do urban life just beyond Shaftesbury Avenue or Broadway, and the plays argue for the necessity of spiritual epiphanies that reject the standards held by those worlds. Hence, an audience's final exit from the auditorium extends beyond the purview of the theater building. If Harry or Celia or Michael need to leave then what pins us in place? Thomas Becket is an anomaly in Eliotic drama for being extraordinarily heroic; the characters in the drawing room dramas are aggressively ordinary (albeit rich), suggesting broad emotional access to their restlessness. Together they imply that the same exits are available to the audience. We, like Celia, might simply pick up and leave.

II. Intractable Spaces and Publics

Prefiguring his experiments with stage space, Eliot pursued two related topics in *Criterion* Commentaries in the late 1920s and 30s: prescriptions for local places of worship and "The Idea of Europe," formulations about how national populations ought to understand their own culture alongside others.[15] Both of these proved thorny and Eliot was unable to engage and sway his intended public. The two ideas are intuitively connected, and Eliot's spatial politics tacitly undergird both, but they remain formally disconnected in separate sections within his *Criterion* Commentaries, as if he was unable to articulate them together. In this sense, the plays allow him to close a gap between religious and political prescriptions that remain distinct from each other in the *Criterion*. Christianity should not remain "on a shelf for reference, like old text-books," he says, but change and mature over time like one's appreciation for the literature of Shakespeare, Milton, or Dante.[16] At the same time, his political vision of international cooperation called for a system wherein "varieties of region and language, and the divergent paths of development" of national cultures and the development of "Nordic, Celtic, Latin and Slavonic languages" would create "significant unity—unity, not uniformity."[17] This emphasis on *unity, not uniformity* drives much of his post-1945 public intellectual work. Drawing on insights from his roles within Lloyds Bank, Eliot saw economic imperatives driving national politics, and he often complained that modern English culture was too obsessed with short-term gains at the expense of metaphysical and cultural losses.[18] The European Idea proves a handy term for him to develop cultural prescriptions outside the realm of politics but overlapping with his understanding of global finance. He called to "all those who are concerned with the general ideas of art, literature and philosophy, as well as the social sciences" but not "politics nor work for politicians."[19] However, since art and culture are tethered to the material realities of politics and economics, adhering to this compartmentalized sphere of reference required a fair amount of intellectual contortion on Eliot's part.

Eliot's sense of Western Civ on the brink of collapse follows from Paul Valéry's decentering observation after World War I that Western Europe was "a small and isolated cape on the western side of the Asiatic Continent" that needed Russian support to win the war.[20] A monolithic arrogance lies behind Eliot's comments about the potential of Anglicanism to redeem humanity, but the essays from the 1920s and 30s show his real struggles to articulate *how* Anglicanism might speak to disenfranchised populations and what "The European Idea" means in practical terms. Eliot declares that "we believe that there is a British idea of culture and a British idea of civilization, both quite distinct from either French or German" and "in this reorganization of the ideas of Europe, the ideas of Britain and the British Empire have their place"—but who does that "we" include beyond Eliot's small circle of literary friends?[21] What purchase do they have on contemporary conversations, and how do these many national cultures hope to fit together without the threat of territorial intrusions? Historical precedents if not current events in the 1930s should have led them to expect territorial wars of expansion within continental Europe. As if throwing up his hands in a representative Commentary from August 1927, Eliot abruptly breaks off and opens a new section on "Ancient Buildings Again" where he insists on the importance of stopping the demolition of some small churches in central London. There too, any definite intervention based on Eliot's own views seems unlikely, and in two brief paragraphs, he notes that more discussion will follow.

Repeated deferrals in the face of disappointment, objections in the negative without positive calls to action—this critical pose seems to have suited Eliot quite well.[22] Eliot's later poetic dramas call for far more difficult and active changes, however, stemming directly from the observations he made in prose. In 1938, in response to England's capitulation in the Munich Agreement, Chamberlain's attempt to placate Hitler's Germany, he declaimed: "Was our society [...] assembled around anything more permanent than congeries of banks, insurance companies, and industries, and had it any beliefs more essential than a belief in compound interest and the maintenance of dividends?"[23] This comment, from the tail end of *The Idea of a Christian Society*, was written during a phase of uncomfortable introspection and "a feeling of humiliation," wherein Eliot found himself unable to "match [Fascist] conviction with [his own, democratic] conviction."[24] He calls this long essay a foray into "constructive thinking" to prepare for the end of the war when the chaos of reconstruction might be usefully managed by religious thinkers and leaders to mediate the development of modern English society.[25] At the same time, Eliot is deeply critical of top-down attempts to manage social and cultural growth of the nation. Commenting upon issues as diverse as pacifism, international finance, Oxford University, and the establishment of arts councils in the UK, Eliot distinguishes between organic formations that are robust "growths" from the grassroots level versus restrictive "constructions from above" or "creation[s] by the power of money."[26] The two impulses—to correct society as a cultural arbiter and to protest cultural arbitration by authority figures—continually come into conflict in his nonfiction.

Despite the confidence of his assertions, Eliot in the 1920s and 30s was a public intellectual who could not influence the general public or impact broader social policies despite cultivating a wide and influential acquaintance, and he had to become comfortable in his role as an outsider to the world of real action and activism. In a sense, his frustration with recalcitrant publics made possible the multivalent theatrical tropes that allow rich forms of otherness to manifest in the poetic drama. Yet another unsuccessful campaign was his opposition to the Music and Drama Bill of 1938 that proposed a centralized National Theatre, which he found sinister enough to equate with Fascist propaganda outlets. In his eyes, creating a National Theatre would impose the appearance of solidarity between Britain and its Indian, African, and Caribbean colonies while glossing over the real problems with Imperial rule.[27] But short of using propaganda to influence subject populations, how might England inspire love for British rule among strident anticolonialists (Ireland had already broken away in 1922, and India insistently demanded freedom in exchange for war help)? How might any ruler actually follow Eliot's prescription in his essay "Machiavelli" that a ruler "cannot govern people for ever against their will" and "must use every means to make them contented and to persuade them that your government is to their interest"?[28] The public commentator withdraws into the role of poet after making these observations, claiming no responsibility for the realms of policy and politics. Even into the post-World War II years, Eliot continued to advocate for locally situated internationalism, particularly in its Christian dimensions. He was leery of internationalist organizations like UNESCO, criticizing them for "grandiose and cloudy schemes for 'producing international understanding'" through top-down infrastructure, in contrast to which he repeatedly tried to anchor his principles in practical suggestions for everyday living.[29] Local churches and Anglicanism, so obviously to him a viable alternative to degraded modern existence, remained an unpopular answer that suited a dwindling number of people. His inability to shape what he considered to be crucial cultural conversations led, perhaps, to his turn to the theater where public engagement took on a more visible form.

In Eliot's drama from the mid-1930s onwards, characters show scant direct concern for nationalism or overtly political problems that worried him in other forums.[30] Harry or Celia privilege their religious growth over political concerns that were central for Machiavelli (or Thomas Becket), but the plays subvert such artificial separation of the individual from broader politics through their domestic architecture and stage space. Eliot toed a tricky line as a public intellectual. Despite his vocal avowal of royalism (which cannot be distanced from racist colonialism), he appears sensitive to accusations of everyday racism. For instance, he writes approvingly of Wilkie Collins's *The Moonstone* (1868), in which "Collins's

Indians are intelligent and resourceful human beings with perfectly legitimate and comprehensible motives," although unfortunately the novel's wide popularity has led to "a great deal of bogus Indianism, fakirs and swamis, in crime fiction."[31] Leaving aside that Collins's Indians may not read as *perfectly* legitimate to Anglophone Indians, such commentary indicates less about the novel under review and more about Eliot's own desire to preempt certain accusations. A handful of such passages do not make Eliot himself into a spokesperson for anticolonialism, and contemporaries like Leonard Woolf or E. M. Forster would not have regarded him as such. However, his wide reading habits, his knowledge of global finance formed from working in Lloyds Bank's Colonial and Foreign department and the Pre-War Enemy Debts department, and even perhaps the Indians he met who did not warm to him (famously including Mulk Raj Anand), meant that Eliot was immersed in the consciousness of colonialism and anticolonialism far more than his pronouncements suggest when taken in isolation.[32]

In the 1930s and 40s, Eliot was content to lecture and write, but his peers in the Moot Society and post-1945 organizations like UNESCO dreamt of more prescriptive changes that would directly organize how people lived, studied, and (in the case of the Moot) prayed. Both these organizations, in their own ways, wished to promote peace and prevent future war; faced with their proposals, however, Eliot saw authoritarianism and anti-individualism disguised as benign policy. The implicit question underlying his public and private divisions with the Moot Society and UNESCO is related to the one that the plays repeatedly, obsessively dramatize through scenes of exit: how to correct society and affect positive cultural change from the ground up? As Javadi and Schuchard relate, Eliot carried out a very public campaign against UNESCO's cultural mission, writing letters to editors of London and Paris newspapers and personal correspondences with his friend, the director-general Julian Huxley, demanding that the organization first define "culture" and then propose "clear and distinct ideas of what we want to do before we set out to do it."[33] He ridiculed the UNESCO project to translate world classics into major languages, which the organization touted as a precursor to global peace, writing that "[t]he suggestion that for everybody to read everybody's classics in translation would promote peace, amity and understanding has no foundation."[34] He even becomes frustrated with UNESCO's aim of "teaching the inhabitants of Haiti and British East Africa to read and write," claiming this a "less urgent task" than attending to necessities of daily living, like providing them with food and shelter.[35] There is bombast and overstatement in Eliot's case against UNESCO, but there is also a pointed criticism of the organization's latent white savior mentality. Eliot's responses to the Moot in the late 1930s and explicitly to UNESCO in the late 1940s arise from a deeply held anti-authoritarianism. In this context, wherein the poet simultaneously faces the difficulty of prescriptive action and the desire to diagnose social ills, I speculate about the plays written simultaneously. Considered in their colonial context, and given their professed secularity, where do his exits from the English drawing room lead us?

III. Where to Next?

The drawing room dramas are interesting precisely because they offer so many exits, repeatedly dramatizing what audiences looking for a Noel Coward-esque joke tend to miss. Harry's decision in *The Family Reunion* to "follow the bright angels" into the desert has the air of a touristic getaway,[36] and when Michael from *The Elder Statesman* takes off for fictional San Marco, where he will save both his soul and his pocketbook with Gomez for his guide, the scene takes on elements of a cloyingly happy ending. As discussed, Celia dies in an even more shocking manner than Thomas in *Murder in the Cathedral*, while Colby Simpkins from *The Confidential Clerk* gives up his political influence to become a suburban church organist. Despite the plays' reticence to overtly declare messages, they all insist upon the importance of difficult, uncomfortable, usually unwise decisions to leave behind the certainties of their worlds. The masses of details about characters, the shaggy dog stories and mythic references, and the ostensibly comedic tone of the drawing room plays distract and obscure the essentially breathtaking radicality of Eliot's proposal: to feel something real and break the chain of normal, complacent actions. Eliot's stage spaces remain steeped in conventional attitudes towards family life, class consciousness, and associated national and political allegiances. Meanwhile, offstage space holds out the possibility of alternate modes of living. These elsewheres are only accessed through dramatic exits by characters who disappear from the intrusive gaze of the audience, leaving behind no clue or key to fully understand their motivations or experiences. In this, the plays adhere strictly to their own sense of private faith. They disallow the idly curious, blocking spiritual epiphanies from the view of a Broadway or Shaftesbury Avenue theatergoer who indulges in thoughts of radical leave-taking for a few hours before returning to the kind of life and aspirations held by the Chamberlaynes et al. They withhold access to *both* non-English spaces (which clearly exist) and explanations of personal faith (unlike Thomas Becket, none of the characters in the drawing room dramas explain their motives except in the vaguest terms). These spaces and experiences both exist as immanent at the "fringe of indefinite extent, of feeling."[37]

I suggest that we follow Eliot's lead to seriously consider the trope of the exit scene as a rejection of extant modern value systems. Eliot locates in these exits not the comfort of a cynic who finds everything wrong and remains where they are (arguably his own position vis-à-vis contemporary London), but the idealized optimism of a convert whose faith turns upon respect for native populations that is inherently anticolonial and anti-hierarchical because it is based upon Christian love, however far the practice of Anglicanism has been from this principle. Such a convert has to contort her way out of the historical collusions between Christianity and colonialist politics to remake her faith into something that it historically has not been. Eliot's English men and women reject "home" and travel far away, never establishing another analogous domestic space, and since he repeatedly describes English home spaces as spiritual traps, this disestablishment is a positive step. While Eliot confined his statements to religious liberation, we might extend the implications of his favorite dramatic trope much farther. Even Colby Simpkins's relatively minor sacrifice of giving up his position as the private secretary to the powerful and titled Sir Claude for the sake of an inner calling entails giving up material privileges that drastically change his life. The plays on the whole blithely transcend such prosaic, materialistic fears and failures.[38] Harry at least hands over Wishwood Manor to his brother, who will presumably refill his American Express account from time to time; but Celia leaps into the unknown with little more than mild encouragement from the psychologist Harcourt-Reilly, rejecting the London drawing room's safeties and capitulations.

Perhaps she imagines that she will help people in the way that a UNESCO worker might, becoming a nurse in a "very austere" order.[39] Eliot offers these unusual departures from the stage of conventional modernity as a mark of spiritual superiority and an aspiration for his audiences.

Eliot's converts repeatedly eschew the term *missionary*, although most audiences have mapped the poet's Anglicanism onto the plays' epiphanies. Eliot's prevarication about the term is disingenuous because, as the *Complete Prose* reveals, the model for Harry Monchensey was a real-life French missionary, Charles de Foucauld. Eliot writes to a friend in 1935: "A great deal of fuss is being made now over Lawrence of Arabia; but if you could get hold of the *Vie de Charles de Foucauld* . . . you would learn something about a much greater man in the same genre."[40] In the years leading up to *The Family Reunion*, the French missionary stayed in Eliot's mind; for instance, in 1938, at a speech for a boy's school, he chooses Brother Charles (as the priest called himself) as the most suitable subject for a lengthy address. He tells them that the French missionary started as an iconoclast who left a wealthy and powerful family legacy because "the desert had done something to him, something to elicit the real man underneath."[41] The desert *does something* to Harry as well, reiterating aspects of a well-known colonialist trope wherein a mystical landscape is privileged over the many people who live in it, but the rest of his discussion moves well away from colonial apologia.

Eliot locates Charles's faith as separate from (if not clearly antithetical to) the aims of the French Foreign League in occupied territory. He relates that Charles studied Arabic and Hebrew in Algiers before taking orders and leaving for an outpost far from the centers of power, a sign that he did not want a major role in the exploitative parts of church culture in colonial Algeria. Instead, the priest applied himself to administering basic medicine to poor villagers, assisting them with local rehabilitation projects, and recording Tuareg culture and poetry. "To make converts was not his first aim, though many converts did come," Eliot says; Charles was an exemplary missionary because he was not like most colonizers, "the unscrupulous money-makers" and "dissolute adventurers" who "prey upon the natives, or whose morality is lower than that of the natives whom they look down upon, or whose religion is non-existent."[42] Charles was eventually captured by "a band of Senussi," but Eliot attributes this violence to European war and not local tribes, saying to the school assembly of young boys: "When the Great War came, it was naturally the occasion for sedition among subject tribes and for raiding activity among those unsubdued." Charles was mistaken for a native and shot by a French guard "almost by accident."[43] Nothing about colonial violence is natural or accidental, but Eliot's articulation informs my sense that the plays are not straightforwardly aligned with British Imperialism. To read them as pro-colonial is a mistake as well as a missed opportunity to mobilize these works through close readings to better political ends.

Specifically, Eliot's account of Brother Charles opens up new lines of thought about his understanding of missionary culture. After his misadventures as "Lawrence of Arabia," T. E. Lawrence remained a British soldier, knowing he had been mistreated and misled by British political leaders but staying part of the imperial organization until his death. In contrast, Eliot's account of Charles explicitly locates the priest outside the French nationalist project. This helps us understand the character of Harry, and it also provides a clue for understanding the more radical decision taken by Celia and the far more disturbing depiction of her final weeks. Like Charles de Foucauld, Celia tries to abandon her national affiliations when she travels to Kinkanja as part of a nursing order. Like the French missionary, she rejects colonial privilege and anticolonial outrage, attempting to locate some third space where she can work within her faith without coercing local populations into political subservience. Celia exits to Kinkanja and then, grotesquely, is forced to make another kind of exit. She, like Charles de Foucauld, might have imagined working as a free agent unbound by extant complicities between Church and state that structure modern empires. However much Eliot praised them, such identifications are difficult if not impossible to achieve or sustain. Eliot's account to the schoolboys ends with a downplayed version of Charles's death, and similarly *The Cocktail Party* brushes aside Celia's second unwilled exit while locating spiritual importance in the first.

Eliot's language delights in stereotypical tropes, from the Sweeney poems to *The Cocktail Party*. However, the outlandish depiction of Kinkanja as a colonial space deflates a foundational conceit of imperialism—that the British, having both loftier ideals and superior practicality, were better suited to govern the colonies than the locals themselves. Instead, the colonies remain intractable to the colonialist mentalities of the British upper classes who occupy the stage in every one of the drawing room dramas. At the same time, although the poet's attention remains fixed on Anglo-American society and culture, offstage imperial spaces pull audience attention away from the stage. The colonialist temper is inherently about codifying, counting, and mapping terrain in order to extract value from distant places, and Eliot resists precisely this kind of knowing through metrics. The known and comprehensible British world stands in stark contrast to the unknown world of *feelings* and the uncanny consciousness of larger motives beyond power, money, and influence. Characters turn away from the prosaic into the arena of feelings, of poetry itself. Thus, in *The Family Reunion*, when Harry takes off from Wishwood Manor for somewhere that sounds like North Africa, Eliot is not simply repeating the colonialist trope of blank spaces on the map familiar to him from Conrad. He does not distinguish between good and bad colonialisms or arbitrate between just and unjust ecocritical and human rights violations carried out in the name of good governance. He consigns the ritzy London apartment, the British manorial system, all the social forms and colonial wealth that prop them up to the same perverseness.

Eliot's final play, *The Elder Statesman*, presents an interesting twist on the theme that might be related to the poet's concurrent experience of happy domesticity: the imaginary Central American republic of San Marco serves as the locus of both the known and unknown, a place where Michael Claverton can grasp at spiritual knowledge as well as a fortune in an erstwhile colony. Michael does not throw tantrums like Harry, nor does he immerse himself in abject work like Celia, and, in this sense, the final play does not question to the same extent the values of British social and material prestige and the means through which it was obtained, its empire.

At the fringes of feeling where Eliot brings audiences to roam, it is worth speculating about the kinds of literary connections that the plays make possible. Eliotic fringe intellectual spaces are not vast empty deserts after all. Taking Harry's exit for a jumping-off point, we locate the story of Charles de Foucauld and the travesties of the FLN on Algeria. We might then trace a line directly from *The Family Reunion* or *The Cocktail Party*, through the biography of Brother Charles, to the large body of postcolonial literature and art that articulates questions of individual faith and national loyalties in the later twentieth century. With feelings as our guide, we might understand Celia's actions as a link to other attempts to locate a humanist position outside the binary of nationalism versus antinationalism. *The Cocktail Party* resonates with works interested in questions of race, ethnicity, gender, and identity broadly, showing the importance of personal faith and the brutal impacts of global politics that inevitably affect such positions.

Tracing transhistorical literary connections can impact our understanding and teaching of literary studies in positive ways, too. The decentering of authorial intent and emphasis on interpretive freedoms championed by Eliot led to the establishment of New Criticism as a dominant disciplinary lens in the field of Anglo-American literary studies, though its outcome was not as democratic as Eliot imagined. New Criticism led to the propagation of a classroom canon that was overwhelmingly white, male, and European—in other words, too much like Eliot himself. Subsequent waves of feminist and postcolonial critics have worked hard to reincorporate historical, cultural, and biographical research into literary studies, in pursuit of re-readings that better suit the needs of a wider audience. Within modernist studies, an increasing awareness of other strands of literary theory has guided scholars to reapproach so-called canonical texts like *The Waste Land* through concepts of multiplicity, simultaneity, and unknowability that were not unique to Eliot but, as Mara de Gennaro recently argues, originated with Aimé Césaire, Édouard Glissant, and C. L. R. James's poetry and theory.[44] Also very recently, modernist studies has been impelled to attend to indigenous voices across the globe and embrace wider perspectives on literature and culture of the long twentieth century. Real *unity, not uniformity* (to borrow Eliot's phrase) means engaging with familiar figures alongside others who are still shut out of, or have exited, critical conversations in modernist studies. Eliot might not occupy a central place in literature classrooms globally for much longer (or anymore), but the argumentative, anti-authoritarian, elitist yet democratic, sometimes wrongheaded poet might well have been excited at the prospect of once again struggling for inclusion in robust discussions of poetry and literature.

Contemporary activist thinking points out that one function of art is to insist upon impossible possibilities, to jog audiences out of our settled senses of what is and can be. Eliot's plays, in all their flawed religious optimism, certainly do that. Together with *Four Quartets*, these late pieces are a sustained attempt to reach past the poet's own public persona and access grassroots-level, utopic spaces of belief and spiritual sustenance. The exit scenes ask us to consider radically foolish actions for their merits instead of their easily predictable ends; as I have argued, Celia's epiphany leads nowhere in material terms, and her exit, decisive as it is, leads to a literal dead end. Celia's renunciation repeats Eliot's formula from *Murder in the Cathedral* of the spiritual clarity that comes from rejecting the limited real world, whatever the cost of such exits. The historical precedents of Thomas à Becket and Charles de Foucauld lead Eliot to treat the importance of being alive in a cavalier manner; but, by allowing non-English places to intrude into the insulated drawing rooms of the dramas, Eliot opens the stage space beyond his own Anglican poetics. Chills and drafts pervade Wishwood Manor onstage and also blow in a global audience's drafty resistance to Eliot's circumscribed concern with England and English peoples.

Notes

1 The writing and revision of this essay was made possible by support from the National Endowment for the Humanities and the New York Public Library's Center for Research in the Humanities.
2 *Sweeney Agonistes*, *Coriolan*, and *Murder in the Cathedral* do not precisely fit the analytic framework I offer here. They do, however, register in different ways the tensions between leaving domestic spaces and remaining tethered to this-worldly concerns. *Sweeney* is a particularly porous fragment, with its rollicking locals, foreigners, soldiers, and the intrusive menace of the Portuguese/Goan Pereira over the telephone.
3 For more, see Julia E. Daniel, "Wind, Rock, Flower, Glass: *The Family Reunion* as Ecodrama," *T. S. Eliot Studies Annual* 3: 69–93 and Patrick R. Query, *Ritual and the Idea of Europe in Interwar Writing* (Ashgate, 2013).
4 *T. S. Eliot: The Contemporary Reviews*, ed. Jewel Spears Brooker (Cambridge University Press, 2004), 384.
5 Richard Findlater, "The Camouflaged Drama" in Brooker, *Contemporary Reviews*, 554–57, 555. There are also more damning responses, often by

academic reviewers writing outside the pressures of journalism, who find in the plays cultural elitism, close-minded religiosity, and racism. I have discussed some of these reviews in "From Humiliation to Epiphany: The Role of Onstage Spaces in T. S. Eliot's Middle Plays," *South Atlantic Review* 82, no. 2 (2017): 59–77.

6   Aarthi Vadde, *Chimeras of Form: Modernist Internationalism beyond Europe, 1914–2016* (Columbia University Press, 2016), 57–58.
7   *Complete Prose* 7:603.
8   *Complete Prose* 7:386.
9   *Complete Poems and Plays*, 434.
10 Brooker, *Contemporary Reviews*, 525.
11 *Complete Poems and Plays*, 420.
12 *Complete Prose* 5:470.
13 This view of the Bengal Famine as a result of British foreign policy is widely accepted in recent years; see Amartya Sen, *Poverty and Famines: An Essay on Entitlement and Deprivation* (Oxford University Press, 1982) for more. I do not mean to prosecute Eliot here but provide a snapshot of his perspective to better locate the spatial possibilities of his plays.
14 I cannot do full justice to this claim in this essay, but reviewing Eliot's comments about political matters in the *Complete Prose* shows that although he did not directly identify with pacifist or anti-racist movements, his discussions of Anglicanism repeatedly center ideas of peace, respect, and nonviolence at the heart of true faith. For instance, he lambasts Aldous Huxley's anti-war pamphlet *What Are You Going to Do about It?* (1936) for detaching a call for peace from religion, arguing that Anglicanism fosters an organic, grassroots sense of equality that would bring true peace whereas Huxley's secular peace paves the way for fascism (*Collected Prose* 5:592). This is a determinedly ahistorical view of a strand of Christianity that is widely understood in modernity as conservative, and, moreover, is closely associated with the imperialist monarchy. The plays are in this sense more historically minded and less idiosyncratic, reflecting twentieth-century realities more fully than Eliot allows in his essays on religion.
15 For an overview of "The Idea of Europe," see Jeroen Vanheste's "The Idea of Europe," in *T. S. Eliot in Context*, ed. Jason Harding (Cambridge University Press, 2011).
16 *Complete Prose* 5:624, 631.
17 *Complete Prose* 7:813.
18 For more, see Matthew Seybold's "Astride the Dark Horse: T. S. Eliot and the Lloyds Bank Intelligence Department," *T. S. Eliot Studies Annual* 1: 131–55.
19 *Complete Prose* 3:157.
20 *Complete Prose* 3:156–57.

21 *Complete Prose* 3:157.
22 For more on Eliot's self-assigned foreigner or "metic" role in English culture, see Jean Michel Rabate, "Tradition and T. S. Eliot," in *The Cambridge Companion to T. S. Eliot*, ed. David A. Moody (Cambridge University Press, 2006) and Matthew Hart, "Visible Poet: T. S. Eliot and Modernist Studies," *American Literary History* 19, no. 1 (2006): 174–89.
23 *Complete Prose* 5:717.
24 *Complete Prose* 5:717. For more on this, see Peter Dale Scott, "The Social Critic and his Discontents," in Moody, *Cambridge Companion to T. S. Eliot*.
25 *Complete Prose* 5:718.
26 *Complete Prose* 5:592, 593.
27 *Complete Prose* 5:610–11.
28 *Complete Prose* 3:115.
29 *Complete Prose* 7:46.
30 Steven Matthews argues that Eliot struggled with a fascination with fascist monomyth in the late 1920s but by the time he abandoned writing *Coriolan* in 1932 he sees nationalism as a false religion that misleads the masses. For more, see Matthews, "'You Can See Some Eagles. And Hear the Trumpets': The Literary and Political Hinterland of T. S. Eliot's *Coriolan*," *Journal of Modern Literature* 36, no. 2 (2013): 44–60.
31 *Complete Prose* 3:15–16.
32 Mulk Raj Anand, *Conversations in Bloomsbury*, ed. Saros Cowasjee (Vision Books India, 2013).
33 *Complete Prose* 7:19.
34 *Complete Prose* 7: xviii–xix.
35 *Complete Prose* 7:45–46.
36 *Complete Poems and Plays*, 339.
37 *Complete Prose* 7:603.
38 We must understand these moves by Eliot within the context of their writing. Eliot's theory of impersonality, for instance, has become a critical commonplace but, as I have hinted here, there are a lot of personal feelings inherently shaping his works, particularly the plays. This is particularly true of *The Family Reunion*, which has changed in critical estimation quite drastically after the opening of the Emily Hale letters. Whittier-Ferguson shows how writing the character of Mary allowed Eliot to expunge the real impact of his epistolary lover from his work. While the play frames Harry as a high-minded ascetic, it is possible to take a far dimmer view of the character; it was much easier for Eliot to imagine the hero for his play than to exemplify the qualities that he praised. For more on this, see John Whittier-Ferguson, "'I would meet you upon this honestly': The Repudiation of Mary in *The Family Reunion*," *T. S. Eliot Studies Annual* 4: 215–28.
39 *Complete Poems and Plays*, 433.

40   *Complete Prose* 5:628n.
41   *Complete Prose* 5:626.
42   *Complete Prose* 5:626–27.
43   *Complete Prose* 5:627.
44   Mara de Gennaro, *Modernism after Postcolonialism: Toward a Nonterritorial Comparative Literature* (Johns Hopkins University Press, 2020).

Religion, Rites, and Emily Hale

Sara Fitzgerald

When T. S. Eliot acknowledged his longtime love for Emily Hale in 1930, he positioned her as a Beatrice-like model of female perfection. Ironically, Hale actually personified the same kind of institutional Unitarianism that Eliot had already rejected, first through his impulsive marriage to Vivien Haigh-Wood in 1915 and then with his decision to convert to Anglicanism twelve years later. Over the decades of letters that followed, the two of them argued over what it meant to be a Christian and whether Unitarians, in Eliot's view, fell short. Hale also stepped down from her pedestal long enough to repeatedly challenge Eliot on why he felt his religious beliefs precluded him from obtaining a divorce so that the two of them could marry.

Eliot's letters to Hale add to the already large body of commentary—both Eliot's own and by others—on the nature of his faith. But because Eliot arranged for the bulk of Hale's letters to be destroyed, scholars will never fully know her side of their religious debates. This paper reviews what *is* known about Hale's faith, based on research into her life, the perspectives of her clergy father and uncle and the congregations they served, as well as the clues that *can* be found in Eliot's letters.

Close family members on both sides of Hale's family were leaders of the turn-of-the century Unitarian denomination, who shared podiums and professional networks with Eliot's relatives. Hale's great-aunt, Sarah Emery Hooper, co-founded the organization that later became the

Women's Alliance of the Unitarian church. When she died in 1915 at the age of 92, Hooper was the only woman to have served as first vice-president of the American Unitarian Association (AUA). (Samuel A. Eliot II, Eliot's cousin and son of the former president of Harvard, was the AUA's president at the time of her death.) Hooper had been an active member of South Congregational Church and was a close friend of its former pastor, the great Unitarian leader Dr. Edward Everett Hale.[1] Her funeral was conducted by the Rev. Edward Cummings, father of the poet E. E. Cummings, another friend of Hale's and Eliot's.[2]

For most of her life, Emily Hale lived within the orbit of two prominent Unitarian clergymen, her father and her uncle. Both graduated from Harvard Divinity School in the late nineteenth century after first pursuing other careers. Hale lived with her father, Edward Hale, until his death in 1918 when she was twenty-six. She remained close to her uncle, John Carroll Perkins, for the next thirty-two years, frequently living or traveling with him before he died in 1950 at the age of eighty-eight.

Hale's father was profiled in the fourth volume of Samuel Eliot's *Heralds of a Liberal Faith* and her uncle contributed to the book, which summarized the lives of some two hundred "Pilots," who served the denomination immediately before and after the turn of the twentieth century. (Samuel Eliot died during the book's final stages, and the work was completed by T. S. Eliot's first cousin, the Rev. Frederick May Eliot.) In his Introduction, Samuel Eliot wrote of this era of church leaders:

> Saints and heroes were, indeed, their forerunners, but they could not conceive of themselves as belonging to a clerical order or to a privileged class invested with special prerogatives. But they *did* belong in an authentic "Prophetic Succession." They were something more than mere transmitters of received opinions and prescribed usages. They preferred immediacy to tradition. They wanted to liberate men from the burdens of dogma and sacerdotalism.[3]

He went on:

> First, these men were all optimists, seed-sowers, believers in growth and progress. Their optimism was not, however, just a

cheerful assumption that, after some fashion, everything was going to come out all right. [...] They *did* brush away a lot of cobwebs. They *did* protest against the awful notions of "total depravity" and "original sin" and a cruel, commercial "atonement," against a view of miracles that implied the suspension of natural law, against the complicated conception of a Triune God. But what they brought into Christian thought was vastly more important than what they expelled. Fundamentally they were builders—bridge builders—interpreting the new to the old and the old to the new. They were more eager to fulfill than to destroy.[4]

Emily Hale's religious outlook was likely shaped by spending the first third of her life with her pastor father. Edward Hale graduated at the top of the Harvard Class of 1879, and was chosen class poet, delivering what was described as a "strikingly original poem" at the class day celebrations.[5] After graduation, he spent three years in Europe, planning to become an architect. When he returned home in 1882, he served for two years as private secretary to Harvard President Charles William Eliot. He then enrolled at the divinity school, graduating in 1886. He served under Everett Edward Hale at South Congregational Church, and also led the Benevolent Fraternity of Churches in Boston and taught homiletics at the divinity school.[6]

As Hale and Perkins began their ministerial careers, their denomination was trying to expand beyond its New England base, and both were called to launch new churches. In Edward Hale's case, it was in the New Jersey suburbs known as "the Oranges." Many Unitarians had moved out to those suburbs from New York City but were forced to gather in private homes as there were no established churches. With the support of the Rev. D. W. Morehouse, the AUA's superintendent of church extension work in the region, the First Unitarian Church of Essex County held its first meeting at the local Masonic Temple in January 1890. Before the end of the year, its members voted to call Edward Hale as their pastor, and in April 1891 he preached his first sermon.[7] Six months later, on October 27, 1891, the Hales' first child, Emily, was born.

Church records show that the congregation defined itself as Christian and practiced communion regularly. Edward Everett Hale presented the congregation with a new "communion set," and Emily's mother donated a communion cup in memory of her parents.[8] A church history prepared at the end of the twentieth century described the early congregation's beliefs this way:

> The core of our present stance—the creedlessness, the search for truth, the emphasis on service rather than salvation—existed already in 1890. [...] Our founding document, the 1890 constitution and bylaws, said, in Article 2, "We associate ourselves together as a Christian Church for the purpose of moral and religious improvement and of promoting truth and righteousness in the world, through the study, practice, and diffusion of pure religion, as taught by Jesus of Nazareth."

A statement, "Our Faith," formulated a few years before the church's founding by James Freeman Clarke, a prominent Unitarian, was posted on the Sunday School's wall. Five points defined his "theology of the future":

- The Fatherhood of God
- The Brotherhood of Man
- The Leadership of Jesus
- Salvation by Character
- Progress of Mankind onward and upward forever.

Prominent local citizens served as early church leaders, including the uncle of Franklin D. Roosevelt and Wilson and Margaret Farrand, parents of Margaret Farrand Thorp, who was born within weeks of Emily and became her lifelong friend. Wilson Farrand later served on the Princeton Board of Trustees.

In March 1892, the congregation purchased the property on Cleveland Street in Orange where the church is still located. The following November, the congregation broke ground on its first chapel. At Edward Hale's proposal, the church changed its worship service to give the congregation a more prominent role, with more singing and reading from the Psalms. Emily's father also urged his church to take stands on social issues.

On February 7, 1893, the *New York Evening Post* reported that he called on his congregants "to use all possible effort [...] to rouse such public indignation as will compel a repeal" of a new law that had legalized gambling on horse racing in New Jersey. After listening to his sermon, the congregation adopted a resolution opposing "the obnoxious law."[9]

But suburban New Jersey was tough territory for evangelizing Unitarians. Twenty years later, the *Newark Evening News* recounted the church's early history under the headline: "Changed View on Unitarians: No Longer Ostracized, as Was Case When Orange Church Was Organized." The congregation, it said, "has come to be recognized as one of the leading churches of the community, overcoming the prejudice that was exhibited toward the denomination when the church was started."[10] For many years, the only local congregation that was willing to co-operate with Hale's church was the Swedenborgians.

Rev. Hale had taught the art of delivering sermons, and he was frequently called on to lecture or participate in services with other faith communities. Two years after he arrived, he spoke at All Souls' Church in Bridgewater, New Jersey, on "A Summer in Jersey."[11] In September 1893, he received a one-year appointment to lecture at Harvard on the subject of Congregational Polity.[12] A year later, he delivered a paper at a Unitarian conference in Baltimore.[13] In 1895, he spoke when the cornerstone was laid for the new temple of a nearby Jewish congregation.[14] His daughter undoubtedly learned some of her own public speaking skills from years of listening to her father.

Five years after he assumed the pulpit, Hale's congregation had grown to sixty-three dues-paying families. In his stewardship pitch that year, he proposed contributing to the Calhoun School, which promoted "civilization and education among the negroes in Alabama," and whose principal had recently appealed to the congregation for support. "The school is not denominational in its teaching," Hale wrote, "but its circumstances are such that it must depend chiefly upon those of our faith to support it."[15] (Seventy years later, his daughter would make a significant gift to a secondary school for Black youths in North Carolina that was started by acolytes of Booker T. Washington.)

During those years, as the wife of a pastor, Hale's mother was also active in church life, playing a traditional leadership role in the congregation's women's auxiliary. In 1896, she spoke to the group about the anti-slavery work of William Henry Furness, a nineteenth-century Unitarian abolitionist; previously she read extracts from "Prof. Adler's discourse on the religious training of the young in which he deprecated parents bringing up children to their beliefs." The reference was likely to Austrian psychiatrist Alfred Adler, a contemporary of Sigmund Freud.[16]

A year later, on April 25, 1897, Rev. Hale submitted his resignation, effective July 1, to return to Harvard Divinity School as an assistant professor of homiletics. The church's board of trustees accepted the resignation "with great regret." But just as the Hales were returning to Boston, tragedy struck: their toddler son, William, died of dysentery, a few days before his second birthday. Hale's mother suffered a breakdown and was institutionalized at McLean Hospital in Belmont, Massachusetts, for the rest of her life. In what must have been a traumatic transition, a few months later her husband began serving as pastor of the First Church of Chestnut Hill in the upscale suburbs west of Boston.

Hale's congregation was made up of socially prominent families, people like the Saltonstalls, the Lowells, and the Lees, who had founded a nearby rural chapel in 1861. One of the Lees was Alice Hathaway Lee, the first wife of Theodore Roosevelt. Mary Lee, another family member, was a contemporary of Emily Hale's who became a journalist and well-known author. In a congregational history, Lee acknowledged that Chestnut Hill was "hetrogeneous [sic] in the extreme." From the families who lived there "in the early days" came, among others, US Senator Leverett Saltonstall; US District Court Judge James Arnold Lowell; Mary Hale Lowell, the countess of Berkeley; Mary Kingsbury Simkhovitch, director of Greenwich House, a New York settlement house; Mary Ursula Burrage, superintendent of Children's Island Sanitarium; and Kenneth Murdock, who joined the English faculty at Harvard soon after Eliot left.[17]

The Chestnut Hill congregation had stopped meeting in 1881, but as the new century approached, the surrounding population was growing "so rapidly that it soon became apparent that the Sunday services in the Chapel could be resumed," according to a later church history. When Rev. Hale arrived in 1897, he "proved to be just the individual needed to get the Church going again."[18] Mary Lee, who knew both Emily and her father, recalled that "Under Mr. Hale's ministry, and due largely to his influence, the congregation became once more a coherent whole." With Hale's leadership, the congregation raised the money to build a larger church. Hale lent his architectural skills to the design of the building, which was dedicated in 1910 (Rev. Samuel Eliot delivered the main address) and still stands today.[19]

As she moved into her twenties, Emily Hale may have been called on to perform some of the traditional roles of a pastor's wife. On New Year's Day 1913, she was one of eight women—including Grace and Rosamond Eliot, granddaughters of the former Harvard president—who served refreshments at a large reception at the AUA's headquarters on Beacon Street.[20] The Unitarian-affiliated Lend-a-Hand Dramatic Club was among the amateur companies with whom Hale also performed during those years.[21]

Eliot's later letters to Hale suggest that he had visited her home and met her father in 1913–14, the years he tried to court her. Early in their correspondence, Eliot recalled attending a performance of *Tristan und Isolde* with her "parents," though that memory may have been faulty, considering that her mother was then institutionalized.[22] When they began their intense correspondence in 1930, it appears Hale told Eliot about her father's sudden death four years after he had left Boston. Eliot responded, "I can understand how close you & your father were" (December 2, 1930). A few years later, when Hale was forty and Eliot was still married, he invoked the memory of her father as he considered the propriety of traveling to visit her in California. "I feel almost as if I were in direct contact with your Father in such matters," he wrote, "and certainly I feel as much consideration for what he would think and feel, as if he were actually present" (May 13, 1932).

The Chestnut Hill church histories provide few details about Rev. Hale's death. "Mr. Hale's health gave way in 1916," Lee wrote, "and he was obliged to be away for many months."[23] The 1986 history reported, "Unfortunately for Mr. Hale and for the Church in 1916 he became seriously ill and went south in an attempt to recuperate."[24] On March 26, 1918, Hale had been scheduled to deliver one of the Holy Week sermons at King's Chapel, the "mother church" of Unitarianism, but may not have appeared, because the *Boston Globe* reported that he died at home the next day "after a few days' illness."[25] Hale's obituaries underscored the many prominent ways he had served his denomination, including editing the *Christian Register* for part of a year, and managing Harvard's Appleton Chapel during the absence of its regular overseer. In 1901, the Unitarians' Meadville Theological School, then located in Pennsylvania, elected him as its president, but he chose not to accept the post.[26]

Hale taught at Harvard until 1906. At the request of the divinity school, he began reconstructing the course lectures of its late longtime dean, the Rev. Dr. Charles Carroll Everett. It was considered an "enormous" task because Hale had to rely solely on notes taken by Everett's students, a younger generation of Unitarian ministers who had been inspired by their professor. Everett's "work on The Science of Thought shows the depth and vigor of his thinking," one Unitarian history concluded, "but his volumes on The Gospel of Paul, Religions before Christianity, Poetry, Comedy, and Duty, suggest the breadth of his inquiries and the richness of his philosophical investigations."[27] After reconstructing one of Everett's courses in *The Psychological Elements of Religious Faith*, Hale added another in *Theism and the Christian Faith*. Hale's preface to the volume provides no clues about his own beliefs, but, as a student, he likely was inspired by Everett's philosophy and teachings and in accord with them if recruited to reconstruct the lectures.

Emily Hale and Eliot later differed in how they viewed the sacrament of communion. He came to believe it should be restricted to those who had had a "proper" Christian baptism in the name of the Triune God. But Hale came of age when the Unitarians were moving toward a less formal, more personal remembrance of Christ's Last Supper. Her father's reconstruction of one of the dean's lectures on baptism and communion read:

> As regards the communion, the fact that the Church has chosen this method to commemorate its founder is enough. It is first of all a service of commemoration; in how intense a form we do not always remember. It goes back without a break to the tenderest moment in the life of Jesus. [...] One should bear in mind that in all that is essential it is a very simple service, and also that it is a service which has been newly consecrated again and again by

the holy men and women, the heroic lives, who in every age have joined in it. Furthermore, it is a symbol both of the profound mysticism which underlies all true religion and especially the Christian religion, and also of the manner in which the daily life of men should be transfigured.[28]

Similarly, in his 1902 book, *Unitarianism in America*, George W. Cook described mainstream Unitarian practices this way:

The last twenty years of the nineteenth century saw an increased use of the simpler Christian rites in Unitarian churches. In that time a distinct advance was made in the acceptableness of the communion service, and probably in the number of those willing to join in its observance. The abandonment of its mystical features and its interpretation as a simple memorial service, that would help to cherish loved ones gone hence, and the saintly and heroic of all ages, as well as the one great leader of the Christian body, has given it for Unitarians a new spiritual effectiveness.[29]

After Edward Hale died, Mary Lee wrote that the Chestnut Hill church would always remember him "for his great earnestness, his genuine friendliness, his finely cultivated intelligence and his deep conviction of the uselessness of war, the truth of which some of us who went overseas in [World War I] came home doubly convinced."[30] Elmer Osgood Cappers, a member of the church's next generation, wrote that Hale's pastorate was "truly a bridge between the Old Chapel and the new Church." After Hale's death, an endowment fund was created in his memory and a stained-glass window installed over the church's main entrance, noting the years of his life and service to the church. Emily later provided a portrait of her father for the minister's study. It depicted, in Cappers's words, "a scholarly man, one who deserved the title 'saintly,' so often given to him in comments by his parishioners."[31]

Rev. Hale was remembered with respect and admiration. According to an unidentified clipping in his file in the Harvard Divinity School's Archives:

> He was peculiarly rich in spiritual graces, and that too, not by inheritance so much as by his own spiritual industry. Never was there a sincerer or a more thorough-going Christian. The precepts which many other ministers only preach were with him personal matters, rules of private conduct in daily operation upon his own life. He recommended nothing that he did not make it a personal duty to practice. His sincerity was transparent.

Describing Hale as a parish minister, the admirer observed, "People knew they could trust him and so they followed him. He spoke to them with an authority which many a greater preacher has utterly lacked, because he held himself under the same authority. [...] He preached not so much with his lips, as by the object-lesson of his own life." But Rev. Hale was also recognized for his skill in homiletics. "He possessed a rare combination of qualifications," the eulogy said, "not only knowledge of the technique, which he conscientiously imparted to his classes, but also the spiritual passion to help, to be of service, to labor for others' benefit, which he unconsciously but none the less effectively imparted."[32]

The death of Hale's father forced her to find a job and sell their home in Chestnut Hill. She left the parish, but religion continued to play an important role in her life. She began working, first as a dorm matron and later as a speech and drama teacher at several women's colleges and private schools that were steeped in a Protestant ethic and featured regular, often mandatory, chapel sessions. When her Simmons College colleague Lucia Briggs discussed hiring Hale at the start of Briggs's long tenure as president of Milwaukee-Downer College, Hale's religious background was a consideration. The college had formed from a merger of two schools, Milwaukee College and Downer College. The former began as the Milwaukee Female Seminary, founded by Lucy Parsons, wife of a Congregational minister, who reached out for help from Catharine Beecher, daughter of the activist Presbyterian minister Lyman Beecher. As she prepared to take the college's helm, Briggs was advised that the college was "a Protestant Christian school and our faculty should be in sympathy with that fact." At the time of its merger in 1895, Downer College's leaders insisted that three-fourths of the college's trustees be members of the Presbyterian or Congregational churches. By the time

Briggs arrived in 1921, the college was still very Protestant in spirit, but formally described as "non-sectarian."[33]

When Briggs broached hiring Hale as a speech and drama teacher, Briggs's predecessor, Ellen Sabin, opposed hiring someone who lacked a college degree. But she let Briggs make her case for Hale's "superior" credentials. Sabin said the candidate's "age and her church" would be considerations. Briggs did not cite Hale's own level of church participation, but said her father was "a Unitarian minister" and "one of the first men in his class at Harvard."[34]

Each school day at Milwaukee-Downer included a mandatory, twenty-minute chapel session, which, Sabin told Briggs, "always consisted of the Scripture reading, a prayer, either read or extemporaneous, one or more hymns, such comment on any subject, religious, educational, political as she considered pertinent," and daily announcements. Sabin noted, "We have never had any objection made on the part of Catholic or Jewish students to being present. I remember, I think, one instance only of a Catholic girl who asked to be excused from attending chapel. [...] I think my Jewish girl never made an objection." During Briggs's years as president, she was remembered for her regular prayer: "Help us to stand for the hard right against the easy wrong."[35] Briggs herself was the granddaughter of a Unitarian minister, but in Milwaukee, Unitarians were harder to find than in Boston. One of Hale's students later recalled that she and Hale had attended a Unitarian church together, and a local Unitarian family had invited them to dinner from time to time.[36]

Hale was often involved with Christmas traditions at the schools where she taught. In her first year at Scripps College in California, she adapted what was described as "an old English Nativity play" for the college's Christmas pageant.[37] Just before Christmas 1933, she co-directed a production of *L'Annonce faite à Marie*, by Paul Claudel, a Frenchman whose verse plays were steeped in the conservative Catholic beliefs he shared with Eliot.[38] At Smith College in 1937, the one school where Hale was *not* in charge of the drama program, she collaborated with the college's Congregational chaplain, the Rev. Burns Chalmers, on an evening service during the Christmas season. It featured three tableaux: "The Prophecy," "The Nativity," and "The Light of the World." The final section included a reading of Eliot's "O Light Invisible" chorus from *The Rock*.[39] At Abbot

Academy in Andover, Massachusetts, Hale's last extended teaching post, her "Christmas reading" was usually featured in the published fall calendar.[40] In December 1956, she directed her senior drama class in a Spanish Christmas miracle story, Gregorio Sierra's *Holy Night*, and was asked to reprise it for the local Catholic church.[41]

The Christmas offerings were most elaborate at Milwaukee-Downer, where English professor Emily Brown directed a large annual production, drawing on Hale's assistance while she taught there. In 1928, Hale's final Christmas in Milwaukee, Brown introduced a new play, *The Little Sanctuary*, based on sixteenth-century Nativity plays. Hale was called on to sing "antiphons" as the Cantor, and to portray the elderly New Testament figure Simeon.[42] Brown was effusive about Hale's performance. "You, yourself, must have felt the silence with which both audiences hung on every word that fell from your lips. Our clergy are loud in praise of the interpretation." Brown said the play revivified "a theme that is sadly neglected in these parlous times."[43]

Hale taught at Milwaukee-Downer for most of the decade before she began her lengthy correspondence with Eliot. The Midwest college's leaders promoted the same kind of liberal education that Eliot had received at Harvard and Oxford, and Sabin had filled her faculty with Congregationalists, Presbyterians, and Episcopalians. Like their New England counterparts, the small liberal arts colleges of Wisconsin "made the tacit assumption that it was the classical curriculum that facilitated their ability both to train the mind to think (to achieve 'mental discipline') and to develop Christian character and devotion of public service," noted one history of the college.[44] Briggs herself was well steeped in that tradition because her father was LeBaron Russell Briggs, who had served as president of Radcliffe and dean of Harvard. Scripps, where Hale taught a few years later, was the second of the Claremont Colleges, founded by Congregationalists, again drawing on the models of Oxford and Cambridge.

As Hale began to travel to Europe in the 1920s, she experienced a range of religious experiences, writing in 1927 about visiting Assisi, Italy, "sacred to the memory of St. Francis and St. Clara," passing a religious procession in a mountain town in Umbria, attending mass with villagers outside of Milan, viewing *The Last Supper*, and accepting hospitality from a priest in a monastery courtyard.[45] A year later, she described attending services at King's Chapel in Cambridge, England, and visiting some of that country's great cathedrals.[46]

After her father died, Hale spent an increasing amount of time in the company of her uncle, John Carroll Perkins. After serving for a few years as a school teacher, he graduated from Harvard Divinity School in 1891, and the following year married Hale's maternal aunt, Edith Milliken. Perkins served a church in Portland, Maine, for more than twenty years, then traveled west to Seattle, founding University Unitarian Church near the campus of the University of Washington and serving as its pastor from 1914 to 1926. During the late nineteenth century, the Unitarians had concluded that targeting college communities was one of their most effective ways of "extending Unitarianism as a modern interpretation of Christianity."[47] In 1922, Perkins received a call to Arlington Street Church in Boston, but decided to stay on in the Pacific Northwest, where, it was felt, his new church and the wider denomination needed his leadership more.[48] Throughout the 1920s, Hale spent several summer vacations in Seattle, and traveled to Europe with her aunt and uncle in 1927, just before Perkins was asked to serve for six months as minister-in-charge of King's Chapel.

Perkins's duties were carefully detailed by the chapel's leaders: he had full responsibility for all the worship services, made arrangements for its daily services, conducted Sunday services when other preachers were present, assumed the pastoral care of the parish, conducted worship services for the Sunday School, and attended church committee meetings. Perkins's term was repeatedly extended for short periods until he was installed as the chapel's minister in 1931. He retired as minister emeritus two years later, but played an important role in the celebrations that marked the chapel's 250th anniversary in 1936. At a service that year that featured a prayer for "the old motherland across the sea," and displayed an antique communion set on the altar, Perkins recalled the history of the chapel, founded as the first Anglican church in the American colonies.[49]

Eliot spent much more time with Hale's uncle than with her father, socializing with the Perkinses during the year he spent at Harvard in 1932–33 and later during his visits to their summer rental in Chipping Campden. Perkins outlived his brother-in-law by more than thirty years, and his conservative theological views likely were closer to Eliot's own. He was interested in church history, and produced the third volume of *Annals of King's Chapel* a few years after he retired. At the time of his death, his successor at that church, Palfrey Perkins, recalled that his late colleague had

> rejoiced in [the chapel's] rich historical background, in the preservation of its ties with the past and with the Mother Country. [...] Though he watched with critical and not always approving eye the more recent developments of Unitarianism, he remained steadfastly loyal to what he delighted to call Unitarian Christianity. Conservative though he was, his alert and active mind kept in close touch with the changing thoughts and activities of the times.[50]

Although Eliot later described Perkins as "a dear old man, but woolyminded,"[51] he seemed to have been more of a conservative religious soulmate to Eliot than Emily Hale was. While Hale was increasingly required to tend to the needs of her aging relatives, there is no indication she fully embraced her uncle's religious views. Notably, she also did not appear to cite the views of her relatives when she asked Eliot why he could not seek a divorce.

After 1930, the relationship between Hale and Eliot evolved mostly through their letters, punctuated by visits on both sides of the Atlantic, some longer and more significant than others. Initially, Hale was likely puzzled by Eliot's decision to become an Anglican, but seems to have been a tolerant listener as he shared his religious opinions. Still, she may have felt uncomfortable about the way his early letters venerated her.

As they began to explore the details of each other's lives, Eliot told her, "No doubt, it is because of my weakness that the discipline and routine of Catholicism is necessary for me, though circumstances prevent my practicing and meditating all that I should; but communion twice a week and Sunday High Mass have become the minimum essential to support me." He told Hale that because she was "naturally in a much higher state of grace" than he was, that she would not need "the detailed precise beliefs that I need" (March 4, 1931).

A few months later, he asked Hale whether she read the Bible or said prayers at bedtime. He added that he got satisfaction out of praying for the persons he cared about, and for the persons they cared about, both living and dead (June 1, 1931). It's not clear whether or how Hale responded. At the end of 1931, Eliot observed that Hale seemed "to have a good deal of work in connexion with the Church" (December 29, 1931). (That letter arrived during the time Hale's uncle was in charge of King's Chapel and she was attending at least some services there.) As Eliot's year at Harvard approached, Hale suggested he could deliver a lecture at that church, and offered "The Influence of the Bible upon English Literature" as a possible topic; Eliot agreed it was a good idea (June 21, 1932).[52]

Eliot's letters to Hale were peppered with references to prayers for her and her relatives, his practices on Catholic holy days (on those days, the letters were usually dated by the religious holiday), and spiritual advice to Hale. In one example of the latter, Eliot expressed concern that she was experiencing an "acute spiritual crisis" in the summer of 1931. The crisis may have actually been a financial one since Hale did not have a regular job. Eliot wrote, "What I want to remind you is that you might, in consequence, be in danger of missing the two great Christian virtues: Humility and Hope; and if you did you would be wandering in the wilderness indeed. [...] Hope, too, is not only a blessed gift but a duty. And Despair is really a sin" (August 11, 1931). The following year, Hale seems to have described Eliot's religious pronouncements as "sermons." Eliot responded, "All they amount to is my reflection upon my own experience and struggles; and when I feel that there is a parallel between your life and mine I am impelled to talk about myself" (May 3, 1932).

After they spent time together and their relationship deepened, they challenged each other about their religious views—probably originating in their differences over whether Eliot could or should divorce Vivien. In February 1933, Eliot wrote, "I prefer a person who has committed almost any sin and had to gain virtue through suffering; and I think the Gospels confirm this." He observed that Unitarianism was an "easy" religion to follow for people who live sheltered lives, and noted it had served his parents' needs. But he believed that "it lets you down" when you move from a Unitarian society. By contrast, "the Catholic faith expects more, and gives more; and it is there to support you when you find yourself isolated, as I have been, in the midst of pagans" (February 27, 1933).

In the same letter, he told Hale that the more he loved her, the more he wanted to quarrel with her over things, both small and large. And that included their religious beliefs. "The fact that I am a Trinitarian, and that you are a Unitarian, matters very much to me. It means a Fight. Of course I mean to win, Very likely I shant." When he entered Catholic households, he felt "in communion" with those people in ways he was not with her, because she would view their beliefs as "degraded superstitions." And, he observed, she did not go to church regularly—or at least as regularly as he did. Yet, he said, "all the things which might seem to divide me more completely from Emily are really things that attach me to her more closely."

They began discussing divorce on New Year's Eve, 1932, when Eliot was visiting her at Scripps College, and it remained a recurring topic for many years. In perhaps his strongest response to Hale's queries about divorce, Eliot wrote in November 1933 that "there is nothing in *this* world that I would not give up without hesitation if I had even the slightest hope that you would accept me as your husband." But, he went on,

> the position of the Church is completely uncompromising about the indissolubility of marriage. [...] I think that my responsibility to society counts more with me. I am—I can say it without the slightest vanity—the most conspicuous layman in the Church to-day, and my defection would be all the more significant because I was not born into it. I should of course be excommunicate, I should no longer take any part in Church affairs, and if I ever raised my voice to speak for the Faith or attack paganism I should meet only with ridicule and contempt.

It would amount, he concluded, to the "triumph of the enemies of Christianity" (November 19, 1933).

While divorce was rare among Hale's friends, it was not unknown to her. Barbara Hinkley, Eliot's first cousin, divorced her husband because of his infidelities and later remarried a divorced man (August 9, 1932). Conrad Aiken and E. E. Cummings, Harvard contemporaries of Eliot's that Hale knew, had also divorced their first wives. Dorothy Elsmith, who provided Hale and Eliot with a private place to meet in the United States, divorced her second husband during World War II. Over the years, Eliot acknowledged that his marriage to Vivien had taken place in a registry office rather than a church, and told Hale about his own infidelities. But he did not share whatever he suspected or knew of Vivien's. Unless Eliot were willing to accuse his wife of infidelity, obtaining a divorce would, he argued, require Vivien to cooperate, and he did not believe that she would (for example, June 1, 1933).

At Princeton, Hale sequestered a significant letter on this topic from Ada Eliot Sheffield, Eliot's sister. In October 1933, Eliot encouraged Hale to reach out to Ada, and his favorite sibling provided her with this advice:

> Your very difficult questions I will answer in accordance with my best understanding of Tom. I think you underestimate the strength of his feeling toward his Church. Mrs. Hinkley believes his change of faith to have been an escape from personal unhappiness. In my own opinion, while this may have played a part, the roots of his conversion go much deeper than that. His writing and his talk all reveal a profound sense of the value of tradition, reaching back far into the past, changing by slow growth, but never breaking with what has gone before. He attends mass with great regularity, makes confession as the Church requires, has attended a religious retreat this fall. He speaks at Church conventions, is active in their counsels, and has three times this summer visited in the homes of leading clergymen. Moreover, the Church is backing him in this most trying step he is taking. If he accepts this backing for a separation, which is the most the Church will endorse, and then, having got this much, were to leave the Church, in order to get a more complete release from his bonds than they would recognize, he would feel himself to be doing something unhandsome.
>
>   This brings me to another aspect of the matter. Were Tom to give up his Church for the sake of a woman—which I do not believe he would ever do—his respect for himself would suffer. This would inevitably end by affecting his feeling for the woman herself, and she would not be happy. [...]

> If you can continue [as] Tom's dearest friend, giving and receiving confidence and affection, you will be a constant source of happiness and strength to him. For you to suggest anything else would, I believe merely cause him added suffering.

Ada acknowledged that "alike as Tom and I are in some respects, we are different in just those respects that make him a devout Anglo-Catholic and me an equally reverent—as I hope—agnostic." Tom, she concluded, "will never again be a Unitarian, and he is a man whose nature craves a religion."[53]

After Hale and Eliot shared an intensely romantic time in London in the final months of 1935, Hale asked Eliot whether there was, as he characterized it, "some tribunal which had the function of handling special cases of unfortunate marriage, and granting dispensation" (March 3, 1936). Eliot continued to try to temper her expectations. "We may and do hope that we may be ultimately united. But we know that there is very little on which to build such a hope" (February 21, 1936). Eliot said he could not foresee that church law or common law would change in a way that would permit his marriage to be dissolved.

But in late 1937, Parliament *did* amend England's civil divorce laws to broaden the grounds for divorce. A divorce could now be granted when a spouse was judged to be incurably of unsound mind and had been continuously under treatment for at least five years. As World War II broke out in fall of 1939, and Hale anticipated another long separation, she raised the topic again. Eliot maintained that the legislation "has no bearing upon it. I am afraid that patience has to have deeper foundations than illusory hopes." He closed, "We must try to submerge our own griefs in those of the world, which were never greater than now" (October 7, 1939).

Hale still pressed back, this time referencing Vivien's institutionalization the previous year. Eliot responded that the Anglican church did not recognize insanity as grounds for divorce unless it could be proved that the spouse was too demented when they wed to be able to make a valid contract. He added, "If I should eventually take advantage of the facilities offered by the State I should be doing something which from the point of view of the Church was morally wrong." This time he added, "I must tell you that I have been very miserable over this correspondence on these subjects; and the self-reproach to which it leads, is much increased by the terror of setting you more firmly in opposition to the Catholic Faith" (November 24, 1939).

Eliot thus continued to fall back on his religious beliefs to deflect Hale's desire to marry. Eliot was also said by some of his biographers to have taken a "vow of celibacy" in 1928, but Jayme Stayer of Loyola University Chicago has challenged that notion, noting that the only vow an Anglican layperson could make at that time was the marriage vow itself.[54]

There are hints that Hale and Eliot sometimes attended church together. During his visit to California, friends of Hale's drove them to a nearby Episcopal church. In October 1935, Eliot, Hale, and the Perkinses attended services at St. George's Chapel in Windsor.[55] Eliot later referenced "the vicar of Campden," presumably the pastor of the Anglican Church of St. James in Chipping Campden, close to the home where they stayed (October 13, 1942). As Eliot was beginning to compose "Burnt Norton" after Hale's longest visit to England, he wrote, "Whenever I go to early Mass, and kneel in the pew in that rather dismal church, I think of the last time—and the first time it was there,—when we knelt together in the early morning; and I am always always conscious of your absence, and I feel that you *ought* to be there with me" (January 16, 1936).[56]

But a quarter-century later, Eliot recalled those experiences differently. In the letter he sent Harvard to coincide with the opening of Hale's letters, he expressed his frustration that he could "never make her understand that it was improper for her, a Unitarian, to communicate in an Anglican church." Eliot claimed Hale was oblivious to "the fact that it shocked me" and he could "not help thinking that if she had truly loved me she would have respected my feelings if not my theology." While they were still corresponding, Eliot expressed his annoyance with clergy who lowered their standards and served communion to Unitarians like Hale. These included the vicars of St. John's Church in Northampton (October 17, 1936) and the church in Campden (October 13, 1942, September 26, 1946). Their conflict broke out most dramatically in the fall of 1946, shortly after a romantic reunion after the war. Hale apparently told Eliot she had taken communion, and he likened it to violating the rules of a private club, rules that he said it was his duty to enforce (September 26, 1946). Over the next two months, they continued to argue over the issue, Hale asserting, in the words of Eliot, that her "whole nature cries out against limiting attendance at the communion table" (November 9, 1946). Communion *was*, in fact, part of Hale's faith tradition, and during her lifetime, Unitarians were becoming increasingly tolerant of how their congregations celebrated it.

Hale's different view of communion was reflected in a remembrance she wrote of a weekend she spent in May, 1936, at Senexet, a Unitarian retreat house in the Connecticut countryside. For Hale, the "height of the retreat" came when she discovered the center's simple, candlelit chapel, where tears came "at once to my eyes. Whether at a communion service, or daily homily, we worshipped a spirit breathlessly close to us, and felt the presence of loved ones whose spirit also was by us. To kneel before the little light on the altar was like coming to the Inn at Bethlehem."[57] Hale's words echo how George Cook characterized what communion meant to Unitarians at the start of the twentieth century, a way to cherish the memory of departed loved ones, such as Hale's father.

An intriguing, undated short story can be found in Hale's papers at Smith College, describing an episode set at what seems to be St. Michael's Church in Beaulieu-sur-Mer, France, an English-speaking Anglican congregation on the French Riviera. (Hale likely visited the church in 1934–35.) The narrator vividly describes the church as "among the precious places which hold the affections deeply, as if a very bit of ourselves were left happily behind to join the blessed company of All Souls who have preceded us." The story describes a Sunday service, attended by the bishop of the diocese. The narrator finds herself dozing off during the sermon, "purely theological, interesting to students of theology perhaps, but frankly disappointing to me on such an occasion." Suddenly, the spell is broken by a "short sharp cracking little explosion, followed by a patter, like fragments of splintered glass." Inexplicably, the "simple small glass cruet that holds the Holy Sacrament" had shattered, leaving "a quiet red pool" on the pavement stones, and the "faint sweet smell of grapes" wafting through the church. The narrator describes how the priests scurried to pretend that nothing unusual had happened. As the service "proceeded reverently," the narrator wonders if the "strange little incident, now so completely and expertly disregarded, had occurred."

At a later reception, the narrator observes to the vicar, "In the old days, it would have been considered an omen for good or for evil." Later, as she walks to the beach, she reflects that "blessings *do* come in strange disguises, as I heard again the sharp patter of the broken glass and smelt the sweet native wine. I recalled, too, my words to the little vicar about omens."[58]

After sharing her story with Eliot, Hale asked whether anything could be done with it. He described it as "an excellently written account of an odd small event—as a record it needs no improvement." While he said he found the story interesting because he knew the author, he asserted that it needed more dramatic intensity, and that could only be accomplished if the wine were "consecrated," a device he felt could not be managed "with good taste" (August 16, 1935).

Following her romantic time with Eliot in England in the fall of 1935, Hale struggled to find a new job and wrestled over her future with Eliot, including their religious differences. She seems to have made a pitch for tolerance, arguing that the Unitarian church was an institution, not a defined belief system. In response, Eliot made a distinction between Christian "behavior" and the label conferred by the rite of baptism. He then added:

> If I were to set myself up as "a better Christian" or as *more* Christian, than your relatives or for that matter my own, I should be guilty both of a confusion of terms and of a mortal sin of pride. [...] When I spoke of baptism, it was merely a statement of fact. I also was baptised as a Unitarian, but I had to be baptised again to be admitted to the Church of England: because Unitarian baptism is not in the Name of the Father, the Son and the Holy Ghost.

Eliot concluded that Hale's views amounted to "a rather intolerant form of tolerance" (March 24, 1936).

During these years, Unitarians were struggling to define themselves as a denomination, and battling over whether to retain references to Christ in their official documents. Hale's uncle later observed (in "A Unitarian Denomination") that at a 1925 Boston meeting, the AUA had voted to eliminate "Christian phraseology" from its bylaws and declared that its purpose was to promote "pure religion." During his Harvard sabbatical, Eliot told Hale that her uncle had given him "a very depressing account of the decay of the Unitarian Church," including "a really abominable heretical saying" delivered by his paternal uncle, Rev. Christopher Rhodes Eliot (May 21, 1933). Over the next quarter-century, Perkins grew increasingly troubled as the denomination broadened its outlook and became less doctrinaire.[59]

Hale continued to write Eliot about religious tolerance. In response, he hoped she would not think "that I undervalue or dispute the fundamental Christianity of people who are not technically Christians." He further hoped that she could distinguish his "personal arrogance" from his "maintenance of impersonal distinctions." He argued that there was a "difference between intolerance, and being *indifferent* to distinctions" (April 7, 1936). That point, however, may have been lost on Hale.

Hale's retreat to Senexet contrasted with those that Eliot made to austere monasteries. Before she went, he told her that the maintenance of complete silence was "a most desirable and necessary rule, in my opinion. One should not be bothered by the personalities of one's fellow-retreaters" (May 18, 1936). But Hale had a different experience. The retreat center was managed by Velma Wright Williams, widow of the Rev. Theodore Chickering Williams, a friend of Hale's father and another leader profiled in Samuel Eliot's *Heralds of a Liberal Faith*. Velma Williams survived her husband by twenty-five years, and was credited in that volume for establishing Senexet House "as a place for spiritual refreshment and the deepening of religious life."[60] The center was a transformed Victorian-era summer home, situated on eleven forested acres. "On a most lovely early spring day," Hale recalled in her essay five years later, "the great pines gave the first welcome—one can never forget the impressiveness of that grove." As Hale described it, the center's ambience was more like that of an attractive bed-and-breakfast inn than a monastery cell. Still, the weekend was an emotional one. Williams, she recalled, presided "like a wise abbess," who placed "her flock" so that "strangers might become friends, congenial spirit meet congenial spirit." Merriment, Hale added, "was the wholesome leaven often at these hours, for she loved quick wit and happy exchange of experiences."

Around that time, Hale accepted a job at Smith College, and Eliot visited her there in the fall of 1936. Afterwards, he told her he was disappointed he had not been able to visit St. John's, the Episcopalian church on the edge of the campus. Hale had begun attending services there, a sign that she may have been trying to better understand Eliot's faith and meet him halfway. After he returned home, Eliot fussed that if she intended "to make communions" there, she should contact the vicar to determine whether she needed "what we call a 'valid baptism.'" He added, "The rule of England is similar to that of the Roman Church; but the Episcopal Church in America is independent and I dare say have (sic) freer regulations" (October 17, 1936). A few weeks later, he said he was happy to learn that Hale *had* been baptized "in the Name of the Father and the Son and the Holy Ghost," but was puzzled why she thought the answer obvious, since he, and he supposed "most Unitarian babes," were not. He could not understand how anyone could be "a Unitarian and a Trinitarian at once" (November 25, 1936). Hale, on the other hand, was puzzled that Eliot did not consider her to be a Christian.

A few weeks later, Eliot wrote, "When you say that 'Unitarians believe' etc. you may be speaking for some Unitarians, but certainly not for those amongst whom I was brought up." Eliot cited the words of the same Unitarian "creed" that had been posted on the wall of her father's New Jersey church, and said he could not call those beliefs Christian. "It may be a 'religion', but it is not the Christian religion." But, he added, "you will realise perhaps that when it comes to discussing theology with *you*, I am on very difficult and delicate ground" (December 16, 1936).

Two months later, Hale told Eliot that she had spoken to Albion Ockenden, the rector of St. John's, about confirmation classes, but did not feel she had the time to go through the process during her first year at Smith. Eliot was sympathetic, but said he hoped she would follow through in the future. "After all," he said, "one cannot go on being a Unitarian and a Trinitarian at the same time" (February 12, 1937). A year later, Hale reported back, seeming to express some disappointment about the classes. Eliot responded sympathetically, suggesting that Ockenden might be "a wise man," but that priests who were "zealous for converts" did not always know how to work with adults from other faiths. Adults, he asserted, should be examined for evidence that they knew what they were doing "and that they realise that what they are taking is a very big step, the most important decision of their lives, and not merely an affirmation of something they have believed already." Eliot acknowledged that in his own case, his priest and the examining bishop "both assumed my qualifications a little too readily. I should have been kept waiting longer." He told Hale he was sure "that you were right to hold back," but that Ockenden's enthusiasm gave her "a greater responsibility to examine yourself and find out as clearly as possible what you do believe and what you don't" (January 28, 1938). Ockenden died later that year and Hale did not seem to pursue Episcopalian religious instruction after that.[61] When she returned to Northampton in retirement, a newspaper story described her as "an active member of the Unitarian Church" and a member of the Northampton Area Council of Churches.[62]

Over the years, Hale also remained connected to the congregations her father and uncle had served. In October 1936, she attended the seventy-fifth anniversary of the Chestnut Hill church, an event that also marked the twenty-fifth anniversary of the sanctuary her father had helped to design and build.[63] During her many summers in Seattle, Hale attended University Unitarian, the congregation her uncle had founded, and performed dramatic programs for its women's auxiliary. In November 1963, she returned to Seattle for the church's fiftieth anniversary.[64] In the late 1960s, she was still listed in the directory of "members and friends" of the Chestnut Hill church, even though she lived in Concord, about twenty miles away.[65] Hale's one and only home of her own was on Church Green, just a few steps from First Parish Church where she worshipped. At her memorial service there on October 16, 1969, her minister recalled that a friend had taken her to church the week before, and that she had been getting ready to attend services on the morning she died, just shy of her seventy-eighth birthday.

In his eulogy, the minister provided an overview of how Hale had practiced her faith over her lifetime: "She was of a line that is properly called traditional, and though I knew (as many of you did) that Emily Hale represented the finest and deepest kind of liberalism (in that she was totally honest, explicitly candid, and a great respector of human reason and freedom) the old and familiar language meant much to her." Hale, he noted, had specified the excerpts from the Book of Common Prayer to be read at her funeral. "One might almost see dear Emily at the moment nodding her solemn assent, and finding serene satisfaction in the antiquity and the preciousness of the sense of everlastingness of these ancient words. I also suspect that Emily would in the midst of her solemness, smile also because happiness and peace possess her." As to why Hale was getting ready to attend church on the morning she died, the pastor concluded,

> She was here I expect for a number of reasons—one of which must have been that her whole life was lived with reverence, and therefore the custom of giving expression to that reverence was a part of her very being. What was most important, however, was not the fact of going to church; it was rather that she had long ago discovered the meaning of her life. [...] She was not a religious lady because you often met her in church. She was a religious lady because she was a religious person to whom the days of her existence were exciting, opportunity-laden and colorful.[66]

After Hale's death, Dorothy Elsmith prepared a memorial remembrance that was distributed to Hale's friends. Elsmith wrote that Hale's Unitarian affiliations "were life-long and firm but never rigid." But Elsmith went beyond the Book of Common Prayer in selecting verses to frame her own document, reprinting a few lines from "East Coker" and "Little Gidding." Elsmith did not identify the poems or the poet. Nor did she explain why she had chosen those particular words. But at a time when well-known Eliot verses were turning up in eulogies and on tombstones all around the world, she also didn't have to.[67]

Notes

1. "Mrs. Sarah Emery Hooper," *Cambridge Chronicle*, February 21, 1914, 12; "Recent Deaths: Mrs. Samuel Thompson Hooper," *Boston Evening Transcript*, February 18, 1914, 7. Hooper's obituaries identified the organization as the "Woman's Alliance." Among her many accomplishments, Hooper also founded the Boston Cooking School and served on the Boston Sanitary Commission.
2. In 1913, Hale, Eliot, and Cummings were all performing with the Cambridge Social Dramatic Club.
3. *Heralds of a Liberal Faith, Vol. IV: Pilots*, ed. Samuel Atkins Eliot (Beacon Press, 1952), xvi–xvii. Two of T. S. Eliot's uncles were also profiled in the book.
4. *Heralds of a Liberal Faith*, 4:xxiii.

5   "Class Day," *Harvard Crimson*, June 20, 1879.
6   First Unitarian Universalist Church of Essex County, "Our Ministers," https://essexuu.org/ministers.html.
7   Paul Axel-Lute, excerpts from a lecture, "Notes on the History of the First Unitarian Universalist Church of Essex County (Orange, New Jersey)," delivered April 30, 2000, https://essexuu.org/history.html.
8   "Notes and Excerpts from the Archives of the First Unitarian Church of Essex County," December 6, 1981, https://essexuu.org/archives.html.
9   *New York Evening Post*, February 7, 1893, scrapbook clipping described in church archives.
10 *Newark Evening News*, January 17, 1910, scrapbook clipping described in church archives.
11 "Here and There," *Bridgewater Courier-News*, November 22, 1893, 1.
12 "Talent at Harvard; List of Lecturers and Instructors for the Coming Year," *Passaic Daily News*, September 28, 1893, 2.
13 "Unitarian Conference Adjourns," *New Brunswick Daily Times*, November 15, 1894.
14 Highlighted from scrapbook, church archives.
15 Rev. Edward Hale appeal letter, February 27, 1896, church scrapbook described in church archives.
16 Alliance notes from church archives.
17 Mary Lee, *A History of the Chestnut Hill Chapel* (published by the History Committee of The First Church in Chestnut Hill, 1937), 43, 70.
18 Elmer Osgood Cappers, *History of the First Church in Chestnut Hill, Newton, Massachusetts 1861–1986* (published by The First Church in Chestnut Hill, 1986), 13. Cappers was described to this author as an amateur historian and some of his facts appear to be incorrect. There seems to be no basis for his assertion that Emily Milliken Hale "gave devoted service to the First Church," since she was institutionalized around the time her husband became pastor.
19 Lee, *Chestnut Hill Chapel*, 41; Cappers, *First Church in Chestnut Hill*, 16.
20 "Unitarians Have 'Open House,'" *Boston Evening Transcript*, January 1, 1913, 6. Hale was close in age to the Eliot cousins, but they appeared to have moved in different social circles.
21 "Table Gossip," *Boston Globe*, April 12, 1914, 66; "Present Twelfth Night," *Boston Globe*, April 26, 1914, 7.
22 Letter of January 20, 1931, Emily Hale Letters from T. S. Eliot, C0686, Manuscripts Division, Department of Special Collections, Princeton University Library. All subsequent letters from this collection cited by date. As this volume was going to press, the full text of the letters became available at https://tseliot.com/the-eliot-hale-letters/letters.
23 Lee, *Chestnut Hill Chapel*, 42.
24 Cappers, *First Church in Chestnut Hill*, 20.

25 "Rev. Edward Hale, Pastor at Chestnut Hill, Dead," *Boston Globe*, March 28, 1918, 6; "Extra Holy Week Services to Be Held in King's Chapel," *Boston Globe*, March 22, 1918, 9.
26 Andover-Harvard Theological Library, Harvard Divinity School, Edward Hale profile, http://library.hds.harvard.edu/exhibits/featured-images/edward-hale; "Harvard Divinity School: The First Hundred Years," https://guides.library.harvard.edu/hds/1st-100/hds/19th-century-faculty. Hale was also offered the job of principal of Phillips Exeter Academy in New Hampshire, which he attended before entering Harvard. *Heralds of a Liberal Faith*, 4:154–55.
27 George Willis Cook, *Unitarianism in America: A History of Its Origin and Development* (American Unitarian Association, 1902), www.gutenberg.org/files/8605/8605-h/8605-h.htm#sn6.
28 Charles Carroll Everett, *Theism and the Christian Faith: Lectures Delivered in the Harvard Divinity School*, ed. Edward Hale (Harvard University Press, 1909), 491; "Preface," by W. W. Fenn, iii–iv; "Editor's Preface," by Edward Hale, v.
29 Cook, *Unitarianism in America*.
30 Lee, *Chestnut Hill Chapel*, 42.
31 Cappers, *First Church in Chestnut Hill*, 21. When an organ was installed in the church years later, the stained-glass window was blocked off; its design is no longer visible from either side.
32 Harvard Divinity School Archives, Edward Hale Folder.
33 Ellen C. Sabin to Lucia R. Briggs, April 30, 1921; May 18, 1921. The letters that the presidents exchanged at the start of Briggs's term are excerpted in "Faithfully Yours, Ellen C. Sabin: Correspondence between Ellen C. Sabin and Lucia R. Briggs from January, 1921 to August, 1921," ed. Virginia A. Palmer, *Wisconsin Magazine of History*, State Historical Society of Wisconsin, 67, no. 1 (1983).
34 Sabin to Briggs, May 18, 1921; Briggs to Sabin, June 2, 1921.
35 Sabin to Briggs, June 29, 1921. Frances Willard Hadley, "From a College Window," Mary Spicuzza Schmal Scrapbook, Milwaukee-Downer College Manuscripts, Lawrence University Archives.
36 Dorothea Packard Barr to Phil Hanrahan, June 27, 1989. The author is grateful to Hanrahan for providing copies of the notes and correspondence he saved from when he wrote his article "T. S. Eliot's Secret Love," which appeared in the summer 1990 issue of *Lawrence Today*.
37 *La Semeuse*, 1933, Scripps College Yearbook, 41.
38 "Acclaim Artistic French Production at Scripps College," *Pomona Progress-Bulletin*, December 13, 1933, 5.
39 Program, "Christmas Service in the Chapel," December 16, 1937, Emily Hale Papers, Smith College Archive, CA-MS-00344, Box 841, Folder 21, Smith College 1937–63 ("Emily Hale Papers" in subsequent notes).

40 See, for instance, "Fall Calendar—1954," *Abbot Academy Bulletin*, series 2, issue 1 (October 1954), 1.
41 Holy Night program, Emily Hale Papers, Folder 2, Abbot Academy, Andover, 1950–57; Emily Hale to Margaret, December 23, 1956, Emily Hale Letters, Other Letters, Box 14, Folder 6, Letters from Emily Hale to Willard and Margaret Thorp.
42 *1930 Cumtux*. Coincidentally, it was around this time that Eliot published his poem "A Song for Simeon."
43 Emily F. Brown to "My dear fellow worker," December 16, 1928, Emily Hale Papers, Folder 7, Correspondence, 1924–59.
44 Lynne H. Kleinman, *The Milwaukee-Downer Woman* (Lawrence University Press, 1997), 6, 31–32.
45 Emily Hale, "Impressions," *Kodak*, November 1927, 10–12.
46 Emily Hale, "Our Faculty in England," *Kodak*, November 1928, 4.
47 Cook, *Unitarianism in America*.
48 Edwin A Start, "Correspondence: Dr. Perkins Reconsiders His Call," *Christian Register*, August 31, 1922, 833.
49 Palfrey Perkins, "John Carroll Perkins," Harvard Divinity School Library, P: H. J. Paton, George F. Patterson, John Carroll Perkins, John E. Powers, Richardson, Robert Dale. Papers, 1920–69, bMS 108, bMS 108/16 (29), Box 16, Folder 29; John Carroll Perkins, *Annals of King's Chapel, Vol. 3: 1895–1940* (Little, Brown, 1940), 179, 194, copy in T. S. Matthews Papers, Princeton University Library, Manuscript Division, Department of Special Collections, C1131, Series 5, Subseries 5a, TSE Working Files, TSE Subject Files, Fo–W, Other Women Folder, Box 43, Folder 7. "King's Chapel 250 Years Old," *Boston Globe*, November 16, 1936, 2. There are slight discrepancies among the chronologies recounting Perkins's career. An essay Hale wrote about her uncle's funeral described the "Holy Communion Table" at the front of the church (Emily Hale, "The Last Honors for John Carroll Perkins," December 26, 1950, Emily Hale Papers, Publications Folder) and https://tseliot.com/the-eliot-hale-letters/appendix.
50 Palfrey Perkins, "John Carroll Perkins," remembrance, John Carroll Perkins folder.
51 "Statement by T. S. Eliot on the Opening of the Emily Hale Letters at Princeton," T. S. Eliot Foundation, January 2, 2020, https://tseliot.com/foundation/statement-by-t-s-eliot-on-the-opening-of-the-emily-hale-letters-at-princeton/.
52 Eliot's talk, "The Bible as Scripture and as Literature," was delivered on December 1, 1932. *Letters* 6:429n.
53 Ada E. Sheffield to Emily Hale, October 22, 1933, Emily Hale Letters from T. S. Eliot, Other Letters, 1895–1957, Letters from Others to Emily Hale, 1895–1943, Box 14, Folder 5; also https://tseliot.com/the-eliot-hale-letters/letters/l270.

54 Jayme Stayer, "What's Missing From the Hale Letters: Canonical and Historical Considerations in Anglo-Catholicism," paper delivered to the American Literature Association, May 24, 2022.
55 *Letters* 7:816n.
56 This church is unidentified, but Lyndall Gordon assumes it is St. Stephen's in Kensington, Eliot's home church. Lyndall Gordon, *The Hyacinth Girl: T. S. Eliot's Hidden Muse* (Virago Press, 2022), 223.
57 "For Senexet, November 5th, 1941," see Emily Hale Papers, Folder 15, Publications, 1928–51, and https://tseliot.com/the-eliot-hale-letters/appendix.
58 Undated, untitled typed story, Emily Hale Papers, Publications Folder, also https://tseliot.com/the-eliot-hale-letters/appendix.
59 John Carroll Perkins, "A Unitarian Denomination," undated paper distributed by the Unitarian Christian Fellowship, Perkins Folder, Harvard Divinity School Library. The paper was written in Perkins's final years because it references a 1947 event.
60 *Heralds of a Liberal Faith*, 4:255.
61 "Rev. Albion C. Ockenden," *New York Times*, August 6, 1938, 13.
62 "Miss Emily Hale Elected President of Woman's Club," *Daily Hampshire Gazette*, April 20, 1961, newspaper clipping, Emily Hale Papers, Folder 1, Biographical Material, 1936–90.
63 Lee, *Chestnut Hill Chapel*, 8.
64 "Unitarians to Note 50th Anniversary," *Seattle Times*, November 20, 1963, 42. Because the celebration was scheduled the weekend President Kennedy was assassinated, the events may not have come off as planned.
65 "Members and Friends of the First Church in Chestnut Hill," Mary Lee Papers, 1834–1982 (inclusive), 1915–49 (bulk), Schlesinger Library, Harvard University, MC 587, Series 1, Subseries G, "History of Chestnut Hill Chapel and related, 1892, 1936–1975," Correspondence, church history writings re: installation of new ministers, Box 39, Folder 9, 1962–70 Folder.
66 "Words from Memorial Service for Emily Hale," T. S. Matthews Papers, Box 43, Other Women Folder.
67 "Emily Hale: October 27, 1891–October 12, 1969," memorial remembrance, Emily Hale Papers, Biographical Materials Folder; Dorothy Olcott Elsmith to T. S. Matthews, January 17, 1973, T. S. Matthews Papers, Series 3: Correspondence, 1931–90, Dorothy O. Elsmith Correspondence Folder, Box 20, Folder 11.

Eliot among the Rag-Pickers
Waste, Hope, and the Ecocritical Imagination in *The Waste Land*

Sarah Kennedy

What are the roots that clutch, what branches grow
Out of this stony rubbish? Son of man,
You cannot say, or guess, for you know only
A heap of broken images, where the sun beats,
And the dead tree gives no shelter, the cricket no relief,
And the dry stone no sound of water.
—T. S. Eliot, *The Waste Land* (1922)

Moulus par le travail et tourmentés par l'âge
Ereintés et pliant sous un tas de débris[1]
—Charles Baudelaire, "Le Vin des chiffonniers,"
Les Fleurs du Mal (1857)

A century is not so very long at all, really, in what Eliot called "the scheme of generation,"[2] let alone the long arc of planetary time. *The Waste Land* continues to be rich and strange even after so much time as a cultural touchstone. Yet as we cast our backward glance over the past hundred years, things look very different from our present realities. To say nothing of the vast social, demographic, and political shifts occasioned by economic and technological change, we now face a globally precarious future in a way that even the devastation of the Great

War did not anticipate. When Eliot published *The Waste Land* in 1922, atmospheric carbon was just over 300 ppm. As of today, it is now at 420 ppm.[3] Anthropogenic climate change has sped up the clock. It is already profoundly altering our world, yet—especially in wealthy nations—the greater part of this seismic upheaval is yet to come. We are haunted by the increasingly dire warnings of the Intergovernmental Panel on Climate Change (IPCC) about climate tipping points, even as we turn or attention to more immediate problems and sources of anxiety, performing a kind of collective inaction. In this age of profound existential uncertainty, what do we cling to? What roots might we clutch, poking out of the stony rubbish? It may be that clinging and clutching are altogether the wrong responses. If so, what other gestures might we turn to, to help us think through—and feel through—our predicament without succumbing to complacency or despair?

There might be good reasons to look in other places for ways through our age of uncertainty, given that there is much in the poem's underlying prejudices and assumptions that we should rightly wish to cast aside. To look back to *The Waste Land* might even be to risk submitting to a nostalgic impulse born of a desire to cast the uncertainties and contingencies of the present era in the reassuringly familiar terms of a retro-*avant garde*. And, after all, *The Waste Land* has been excavated, picked over, scavenged and exhausted by exegesis, interpretation, pastiche, and reification; subsumed into its own apparently determining vision of the crumbling monuments of Western culture. Yet even this anxiety—that there is nothing left of use to say about the poem—is itself nothing new. Sixty years ago, the great poet and literary critic Randall Jarrell complained that Eliot's poetry was lost to us, already buried fathoms deep under the weight of its cultural pre-eminence.[4] Indeed, anxiety about its own belatedness permeates Eliot's poem, as Anthony Cuda demonstrates in his perceptive meditation on the hyacinth garden.[5] The sense that it is already "too late" is one of the things that makes *The Waste Land* feel so perennially modern.

Jahan Ramazani's recent reimagining of *The Waste Land* as "world elegy," clearly shows the enormous and continuing importance of the poem to contemporary poets writing about the great acceleration of the Anthropocene.[6] Ramazani sees *The Waste Land* as a crucial progenitor in a developing genealogy of elegy linking "the short history of poems preoccupied with the dire effects of anthropogenic climate change" to a longer tradition of poetry in "mourning for the world."[7] He argues that the poem's historical and geographical expansiveness—the transnational reach of its allusions—together with its entanglement with various canonical elegiac elements serves "to establish a literary space for mourning on a global scale.[8] Although my focus is less on the elegiac dimension of the poem and its reconfigurations in contemporary poetry, I share Ramazani's sense of *The Waste Land* as an uncannily prescient response to the emotional and ecological complexities of our own moment. My work in mapping the recombinatory affective territories of *The Waste Land* as encoding a postcolonial and posthuman "solastalgia," or climate grief, is in dialogue with his reading of the poem as world elegy and ecocritique. Both readings offer, I think, an emancipatory vision of the poem founded in hope.

In what follows, I read *The Waste Land* as a proleptic instance of solastalgia. I argue that in its rendering of waste as both *topos* and *temporality*, the poem creates a space not only for mourning, but for understanding the peculiar affective ecology of our own time. Its complicated and—I think—evolving relationship to the environmental and postcolonial offers a mechanism for renewal in our thinking through the challenges of the contemporary crisis of the Anthropocene.

I. (Re)reading the Ruins

Early eco-criticism tended to disregard Eliot's work as unyieldingly anthropocentric. Yet the past thirty years—and in particular the "green turn" in modernist studies in the new millennium—have seen *The Waste Land* approaching the status of a seminal ecocritical text.[9] Writing on the environmental imagination in 1995, Lawrence Buell declared *The Waste Land* "one of the first canonical works of modern Anglo-American literature to envision a dying society in the aftermath of world war."[10] Ecocritical analyses of the poem tend to draw on this observation in focusing on the poem's post-pastoral imagery of abjection and excess and its critique of consumption and urban capitalist sterility. As Gabrielle McIntire observes, "*The Waste Land* depicts a culture and a society in which we are no longer able even to think the 'natural' as undefiled."[11] A related strand of recent scholarship concerns Eliot's organicism. Jeremy Diaper, for example, explores Eliot's "profound and prolonged attention to various agrarian, agricultural, and environmental concerns."[12]

In confluence with such re-evaluations, it is time to revisit the poem as an affective ecology. In its mobile, transnational representations of ruin and waste as process and outcome (that is, both temporality and topography) *The Waste Land* models and formalizes the dynamics of the current era. The poet and literary critic Susan Stewart has written a great deal about the figurative possibilities of ruins in Western culture. She argues that the "power of ruins and ruin images to bestow lessons has to do with the fact that they are read—both in themselves, as presences, and as representations."[13] As the exemplary modern poem of ruin, *The Waste Land* is, likewise, both presence and representation. The poem is like a Buddhist koan: old and yet self-renewing; it can hold multiple, mutually incompatible truths within its shifting, shimmering atmosphere. And, like a koan, it has the inexhaustible capacity to tell us new things about ourselves and our situations, even as those things, and those selves and situations change and evolve over time. The literary scholar Robert Pogue Harrison rather movingly describes poets as scryers forecasting changes in the weather and characterizes "modern poetry at its best [as] a kind of spiritual ecology." "Like oracles," he says, "the meaning of their message becomes fully manifest only after the events it foretells have unfolded."[14]

Waste is contiguous with ruin. Both words slip easily between their noun and verb forms, between the processes of degradation and exploitation that result in an unwanted and unlovely remainder, and the vestigial matter itself. *The Waste Land* is pervaded by the cultural, spiritual, political, and aesthetic waste of the past, which it can neither dispose of nor assimilate. Although the fragments are assembled into new patterns—invoking Pound's famous phrase 'Make it new!' as the modernist cause célèbre—they are patterns that retain their brokenness and fissures, like the ruined beauty of Japanese kintsugi pottery, which repairs broken ceramics with seams of gold, tracing the marks of fragmentation and turning them into a web of imperfect connection and contingency. It is little wonder, then, that one of the founding practitioners in the field of waste studies regards *The Waste Land* as a model waste text in its struggle with "irreconcilable" cultural waste. In her wide-ranging study of waste literature,

Susan Signe Morrison writes that "the metaphors of cultural recycling—in concepts such as intertextuality, *bricolage*, and appropriation—become theoretical ways of justifying and explaining literary detritus" in historical circumstances where "originality is virtually impossible."[15] In his work on modernism, technology, and the body, Tim Armstrong similarly finds in *The Waste Land* a "simultaneous fascination with, and revulsion from, waste," which he defines as "both the abject and a valuable surplus which enables culture to continue, creating its own moment as it orders its abjection. There can be no production without waste."[16]

I want to build on this analysis, situating my reflection on the poem at the nexus of literary criticism and cultural ecology. Cultural-ecological approaches, as Hubert Zapf notes, assume "that imaginative literature deals with the basic relation between culture and nature in particularly multi-faceted, self-reflexive, and transformative ways," producing "an 'ecological' dimension of discourse precisely on account of its semantic openness, imaginative intensity, and aesthetic complexity." According to this way of approaching texts, a poem like *The Waste Land* is "a form of cultural knowledge in [its] own right."[17] That knowledge extends outwards to incorporate the poem's reception, its cultural freight; its centrality as a node in a network of literary and extra-literary culture. The poem's cultural knowledge and prescience can be further explored by drawing on the emerging field of waste studies, which takes waste in all its materialities and figurations as a field of literary and cultural analysis, and which has arisen as a response to the imminent dangers of the climate crisis.

Just as waste breaks down, degrades, or changes form, waste as an organic system of representations tends to break down purities and differences. Where hygiene keeps things clean and separate, waste contaminates. In place of what Robert Harrison calls "the logic of distinction,"[18] waste-spaces participate in a horizontal, metonymic logic of connection through contamination. Susan Signe Morrison observes that the field of waste studies attends to this "metonymic charge by looking at texts as a series of non-hierarchized literary actants."[19] This structuring pattern is consistent with the rhizomatic structures explored in the post-structuralist philosophy of Deleuze and Guattari, and with other planar and trans-species networks, such as the entangled underground fungal ecosystems explored by Merlin Sheldrake.[20]

With increasing attention being paid to our organic entanglements, it is important that our thinking encompasses the forms, flows, and networks created by waste as a kind of shadow-ecosystem. Such consciousness has wide implications for how we interpret—and interact with—the world. Writing about the urgent need to reassemble the social, Bruno Latour writes that "Hermeneutics is not a privilege of humans but, so to speak, a property of the world itself. The world is not a solid continent of facts sprinkled by a few lakes of uncertainties, but a vast ocean of uncertainties speckled by a few islands of calibrated and stabilized forms."[21] Latour's pioneering work in the development of Actor-Network-Theory asks us to attend to the "*in-between*," the "not hidden, simply *unknown*" entanglements from which the world in all its complexity is constituted, and which, he says, "resembles a vast hinterland providing the resources for every single course of action to be fulfilled, much like the countryside for an urban dweller, much like the missing masses for a cosmologist trying to balance out the weight of the universe."[22]

My suggestion, then, is that the "waste matter" of *The Waste Land* exists as a sort of living repository of cultural knowledge; a warning and resource in dark and darkening times. I want to explore this possibility by thinking about waste as topography and temporality. First, however, I want to spend a few moments setting out the peculiarity and power of the poem's emotional prescience. In doing so, I suggest that its force as an affective ecology is grounded in its explicitly prophetic vision and fear at the failure of foresight.

II. "Fear in a handful of dust": *The Waste Land* as Eco-Prophecy

We enter the poem's wasteland and the space of prophecy it opens up through the poem's title, and the notions of 'waste' that it conjures with. Thinking through the 'waste' of *The Waste Land* enables us to give particular form and potency to Harrison's conceptualization of poets as meteorological prophets, and in turn to read the climatic conditions of the Anthropocene in the weather patterns of *The Waste Land*. Eliot's poem can be read as a barometer, detecting changes in atmospheric pressure, and as a hygrometer, measuring the presence of water.

To read *The Waste Land* in this way is not so much to read against the grain, but to read its granularity; to move from the metaphors of craft embodied by the woodcarver's art to the practice of geomancy, which is the reading of signs in the patterns of dust and sand (literally, "foresight by earth"). The poem seems self-aware in anticipating this. It begins with an oracle, in its invocation of the Cumaean Sybil in the epigraph from Petronius, albeit an exhausted and despondent one. Eliot tells us that "What Tiresias *sees*, in fact, is the substance of the poem,"[23] but we might well find this to be equally true of the Sybil. Recall that when the god Apollo asked the Sybil how long she wished to live, she answered him by picking up a handful of sand and saying that she wished to live for as many years as she held grains of sand. Ovid tells us that Apollo granted her wish but punished her refusal of his sexual demands by allowing her body to waste away while her immortal spirit endured and she became, like Tithonus, a chirping creature, hybrid and insect-like. Her story is one of violation, and the violence of survival; of being an unwilling witness to the passing of worlds and eons; of living through interesting times. "Fear in a handful of dust" indeed.[24]

The Sybil is herself a reader of the environment—in fact, we might go so far as to understand her as a diminished earth deity. Her method for foretelling the future is a form of geomancy. She discerns the singing of the fates in the voice of the wind, then writes down her kennings on oak leaves arranged inside the entrance of her cave. When the wind blows, the leaves are scattered; the Sybil's prophecies are dispersed in fragments, to be recombined in new patterns by the aleatory movements of the air.[25]

Although she does not prophesy within the scope of Eliot's epigraph quoting from the *Satyricon*, nor does she make any utterance beyond expressing her desire to die, the Sybil has a unique vantage point somewhere in the liminal space of the epigraph, yoked to the poem yet (unlike Tiresias) apparently set apart from it. In her own story—as well as within the paratextual framing of Eliot's poem—the Sybil has a perspective that is both diachronic and simultaneous. Flooded by history, she presides over the poem's "heap of broken images,"[26] a demi-goddess of the ash heap positioned, as Slobodan Paich says, in "a place where the mother earth and the underworld are *near and exuding*."[27]

The haunting lines that open "The Fire Sermon," the third part of *The Waste Land*, could be spoken by the Sybil, although the poem is too lithe to allow us to anchor the lyric voice so firmly:

> The river's tent is broken: the last fingers of leaf
> Clutch and sink into the wet bank. The wind
> Crosses the brown land, unheard. The nymphs are departed.[28]

Whomever is speaking, if we think of the Sybil's method of divination, listening to the wind (now unheard) and writing on leaves (sinking into detritus) these lines seem to speak to a terminal fear—the failure of foresight. They hover disquietingly between description and prophetic vision. They are simultaneously diagnostic and cautionary, depending on one's readerly relation to the poem's unsettled temporality. The lines' attentiveness to the changing quality of the environment runs deeper than anti-pastoral atmospherics. The passage has something of the almanac about it. Like the almanacs used by farmers, sailors, and even astronomers, which contained seasonal and celestial information such as weather forecasts, dates for agricultural planting, planetary rising and setting times, and the hours of the tides, it marks an attempt to chart and therefore anticipate environmental change within the cycle of known variation. The pathos of the passage lies precisely in its sense of the brokenness of such cycles, and the fear—both ancient and modern—that *this time* the wheel may no longer turn. This fear is existential: it encompasses the physical and the metaphysical. In keeping with the circulating logic of waste flows, the forward-looking fear of prophecy's failure that so marks *The Waste Land* also appears as a retrospective counter-movement in the poem's primary affective quality: the feeling of unbelonging in a ruined home, to which I now turn.

III. Solastalgia: The Pain of Unbelonging

In 2003, the Australian environmental philosopher Glenn Albrecht coined the term "solastalgia" to describe "the pain or distress caused by the ongoing loss of solace and the sense of desolation connected to the present state of one's home and territory." He writes that solastalgia is

> the existential and lived experience of negative environmental change, manifest as an attack on one's sense of place. It is characteristically a chronic condition, tied to the gradual erosion of identity created by the sense of belonging to a particular loved place and a feeling of distress, or psychological desolation, about its unwanted transformation.[29]

Solastalgia is the homesickness you have when you are still are home. It is the pain of un-belonging and estrangement from the world that we still inhabit, which is changed irrevocably from the world that we loved.

The denizens of *The Waste Land* are—like the Sybil—beset with the pain of creatures living in a world that has become intolerable, whether we attend to the neurasthenic woman in *A Game of Chess* for whom the wind under the door represents an unbearable environmental intrusion; or Marie, entombed in a Europe she no longer recognizes; or Stetson, who must fend off beasts intent upon desecrating his burial ground; or the melancholic Thames daughter, born (and borne) by the water, but now broken and marooned, speaking elegies for her lost river and able to "connect/Nothing with nothing."[30] These figures live out their lives under the sign of the "Lady of the Rocks,/The lady of situations"[31] in a landscape of echoes, of "reminiscent bells," "empty cisterns and exhausted wells."[32] Shaken by the rumble of "dry sterile thunder without rain,"[33] it is a composite landscape subject to multiple forms of desertification:

> Here is no water but only rock
> Rock and no water and the sandy road
> The road winding above among the mountains
> Which are mountains of rock without water
> If there were water we should stop and drink
> Amongst the rock one cannot stop or think
> Sweat is dry and feet are in the sand[34]

In developing the concept of solastalgia, Glenn Albrecht acknowledges an intellectual debt to the work of the Australian farmer, children's author, and ecological philosopher Elyne Mitchell.

Written with insights sharpened by drought, in an environment shaped by desertification, Mitchell's *Soil and Civilization* (1946) argues that "divorced from his roots, man loses his psychic stability."[35] In its symbiotic focus on desertification and the health of soil as mirroring the life of the human organism, Mitchell's book echoes Eliot's contemporary preoccupations with agrarianism and his engagement in the 1930s and 40s with figures like Viscount Lymington, 9th Earl of Portsmouth, a founding member of Kinship in Husbandry (a precursor to the Soil Association). Jeremy Diaper provides a detailed book-length account of Eliot's organicist engagements and notes the "striking" similarity between the desert symbolism present in *The Waste Land* and "its later connotations in specifically agricultural and organicist discussions."[36]

To apply the concept of solastalgia as a description of the emotional character of *The Waste Land* is therefore not entirely the exercise in critical anachronism it might seem, given that its roots can be traced to a set of social and environmental concerns very closely aligned to Eliot's authorial preoccupations. In relation to the more specifically affective character of solastalgia, prior to writing *The Waste Land* Eliot was already well versed in the theories and work of the pioneering sociologist Émile Durkheim, whose concept of *'anomie'* (or 'normlessness')—a kind of social uprootedness and disconnection—has strong affinities with solastalgia. Eliot had used Durkheim's concept of "collective and individual representations" in writing his own essay on "The Interpretation of Primitive Ritual" while at Harvard in 1913–14,[37] and reviewed the 1916 English translation of Durkheim's *The Elementary Forms of Religious Life* (1912) twice, in August 1916 and January 1918.[38] Although Durkheim developed 'anomie' in his 1897 book *Suicide* as a way to characterize a deep sense of individual alienation from social values and structures, the term is also haunted by collective experiences of alienation and dispossession suffered in colonized countries. We should note that Durkheim's theories—which were highly influential on modernist thinkers—drew on anthropological work attempting to record the experiences of Aboriginal Australian peoples who had been displaced from their land and traditional way of life. The concept of "anomie," like the later Australian coinage "solastalgia," are thus both shaped by the impacts of colonization and colonial exploitation.

This antipodean dimension—to which I shall return later on—offers an important counterpoint to the more parochial scope and reactionary politics of much of the British organicist movement of the 1930s and 40s. Organizations like Kinship in Husbandry coalesced out of an array of groups concerned with English identity in the 1930s, such as English Mistery and the English Array. Despite its name, and unlike many of the most prominent figures in the British organicist movement, Mitchell's eco-philosophical concerns with desertification are not shadowed by "blood and soil" affiliations with the far right.[39] Although her warnings about desertification are grounded in the challenges faced by settler–colonists in the Australian environment, her concern—like Durkheim before her—is to articulate a more general socio-spiritual dynamic based on ecological observation and affective introspection. Although it was written more than two decades before Mitchell's work, *The Waste Land* encodes just such a globally concerned process pattern of observation and introspection. In his study of the cultural meaning of forests, Robert Harrison argues that "Poetry does not only monitor spiritual states of being, or what one used to call the 'spirit' of an age; it also registers the spiritual effects of a changing climate and habitat."[40] He points out that "the figurative and literal meanings of 'wasteland' are mirrored by one another [...] desertification in the literal sense is the 'objective correlative'" of the figurative wasteland.[41]

The Waste Land is a document of the fluid correspondence of states of health between the microcosm of the soul and the macrocosm of the world. Through a process akin to what Ramazani calls "intergeographic layering,"[42] the poem surveys multiple ecosystems in varied states of "biomic" ill-health. Although its figuring of place accords an importance to the local and specific, the poem is ultimately less interested in place as an instrument of political confinement than it is in drawing implicit connections between the fragmented and diseased environments of the cities, plains, mountains, oceans, rivers, deserts, and jungles across which it ranges. *The Waste Land* is prescient in its apprehension of each of these landscapes as sites of waste, a view that chimes with contemporary understandings of the interactive and recombinant features of ecosystems. The following section explores and historicizes the poem's conceptualization of waste topography and temporality.

IV. Waste Land as *Topos* and *Temporality*

In her comprehensive history of the concept of wasteland, Vittoria Di Palma argues that the modern wasteland is primarily

> a category of land [...] united not by consistent physical qualities—whether topographical or ecological—but, rather, by their absence. The wasteland is defined not by what it is or what it has, but by what it lacks: it has no water, food, or people, no cities, buildings, settlements or farms. [...] In its most general sense it stands in for any place that is hostile to human survival.[43]

This makes the wasteland the key *topos* for imaginative consideration of the mutations in our world and climate that we are now facing.

Yet the history of the waste land as representative space of inhospitable emptiness and desolation is complex and shifts with the changes in cultural attitudes to wilderness and agrarian technologies. Up until the fifteenth century, and the process of enclosure and despoliation begun then, wastelands were crucial to the rural economy of Britain. The waste theorist Susan Morrison observes that until the early modern period wastelands "were communal areas for grazing, gathering wood, and collecting herbs for medicine. It was the space, Myra Hird says, of the 'productive remainder,' where poorer members of society could find sustenance in this 'social safety net.'"[44] Sustainability (rather than capitalist surplus) is embedded in the concept of the productive remainder, which prizes but does not exploit the weeds and wayside matter of the wasteland. This earlier vision of the waste inverts the modern trope of desolate solitude into one of community and fecundity.

In the time of Eliot's Romantic precursor Percy Shelley, wastelands were places of possibility. In keeping with the expansive spatial assumptions of colonial powers in the early nineteenth century, Shelley writes in *Julian and Maddalo: A Conversation* (1818–19):

> I love all waste
> And solitary places; where we taste
> The pleasure of believing what we see
> Is boundless, as we wish our souls to be[45]

Eliot's wasteland retains a vestige of Shelley's formulation in its interest in fluidity, hybridity, metamorphoses, proteanism, and other dynamics of the undetermined imagination. However, Shelley's assumption that waste is necessarily capacious, unclaimed, and open to pleasurable exploitation is entirely absent from Eliot's vision.

The word "waste" is related to the word "vast," as well as to "devastation." Its etymological bedrock is formed in the paradoxical mingling of surfeit and loss. We can think of waste, like its metonymic cognates, weeds and wilderness, as surplus or byproduct—as that which is unneeded, unnecessary, or unclaimed. But we also tend to frame discourses of waste in terms of loss or ruin, as a process of extraction or exhaustion of resources or potential. In the Anthropocene, "waste land" is the designated fate of places that are exploited, unwanted, and unseen. It is interesting then, that Phlebas the Phoenician, who escapes the waste land via his death by drowning "Forgot the cry of gulls, and the deep sea swell/And the profit and loss."[46] In death, Phlebas escapes the central paradox of the waste land, and the maddening compulsion to attempt a balancing of the metaphysical accounts. He is himself subject to the recombinatory imperatives of the cycles of death and wasting; his presence retained in the poem's consciousness in parentheses "(Those are pearls that were his eyes. Look!)"—an imaginative surplus displaced from the materiality of the wind-swept sea into the transhistorical realm of culture.

We can read *The Waste Land* as encoding the historical failure of the social-ecological safety net, in the loss of the communal spaces and Edenic imaginaries of the commons. Yet Eliot's early imaginative conceptualizations of wastelands tend to veer away from a nostalgic vision of the rural commons (that comes later, of course, in the Somerset of "East Coker" and in the discourse of organicism). Instead, *The Waste Land* is structured around an axis of aridity that stretches from the "cracked earth" of scoured and "endless plains"[47] to the "brown fog" of London Bridge.[48] In the basalt plains and dry rocks of *The Waste Land*, as in its polluted urban agglomeration of refuse and disappointment, *The Waste Land* is global in its concern. It confronts us with places of habitation rendered barren and uninhabitable, and with the dilemma faced *après le déluge*: how to live after apocalypse.

As this dilemma suggests, wastelands are engulfed in their own temporalities—both timeless and indelibly marked by time and historical change. Di Palma teases out this paradox, asking:

> How can we understand the fact that "wasteland" is a term used to refer to land […] which is as yet unmodified by civilization, and to land, […] which has been consumed and exhausted through industrial excesses? *In other words, how can wasteland be culture's antithesis, as well as its product?* One answer is that in both cases, wasteland is a landscape the resists notions of proper or appropriate use.[49]

Di Palma relates that in English the term "wasteland" was at first "most often found in English versions of the Old Testament, New Testament, and Lives of the Saints, used to translate the Latin *desertus* or *solitudo*. *Desertus* (or *terra deserta*) and *solitudo* imply an emptiness; they are lands characterized by absence"[50]—as in the long-lived legal fiction of "terra nullius," which facilitated the British invasion and settlement of Australia as an "empty territory." In these early usages, the wasteland is consistently described as an uninhabited place. As the Australian poet and activist Judith Wright once noted, a primeval waste is a daunting expanse, a place "in which the avenging agriculturalist who had lost his skills at tracking and finding his way could easily get lost or 'bewildered.'"[51] Noting the strange and looping temporality of ecological devastation, Wright observed that "By the time Australia was brought under the yoke of tribute to Europe, the first cultivated areas in the eastern Mediterranean, and in other places, had themselves reverted to wilderness in the sense of having been laid waste—this time by the effects of agricultural methods and the clearing of forests."[52] *The Waste Land* elides these different timescales and places—or rather, it brings them into messy contact. "Jerusalem Athens Alexandria/ Vienna [and] London" are drawn into a composite hallucination,[53] the "Unreal City" over the mountains,[54] that "cracks and reforms […] in the violet air."[55] Similarly, the "endless plains," and "cracked earth/Ringed by the flat horizon only"[56] of the poem's desert hellscape are the biblical deserts of Sinai, the cold plains of Himavant, and the arid redness of the Australian Outback.

V. Red Rocks: *The Waste Land* and Indigenous Knowledge

In "The Burial of the Dead," we encounter:

> A heap of broken images, where the sun beats,
> And the dead tree gives no shelter, the cricket no relief,
> And the dry stone no sound of water. Only
> There is shadow under this red rock,
> (Come in under the shadow of this red rock)[57]

The biblical overtones of this passage and the echo of Eliot's 1915 poem "The Death of Saint Narcissus"— "Come in under the shadow of this gray rock"[58]—suggest the deracinated barrenness of Renaissance depictions of the saints in the desert. On this reading, the "red rocks" are those of Ezekiel and Ecclesiastes, as reflected in Eliot's notes to *The Waste Land*. This ready etymology seems to me to occlude another fruitful context for re-considering the poem. In their notes to *The Waste Land* the editors of Eliot's *Poems* (2015) are not much interested in the allusive possibilities of Eliot's "red rocks," except to quote Eliot as saying that the symbolism, such as it might be, was "wholly spontaneous."[59] Yet it seems likely that Eliot was thinking of the red rocks of the Australian interior, idealized as a drought-ridden desert *topos* both ancient and modern.

In 2007, Caroline Patey identified striking lexical correspondences between sections of *The Waste Land* and the evocation of desert sandstone plains in passages from Baldwin Spencer and Frank Gillen's anthropological studies of the Aboriginal peoples of Central Australia,[60] concluding that "the deserts of *The Waste Land*, endlessly thirsty and sunny […] owe a lot to the Alice Springs landscape."[61] Spencer and Gillen were an important source for James Frazer's work in comparative mythology, and informed Durkheim's study of so-called primitive religion. As Patey points out, Eliot had read and admired Spencer and Gillen's work.[62] In "War Paint and Feathers," a review published in the *Athenæum* in October 1919, Eliot advises his readers that "one ought, surely, to have read at least one book such as those of Spencer and Gillen on the Australians."[63]

In *The Northern Tribes of Central Australia* (1904), Spencer and Gillen write:

> A few miles to the north of Barrow Creek the hills cease, and for about thirty-five miles the country is as desolate as possible. It is absolutely flat, with not a trace of even a dry water-course, and but little vegetation. Stunted gums, porcupine and spear grass thinly cover the sandy plains. It is quite a relief to come once more into mulga country, and then, some twenty miles further on, the low Davenport Range is crossed. The main part of it is formed of quartzite, but in the heart of the range, and extending roughly east and west, is a valley filled with granite, which has weathered into large boulder-shaped masses of such a striking form that the place is known as the Devil's Marbles. Low ridges of granite run in various directions along and across the valley, and on some of these the huge boulders are poised like rocking stones.[64]

Later, they describe a scene that I think has direct bearing on the "red rock" moment in *The Waste Land*. Spencer and Gillen relate the testimony of an elderly Thungalla man who was the subject of a revenge hunt by white settlers who wanted to murder him for the killing of white men in an earlier attack on a cattle station:

> He told us one day how [...] he had been caught sight of and pursued and had only saved himself by hiding in the crevice of some rocks under the friendly shelter of a bush, behind which he crouched in fear and trembling until his pursuers, little thinking that they were so close to him, had passed by.[65]

I find it both poignant and fascinating that the crouching, fearful figure under *The Waste Land*'s red rock may in fact be an indigenous figure.

Whatever its author's relationship to his sources, the text of *The Waste Land* holds within its rocky topography a crucial but occluded scene of indigenous knowledge and its foreclosure. In the sense of danger and the missed encounter between different orders of understanding, the red center of the poem becomes absorbed into the wasteland of the modernist Western cultural imagination as a figure of threat, barrenness, and spiritual aridity. From a contemporary vantage point—and at a time when indigenous knowledge of environmental systems is increasingly being sought as a corrective to industrial practices—this is a painful irony. The poem's not-quite interplay of showing and seeing gestures to forms of cultural blindness that are yet to be fully overcome. Lacking the cultural knowledge to survive in the outback, white anthropologists looked upon the desert and saw a wasteland. Where the landscape offered more immediate sustenance, the same eyes—like Shelley's—saw wild, unpeopled possibility. As the ethnographer Deborah Bird Rose writes, "in general, settler ideology did not recognize Aboriginal land management, and did not recognize landscapes as the product of Aboriginal knowledge and labour. Settlers in their first years harvested the productivity which was the fruit of Aboriginal people's labour. The appropriation was unknowing and unthinking, and it was short term."[66]

That the primal wasteland is a place defined by nothingness and emptiness is its tragedy, as well as its potential salvation, like the crooked tree in the Chinese proverb spared the axe by virtue of its uselessness as timber.[67] This analogy should spur us to attend to the constructed nature of values such as emptiness and utility, and to re-think the discourses of appropriate use that underlie the concept of wasteland. When white settlers mistook the Australian landscapes managed by Aboriginal people for unpeopled but fruitful wilderness, they were as blind as the explorers who ventured into the searing deserts of the hinterland but failed to see their fecundity and mystery—that is, they had the experience but missed the meaning.

VI. Recuperating Sites of Forgetting

The Waste Land's concern with spiritual misrecognition—with misprision as to value—involves the poem in a political discourse around what landscape features, animals, human individuals, and communities are considered surplus and expendable. In her 1966 book, *Purity and Danger*, Mary Douglas theorized waste expansively, as "matter out of place."[68] Douglas connected this understanding of waste as displaced matter with practices of social hygiene and purification, thinking through the ways in which groups (like Australian indigenous people hunted and displaced) become marginalized, designated as waste, rendered invisible, and ultimately excised from the community of the human.[69]

The "hooded hordes swarming/Over endless plains, stumbling in cracked earth"[70] are the discarded and dehumanized, rendered an indistinct mass as they disappear through gaping fissures as cities turn to rubble and towers fall in the "violet air."[71] Ants swarm, as Eliot conveys all too viscerally in the martyrdom of Celia in *The Cocktail Party*. So do bees, wasps, and locusts. To describe the hooded hordes as swarming is to use the rhetoric of biblical nightmare to frame human beings as vermin. The poem's immersion in Dante's *Inferno*, and repeated gesturing towards the reader's complicity suggests that this dehumanization is being presented critically, as a form of admonition.

The poem sets this terrifying vision of dehumanized otherness against more prosaic portraits of expendable humanity: the people lost, worn, and ruined in recognizable modern cities, creeping through the undergrowth of the urban environment and stalled in dimly lit rooms. These are figures like Mr. Eugenides, the Smyrna merchant, eking out a seedy existence on the edge of a criminal underworld, as well as the "typist home at teatime."[72] Reduced by the structures of her society to a series of functions, secretarial and sexual, she is used, and exhausted, by the young man who requires no response because he does not see her as a person. Lil, too, is a poignant figure of waste. Worn out by childbearing, she disposes of a surplus pregnancy but in doing so is made to suffer a further bodily wasting, brought on by the chemist's pills. The conversation between the two women in the pub ahead of Albert's arrival is structured around a series of attempts to shore up the social and domestic order against calamitous loss and leakage—of teeth, youth, children, desire, and sexual fluids. Albert, about to be demobbed, must be protected from knowledge of this hidden economy of biological and psychosexual waste.

The waste theorist Myra J. Hird tells us that "Western landfills are sites of forgetting."[73] We might revise this to say that landfill, like the ash-heap of history, is a site embodying the fantasy of forgetting, even as the act of attempted repression entangles us more intimately with our waste. The landscape of Eliot's poem is an environment in which waste inexorably circulates and infiltrates. In its most easily identifiable form, it is evoked as the detritus of summer nights, the rubbish and refuse left over as "empty bottles, sandwich papers [...] cardboard boxes, cigarette ends"; evoked, but absent from the suspended present of "The Fire Sermon."[74] It exists as an atmosphere of decay, in the rat-infested environs, and in the flow of the ruined river itself, a river that "sweats/Oil and tar."[75] The sense of ennui, desperation, and despair are symptoms of entropic wasting. As Hird says, "waste flows are always contingent, uncertain and temporal. Not only does waste at times exceed its mundane cultural, economic, and symbolic governance [...] but waste may physically leak, spill, seep, corrode, slip, collapse or explode, contaminating groundwater, soil, the atmosphere, and organisms."[76]

In repeatedly recalling us to the localized and the particular, the poem makes an ethical demand of its critics to attend to the specificity and distinctiveness of histories embedded in locality, and to the variance and richness of the lives in what to us might be "other places." Without this kind of attentiveness, we risk repeating the mistakes of the colonists entering the Australian hinterland, with their lazy obliviousness, their effacement of others, and their impoverishment of vision. The poem resists such tendencies, just as it resists the aestheticization and commodification of ruin—and therein lies some of its radical potential. The flow of waste mirrors other, less tangible flows, like the flow of capital through London's financial district. After laying waste to the Thames in their summer carousing, made possible by the wealth generated by the circulating currency in the financial system, the erstwhile "loitering heirs of City directors" have departed, leaving "no addresses."[77] The circus has moved on. Despite the apparently seasonal underpinnings of the pattern articulated in this passage—beginning with summer nights and ending with "a cold blast"[78]—the Thames daughter's lament operates in conjunction with a slower, submerged, and perhaps more insidious flow of waste.

In "*The Fire Sermon*," the poem unfolds a scene of wasteland on the urban fringe, rendered unbearable—if not wholly unlivable—by industrial efflux. Here, a figure sits in the murky twilight on the banks of the canal, vestige of a river shaped to human purpose, ruminating on the wreckage that surrounds him:

>A rat crept softly through the vegetation
>Dragging its slimy belly on the bank
>While I was fishing in the dull canal
>On a winter evening round behind the gashouse

> Musing upon the king my brother's wreck
> And on the king my father's death before him.
> White bodies naked on the low damp ground
> And bones cast in a little low dry garret,
> Rattled by the rat's foot only, year to year.[79]

His locale is dead or dying, a charnel house of impoverished human ambitions, "behind the gas-house." Now defunct, gashouses were foul-smelling sites for the manufacture of synthetic fuel gases. Unlike natural gas, this is gas produced through the gasification of combustible materials, most often coal. Coal gas was being made and sold commercially in Great Britain from the early decades of the 1800s, and was still a marked feature of Eliot's time.[80] As in *The Waste Land*, most early gashouses were located in poorer urban areas, beside rivers or canals so that the coal could be brought in by barge. The coal would be heated to the point where it emitted gases, including unwanted sulfur, ammonia, and naphthalene, which accounted for the diabolical smell of the gashouses. The toxic residues produced from this process were often then drained out into the river as post-industrial effluent. The earliest process of coal gas purification was known as the "wet lime" process, a process that produced as residue a substance known as "blue billy," one of the first true toxic wastes. The presence of blue billy (with its characteristic color, a Prussian Blue) in industrial waste sites is still a key indicator of contamination today. The stuff is so toxic it cannot be treated or mitigated but must be encased in concrete or circulated to a different site.

The Ferdinand figure fishing in the "dull canal" is thus situated in a habitation zone already rendered hostile to life by poisonous gases from manmade emissions. In the circulating logic of waste, with its continuing materiality and potency, our present is burdened by the effluent of this industrial past.[81] As Morrison observes, "synchronic time frequently characterizes waste literature, where the dregs from the past inexorably materialize."[82] The temporality of waste, its circularity and latency, means that we are trapped in an always-already condition. It is a condition bound up with the very act of reading; what Julian Wolfreys call the experience of "it *is still not yet what it already is*."[83] In the Anthropocene, the "withered stumps of time" are "told upon the walls."[84] The contaminating event that created the waste land—what Paul Virilio calls "the primal accident"[85]—mirrors the biblical Fall. The poem reflects this process as the fishing figure returns at its conclusion, this time as the Fisher King. But the lands cannot simply be put in order. The forgotten or obscured stain upon the land continues to leach poison. The run-off from Eliot's gashouse is still buried beneath the soil of twenty-first-century London.

VII. Conclusion: Shall We Set Our Lands in Order?

As horrifying as this fact is, it should also give cause for hope. It suggests that we are equally unknowing about the regenerative conditions already extant within the wasteland. The wasteland's patterns of creation and gestation are unpredictable, accidental, and often unintended by human actors, as well as being largely unobserved.

"Not-seeing" is at the core of *The Waste Land*, in the tropes of Tiresius's blindness, in the failure of sight in the moment of revelation with the hyacinth girl, and in the agonized questioning in "A Game of Chess": "'Do/ You know nothing? Do you see nothing? Do you remember/'Nothing?'"[86] The waste population of the poem is constituted by a fragmentary, distributed network of individuals casting about for meaning, boats beating against the tide of despair. The poem repeatedly gestures to a future revelation obscured from sight in the poem's present and requiring a commitment that shakes the heart with "the awful daring of a moment's surrender."[87] The "something" that the poem carries on its back, that Madame Sosostris is "forbidden to see,"[88] is the patterning of our collective future.

This opens the way for a forward-thinking consideration of the waste-effects of our present. William Viney suggests that waste allows us access to a narrative and imaginative mode of thinking through the multiple temporalities at stake in our projection of future ruins, which may help us to imagine entirely different types of future.[89] Di Palma tells us that "the emptiness that is the core characteristic of the wasteland is also what gives the term its malleability, its potential for abstraction; a vacant shell, it lies ready to include all those kinds of places that are defined in negative terms, identified primarily by what they are *not*."[90] Eliot's poetry often throws up such moments of potential hidden in vacuity. It is present in

"Gerontion," which Eliot considered as something of a preface to *The Waste Land*,[91] where "Vacant shuttles/Weave the wind";[92] and in "The Dry Salvages" figuring of the ear as "the vacant shell of time," in a section of the poem that looks back to an earlier sea voyage, excised from a draft of *The Waste Land*.[93]

When viewed across the whole span of Eliot's art, these instances are connected with a kind of pregnant absence that anticipates the miracle of the Incarnation, a typological relation revealed most explicitly in Eliot's 1928 poem, "A Song for Simeon." In Eliot's pre-conversion poetry, such possibilities are still latent, hidden beneath the grime, and passed over by the "dirty hands" and "broken fingernails" of "humble people who expect/ Nothing,"[94] like the image that concludes his earlier poem "Preludes," where "worlds revolve like ancient women/Gathering fuel in vacant lots."[95] These figures gesture back to the rag-pickers plying their trade in the *labyrinthe fangeux* of nineteenth-century Paris in Baudelaire's "Le Vin des chiffonniers" ("The Rag-Picker's Wine"). Ground down by age and decrepitude, they stagger under the weight of their debris ("Moulus par le travail et tourmentés par l'âge/Ereintés et pliant sous un tas de débris").[96] Baudelaire's muddy labyrinth, where humanity swarms in seething ferments ("l'humanité grouille en ferments orageux"), suggests the same ungovernable capacity for creation out of ruin as Eliot's 1917 prose work "Eeldrop and Appleplex," in which London is a scene of tropical ferment, "dusty above and moldy below; the tepid air swarmed with flies."[97]

Even in its impoverished form, the wasteland operates as a model of new-seeing—of recognition or intuition of "some infinitely gentle/Infinitely suffering thing" hidden among the ruins.[98] Its future is obscured, yet *The Waste Land* concludes with gestures of care and preservation, however disrupted, modest, or ambiguous. In its awareness of the need for repurposing, salvage, and preservation of that which has been thought lost, squandered, or obscured, the poem helps us to think through (and perhaps to dwell in) the particular emotional tenor and existential necessities of our time.

Notes

1 Ground down by labor and tormented by age,/Exhausted and bending under a pile of debris (my translation).
2 *Poems* 1:201.
3 Data taken from The Keeling Curve, Scripps Institution of Oceanography, University of California San Diego. See https://keelingcurve.ucsd.edu.
4 See Randall Jarrell, "Fifty Years of American Poetry," in *The Third Book of Criticism* (Farrar, Straus and Giroux, 1969), 314–15.
5 See Anthony Cuda, "Back, Late, from the Hyacinth Garden," *T. S. Eliot Studies Annual* 4: 57–71.
6 See Jahan Ramazani, "Burying the Dead: *The Waste Land*, Ecocritique, and World Elegy," *T. S. Eliot Studies Annual* 4: 7–23.
7 Ramazani, "Burying the Dead," 7.
8 Ramazani, "Burying the Dead," 8.
9 See, for example, Gabrielle McIntire, "*The Waste Land* as Ecocritique," in *The Cambridge Companion to* The Waste Land, ed. Gabrielle McIntire (Cambridge University Press, 2015), 178–93. For recent ecocritical reconsideration of the place of Eliot—and modernism more broadly—within the environmental imagination, see Elizabeth Black, *The Nature of Modernism: Ecocritical Approaches to the Poetry of Edward Thomas, T. S. Eliot, Edith Sitwell and Charlotte Mew* (Routledge, 2017); and Etienne Terblanche, *T. S. Eliot, Poetry, and Earth: The Name of the Lotos Rose* (Lexington Books, 2016). See also Matthew Griffiths, "Climate Change and the Individual Talent: Eliotic Ecopoetics," *symploke* 21 (2013): 83–95 for a complementary ecocritical account of Eliot's criticism.
10 Lawrence Buell, *The Environmental Imagination: Thoreau, Nature Writing, and the Formation of American Culture* (Harvard University Press, 1995), 288.
11 McIntire, "*The Waste Land* as Ecocritique," 182.
12 Jeremy Diaper, *T. S. Eliot and Organicism* (Clemson University Press, 2018), 1. See also Alexandra Harris, *Romantic Moderns: English Writers, Artists and the Imagination from Virginia Woolf to John Piper* (Thames Hudson, 2010).
13 Susan Stewart, *The Ruins Lessons: Meaning and Material in Western Culture* (University of Chicago Press, 2020), 4.
14 Robert Pogue Harrison, *Forests: The Shadow of Civilization* (University of Chicago Press, 1992), 149.
15 Susan Signe Morrison, *The Literature of Waste: Material Ecopoetics and Ethical Matter* (Palgrave Macmillan, 2015), 158.
16 Tim Armstrong, *Modernism, Technology, and the Body: A Cultural Study* (Cambridge University Press, 1998), 70–71. See also Rachele Dini,

Consumerism, Waste, and Re-Use in Twentieth-Century Fiction: Legacies of the Avant-Garde (Palgrave Macmillan, 2016).

17 Hubert Zapf, "Cultural Ecology of Literature—Literature as Cultural Ecology," in *Handbook of Ecocriticism and Cultural Ecology*, ed. Hubert Zapf (De Gruyter, 2016), 139.
18 Harrison, *Forests*, x.
19 Morrison, *The Literature of Waste*, 6. See also Thomas Claviez, "Done and over with—Finally? Otherness, Metonymy, and the Ethics of Comparison," *PMLA* 128 (2013): 608–14.
20 See Merlin Sheldrake, *Entangled Life: How Fungi Make our Worlds, Change our Minds, and Shape our Futures* (Vintage, 2020).
21 Bruno Latour, *Reassembling the Social: An Introduction to Actor-Network-Theory* (Oxford University Press, 2005), 245.
22 Latour, *Reassembling the Social*, 244.
23 *Poems* 1:74.
24 *Poems* 1:55.
25 A seventeenth-century Dutch oil painting *The Sibyl Agrippina* by Jan van den Hoecke depicts this (other) Sibyl as a black woman holding a scourge, scroll, and crown of thorns. Although she is not the Cumaean Sibyl, she offers something to our imagining of the historical Sibyls, and I like the off-kilter consonance of the Latin inscription, which reads "Siccabitur ut folium"—"he will be shriveled like a leaf," with the crown of thorns presaging the passion of Christ and displacing the wasting that the Cumaean Sibyl suffers onto a different, post-Classical future.
26 *Poems* 1:55.
27 Slobodan Dan Paich, "Ambiguity of Center and Periphery and the Middle Sea," in *Light Colour Line—Perceiving the Mediterranean: Conflicting Narratives and Ritual Dynamics*, ed. Thomas Dittelbach and Ágnes Sebestyén (Georg Olms Verlag, 2016), 14. My emphasis.
28 *Poems* 1:62.
29 Glenn A. Albrecht, *Earth Emotions: New Words for a New World* (Cornell University Press, 2019), 38–39.
30 *Poems* 1:66.
31 *Poems* 1:56.
32 *Poems* 1:70.
33 *Poems* 1:68.
34 *Poems* 1:68.
35 Elyne Mitchell, *Soil and Civilization* (Halstead Press, 1946), 4.
36 Diaper, *T. S. Eliot and Organicism*, 14.
37 "The Interpretation of Primitive Ritual" (1913), *Complete Prose* 1:110.
38 "Durkheim. An unsigned first review of *The Elementary Forms of the Religious Life* […] by Émile Durkheim" (1916), *Complete Prose* 1:420–24; "Second review of *The Elementary Forms of the Religious Life*, by Émile Durkheim" (1918), *Complete Prose* 1:670–72.

39 British organicist figures like Gerard Wallop (Viscount Lymington), Jorian Jenks, and Rolf Gardiner all had links to the British Union of Fascists. See Richard Moore-Colyer and Philip Conford, "A 'Secret Society'? The Internal and External Relations of the Kinship in Husbandry, 1941–52," *Rural History* 15, no. 2 (2004): 189–206. For an account of the more politically varied forms of organicism in Australia, see Andrea Gaynor, "Antipodean Eco-nazis? The Organic Gardening and Farming Movement and Far-right Ecology in Postwar Australia," *Australian Historical Studies* 43, no. 2 (2012): 253–69.
40 Harrison, *Forests*, 149.
41 Harrison, *Forests*, 261.
42 Ramazani, "Burying the Dead," 12.
43 Vittoria Di Palma, *Wasteland: A History* (Yale University Press, 2014), 3–4.
44 Morrison, *The Literature of Waste*, 100.
45 Percy Bysshe Shelley, *The Major Works*, ed. Zachary Leader and Michael O'Neill (Oxford University Press, 2009), 213.
46 *Poems* 1:67.
47 *Poems* 1:69.
48 *Poems* 1:63.
49 Di Palma, *Wasteland*, 3; my emphasis.
50 Di Palma, *Wasteland*, 3.
51 Judith Wright, "Wilderness, Waste and History," in *Judith Wright: Selected Writings*, ed. Georgina Arnott (Latrobe University Press), 231.
52 Wright, "Wilderness, Waste and History," 232.
53 *Poems* 1:69.
54 *Poems* 1:63.
55 *Poems* 1:69.
56 *Poems* 1:69.
57 *Poems* 1:55.
58 James E. Miller Jr., *T. S. Eliot: The Making of an American Poet, 1888–1922* (Penn State University Press, 2005), 247.
59 *Poems* 1:606.
60 Baldwin Spencer and Francis James Gillen, *Native Tribes of Central Australia* (Macmillan and Co., 1899) and *The Northern Tribes of Central Australia* (Macmillan and Co., 1904).
61 Caroline Patey, "Whose Tradition? T. S. Eliot and the Text of Anthropology," in *T. S. Eliot and the Concept of Tradition*, ed. Giovanni Cianci and Jason Harding (Cambridge University Press, 2007), 167. See also Matthew Griffiths, "Climate Change and the Individual Talent," *Symplokē* 21, nos. 1–2 (2013): 83–95.
62 Patey, "Whose Tradition?," 165.
63 *Complete Prose* 2:138.

64 Spencer and Gillen, *The Northern Tribes of Central Australia*, 5.
65 Spencer and Gillen, *The Northern Tribes of Central Australia*, 185–86.
66 Deborah Bird Rose, *Nourishing Terrains: Australian Aboriginal Views of Landscape and Wilderness* (Australian Heritage Commission, 1996), 75–76. See also Stephen Muecke, "Devastation," in *Culture and Waste: The Creation and Destruction of Value*, ed. Gay Hawkins and Stephen Muecke (Rowman & Littlefield, 2003), 117–27.
67 The story is "The Useless Tree," from the *Zhuangzi*, attributed to the fourth-century philosopher Zhuang Zhou. I first encountered this story in Jenny Odell, *How to Do Nothing: Resisting the Attention Economy* (Melville House, 2019), p. xv.
68 See Mary Douglas, *Purity and Danger* (Routledge, 1966), 2.
69 For a more recent theorization of debility as a categorical assemblage that designates individuals and populations as available for injury, see Jasbir K. Puar, *The Right to Maim: Debility, Capacity, Disability* (Duke University Press, 2017). I am grateful to Galen Bunting for introducing me to Puar's work.
70 *Poems* 1:69.
71 *Poems* 1:69.
72 *Poems* 1:63.
73 Myra J. Hird, "Waste, Landfills, and an Environmental Ethic of Vulnerability," *Ethics & the Environment* 18, no. 1 (2013): 105.
74 *Poems* 1:62.
75 *Poems* 1:65.
76 Hird, "Waste," 105–24.
77 *Poems* 1:62.
78 *Poems* 1:62.
79 *Poems* 1:62.
80 It was only after the nationalization of the gas industry in England, Scotland, and Wales in 1949 that serious attempts were made to switch from coal gas (or "town gas" as it was also known) to natural gas. Exploration of natural gas fields in the North Sea first took place in the 1960s and the North Sea gas supply only became operational after Eliot's death in 1965. The last gasworks in Britain closed in 1981. See Russell Thomas, *Gasworks Profile A: The History and Operation of Gasworks (Manufactured Gas Plants) in Britain Gasworks* (CL:AIRE, 2014).
81 For an account of the ways that "trash and trauma press [...] closely together" in a variety of modern and contemporary texts, see Patricia Yaeger, "Trash as Archive, Trash as Enlightenment," in Hawkins and Muecke, *Culture and Waste*, 108.
82 Morrison, "Waste in Literature and Culture: Aesthetics, Form, and Ethics," *EuropeNow* (2019), www.europenowjournal.org/2019/05/06/waste-in-literature-and-culture-aesthetics-form-and-ethics/.

83 Julian Wolfreys, *Readings: Acts of Close Reading in Literary Theory* (Edinburgh University Press, 2000), 130.
84 *Poems* 1:58.
85 See Paul Virilio, "The Primal Accident," in *The Politics of Everyday Fear*, ed. Brian Massumi (University of Minnesota Press, 1993), 211–20.
86 *Poems* 1:59.
87 *Poems* 1:70.
88 *Poems* 1:56.
89 See William Viney, *Waste: A Philosophy of Things* (Bloomsbury, 2014).
90 Di Palma, *Wasteland*, 3–4; emphasis original.
91 Ricks and McCue quote Irmgard Lehmann's account of a reading Eliot gave at Bryn Mawr in October 1948: "He defined 'Gerontion' as a kind of preliminary stage to *The Waste Land*, from which he read out the fifth part What the Thunder Said." *Poems* 1:468.
92 *Poems* 1:32.
93 *Poems* 1:340–43. The passage excised from *The Waste Land* draws on the Ulysses canto in Dante's *Inferno*, as well as its iteration in Tennyson. *Poems*, 1:681. Reminiscent of Coleridge's *Rime of the Ancient Mariner* in its visionary descent into a maritime hell, and of Franklin's lost expedition to locate the Northwest Passage in its terminal encounter with ice floes and polar bears, the passage depicts an ill-fated sea voyage charting a course "From the Dry Salvages" up the eastern coast and past "the farthest northern islands." With a language of warning bells, rolling seas, breakers, and roaring waves in which the "sea with many voices/Moaned all about us," the passage is clearly the progenitor of "The Dry Salvages." Like the later poem, the early draft features phantasmal siren voices in the rigging: "I thought I saw in the fore cross-trees/Three women leaning forward, with white hair/Streaming behind, who sang above the wind/A song that charmed my senses, while I was/Frightened beyond fear." *Poems* 1:340–42.
94 *Poems* 1:66.
95 *Poems* 1:17.
96 Charles Baudelaire, *Complete Poems*, translated by Walter Martin (Carcanet, 2006), 272. I am grateful to Dr. Ria Banerjee for drawing this connection to my attention.
97 *Complete Prose* 1:528. See "Eeldrop and Appleplex," *Little Review* 4, nos. 1 and 5 (May and September 1917), reprinted in *The Little Review Anthology*, ed. Margaret Anderson (Hermitage House, 1953), 105.
98 *Poems* 1:16.

The Unnatural Excesses of T. S. Eliot

Leonard Diepeveen

> Come to lunch on Sunday. Tom is coming, and, what is more, is coming in a four-piece suit.
>
> —Virginia Woolf to Clive Bell,
> as reported by Clive Bell[1]

Among the more telling moments of early twentieth-century music are the opening measures of Stravinsky's *The Rite of Spring*. This is a bit surprising, perhaps. These measures do not have the cachet of the more apocryphal stories surrounding the work's 1913 Paris premiere: reports from the audience, Stravinsky's own descriptions, those of Nijinsky, or of the musicians. And those whispery early bars are soon eclipsed by Stravinsky's overpowering orchestration—120 instruments, five of each wind instrument,[2] and heavy on the percussion, creating a decibel level well beyond the norm of even the most excited orchestral pieces.

But those ghostly, wavering moments of the opening wind solo point to something essential in modernism, and, indirectly, in T. S. Eliot. In their odd straining, these familiar measures are more polemical than decorative. That odd, wavering wind solo at the beginning is confusing. It is clearly under stress, with the result that it's hard to figure out what instrument is making these sounds. This is purposeful: Stravinsky's score has the woodwinds and strings in particular play at the extreme high edges of their range, playing beyond their comfort zone, creating a straining sound, distorting a register, stretching a norm—a stretching that also characterized the original choreography. What one hears at the beginning of *The Rite of Spring* is a bassoon, playing at the extreme end of its register, well beyond the limits of its sweet spot, a spot every instrument and voice has. This stretching was, and remains, disorienting. As oboist Louis Speyer, who performed at the premiere, reports, "Already the introduction was a surprise, a bassoon in that register, we all looked and even some composers present asked if it was a saxophone."[3] Music critics took note, taking to task the piece for its "exaggerated elements,"[4] always citing the excess that was at its center. Florent Schmitt, music critic for *La France*, asserted:

> M. Igor Strawinsky's music, by its frenetic agitation; by the senseless whirl of its hallucinating rhythms; by its aggregations of harmonies beyond any convention or analysis, of an aggressive hardness that no one—not even M. Richard Strauss—had dared until now; by the obsessive insistence of its themes, their savor and their strangeness; by seeking the most paradoxical sonorities, daring combinations of timbres, systematic use of extreme instrumental ranges; by its tropical orchestration, iridescent and of an unbelievable sumptuosity; in sum, by an excess, an unheard-of luxuriance of refinement and preciosity, the music of M. Igor Strawinsky achieves this unexpected—but intentional—result, that it gives us the impression of the darkest barbarity.[5]

The bassoon's odd timbre, by its very oddity, becomes polemical. It goes beyond the bounds of the normative by increasing, straining, adding: this is excess. In consequence, the high bassoon register elicits from its audience a different kind of attention—a disorientation, and a consequent attempt to place something. This kind of stress has surprising consequences, and not just for emotional affect. Different from the excesses we experience outside of art, excess in art raises questions of sincerity and naturalness, and precipitates a turn to a strange kind of analysis. Art excess is polemical, and it was everywhere early in the twentieth century. Not an isolated moment, Stravinsky's work was part of a larger conversation that was central to modernism, and it included T. S. Eliot as an important participant.

***

While *The Rite of Spring* (along with Joyce's *Ulysses*) has rightly been seen as an impetus for Eliot's use of ancient sources as an interpretive frame for modern culture, it is also central to his uses of excess. By the time *The Rite of Spring* came to London eight years later, it had shed its original outrageous choreography, replacing it with something more sedate. But the original orchestral score remained, and that is what attracted Eliot's attention. In his "London Letter" to *The Dial*, Eliot wrote, the music:

> struck me as possessing a quality of modernity which I missed from the ballet which accompanied it. [...] Whether Strawinsky's music be permanent or ephemeral I do not know; but it did seem to transform the rhythm of the steppes into the scream of the motor horn, the rattle of machinery, the grind of wheels, the beating of iron and steel, the roar of the underground railway, and the other barbaric cries of modern life; and to transform these despairing noises into music.[6]

Eliot's attempt to tie Stravinsky's excesses to modern life was not idiosyncratic. Art in the early twentieth century was often understood to have a mimetic relationship to a new surrounding mass culture. Pound, for example, contrasted life in the modern city versus the nineteenth-century village:

> The life of a village is narrative; you have not been there three weeks before you know that in the revolution et cetera, and when M le Comte et cetera, and so forth. In a city the visual impressions succeed each other, overlap, overcross, they are "cinematographic," but they are not a simple linear sequence. They are often a flood of nouns without verbal relations.[7]

Further, Eliot's applause for Stravinsky wasn't just a momentary expression of his appreciation for another artist's work. Pointed moments of excess, with Stravinsky figured as an overload of sensations, are also what drew Eliot to the metaphysical poets, whose work he admired for its "elaboration [...] of a figure of speech to the furthest stage to which ingenuity can carry it."[8] And it wasn't just as a critic that Eliot explored the uses of excess. By the early 1920s, he had also been working with excess in his own poetry, especially in *The Waste Land*, creating startling moments where the texture or tone seems exaggerated, out of place. Consider these stanzas from "Mr. Eliot's Sunday Morning Service":

> Polyphiloprogenitive
> The sapient sutlers of the Lord
> Drift across the window-panes.
> In the beginning was the Word.
> [...]
> The sable presbyters approach
> The avenue of penitence;
> The young are red and pustular
> Clutching piaculative pence.[9]

The puzzling narratives in this and other quatrain poems are entangled with their excesses. Coupled with the startling immediacy of the present tense, the diction stretches well beyond the conventional, surpassing most readers' vocabularies. Add to that these poems' unusual but heavily precise naming, along with the rapid narrative shifts in the Sweeney poems and others, readers are left with bewildering narratives and extreme psychological situations—a cumulative, disorienting effect.

Eliot's interest had surfaced even earlier, in *Prufrock and Other Observations*, concerning which a reviewer argued that the poems "have the willful outlandishness of the young revolutionary idea" and that they "[miss] the effect by too much cleverness. All beauty has in it an element of strangeness, but here the strangeness over-balances the beauty."[10] The motivation for this reviewer's response can be seen in the narrative and diction of "Mr. Apollinax," where an odd eruption of overwrought diction creates a highly mannered work, in which idiosyncratic names and double rhymes, flirting with the upper registers of what is normative, draw attention to their oddity:

> In the palace of Mrs. Phlaccus, at Professor Channing-Cheetah's
> He laughed like an irresponsible fœtus.[11]

Double rhyme is excessive in English, often leading to the destabilizing tone and affects of humor and irony, with sound overshadowing sense. Form abets function here; the rhyme works in sync with the behavior of Mr. Apollinax, who is sketched in as overdone, outsized, perhaps threatening. He, and many of Eliot's other characters in these early poems, are caricatures—stylized individuals who have been reduced to a few attributes, attributes which then are heavily exaggerated. Because exaggeration amplifies *and* simplifies the semiotic code of its source, its pointing back to a violation of a norm at times works as a caricature of the norm. This strategy of excess was part of a prominent modernist conversation. The list of modernists who employed caricature (which at times entangled a sketchy relationship with primitivism) includes Ezra Pound, Wyndham Lewis, Edith Sitwell, Pablo Picasso, and Miguel Covarrubias.[12]

For Eliot, the apex of excess's effects, of course, lies in *The Waste Land*. Heavy reliance on foreign languages, a plethora of quotation and paratactic shifts, and a knowledge of arcana—even the notes to the poem seem overdone, sometimes comically so. Eliot's poem was understood by early readers not just as knowledge, but as an excessive *display* of knowledge—knowledge attracting attention to itself, an insecure and unnatural knowledge that for some British reviewers was typically American. The demands on Eliot's readers were significant. As Gorham Munson pointed out in 1924:

> To win a complete understanding of "The Waste Land," the reader must scan eleven pages of notes, he must have a considerable learning in letters or be willing to look up references in Milton, Ovid, Middleton, Webster, Spenser, Verlaine, St. Augustine, etc., etc., in order to associate them with their first context, he must read Latin, Greek, French and German, he must know Frazer's "Golden Bough" and steep himself in the legend of the Holy Grail,

studying in particular Miss Weston's "From Ritual to Romance."
The texture of "The Waste Land" is excessively heavy with literary
allusions which the reader of good will, knowing that it is not
unjust to make severe requisitions upon his knowledge, will diligently track down.[13]

This list of stuff was echoed by other reviewers as well, but it wasn't just an apparent sense of required knowledge that made this poem excessive. The quotations are accompanied by a heavy use of paratactic structures, in which excessive allusion is accompanied by excessive rapidity of movement. *The Waste Land* exhibits extremely jarring transitions and overuse of ellipses and parataxis in comparison to cultural standards of the time. The poem's ending lines are the apotheosis of this aesthetic:

> I sat upon the shore
> Fishing, with the arid plain behind me
> Shall I at least set my lands in order?
>
> London Bridge is falling down falling down falling down
>
> *Poi s'ascose nel foco che gli affina*
> *Quando fiam uti chelidon*—O swallow swallow
> *Le Prince d'Aquitaine à la tour abolie*
> These fragments I have shored against my ruins
> Why then Ile fit you. Hieronymo's mad againe.
> Datta. Dayadhvam. Damyata.
>
> Shantih shantih shantih[14]

These straining, overloaded lines achieve their effects by overwhelming readers, much like, as Harold Monro pointed out, "a drawing that is so crowded with apparently unrelated details that the design or meaning (if there be one) cannot be grasped until those details have been absorbed into the mind, and assembled and related to each other."[15] At this point in his career Eliot's poetry was all a bit of a stretch. John Crowe

Ransom argued that in *The Waste Land* Eliot's "intention is evidently to present a wilderness in which both he and the reader may be bewildered, in which one is never to see the wood for the trees."[16] The poems were mannered, even, to some, unnatural.

***

These moments are familiar, but to understand the kind of *work* do they do necessitates a turn to the academic study of excess, which has been circumscribed by four basic approaches: those of Kant's sublime, of Kristeva's abjection, of Bataille's accursed share, and of camp/consumerism. To briefly sketch these out: versions of excess as resulting from the sublime stem from either Edmund Burke or Immanuel Kant, who work with basically the same ideas. The sublime, for Kant, is that which is excessive, beyond our reach:

> The sublime is that, the mere ability to think which shows a faculty of the mind surpassing every standard of sense. . . .
>
> Nature is . . . sublime in those of its phenomena whose intuition brings with it the idea of its infinity. This last can only come by the inadequacy of the greatest effort of our imagination to estimate the magnitude of an object. [...] Therefore it must be the aesthetical estimation of magnitude in which the effort toward comprehension surpasses the power of the imagination.

Kant's sublime leads to an inevitable and instable affect:

> The feeling of the sublime is thus a feeling of displeasure from the inadequacy of the imagination in the aesthetic estimation of magnitude for the estimation by means of reason, and a pleasure that is thereby aroused at the same time from the correspondence of this very judgment of the inadequacy of the greatest sensible faculty in comparison with ideas of reason, insofar as striving for them is nevertheless a law for us.[17]

Sublime's excesses, then, go beyond a norm to reveal our inadequacies, and our inadequacies are—for a moment anyway—a source of pleasure.

Related, but with a distinct turn to the body and *dis*pleasure, is the abject, as theorized by Julia Kristeva:

> These body fluids, this defilement, this shit are what life withstands, hardly and with difficulty, on the part of death. There, I am at the border of my condition as a living being. My body extricates itself, as being alive, from that border. Such wastes drop so that I might live, until, from loss to loss, nothing remains in me and my body falls beyond the limit—*cadere*, cadaver.[18]

An encounter with abjection is specific, jolting, and jostles one into a realm of excess, an experience of not being governed by the linguistic, but instead having been placed in the preverbal, and a weird form of ecstasy. From Kristeva's theory arise some related concepts: of transgression, terror, violence, the monstrous, and the uncanny. Distinguishing cause from effect is important here: for Kristeva, the abject is the thing that produces excess. Excess is an affect, and, like Kant's sublime, it is more emotional than rational.

A third approach, that of Georges Bataille, begins from a more abstract point than either Kristeva or Kant does. Bataille's idea of the "accursed share" points in multiple directions, but basically argues that every culture has an excess that must be wastefully spent:

> Human activity is not entirely reducible to processes of production and conservation, and consumption must be divided into two distinct parts. The first, reducible part is represented by the use of the minimum necessary for the conservation of life and the continuation of individuals' productive activity in a given society; it is therefore a question simply of the fundamental condition of productive activity. The second part is represented by so-called unproductive expenditures: luxury, mourning, war, cults, the construction of sumptuary monuments, games, spectacles, arts, perverse sexual activity (i.e., deflected from genital finality)—all

these represent activities which, at least in primitive circumstances, have no end beyond themselves.[19]

Unlike the other two, Bataille directly does take on art, art as a culture's excess, as a supplement; however, he quickly turns art's excess into something metaphorical, and not fundamentally different from other aspects of human life. Of course, art and poetry are always inherently excessive, if we determine the starting point (the non-excessive in language) as pragmatic communication. But because Bataille sees art as *inherently* excessive, he doesn't differentiate one artwork from another. Excess for him is the ontological basis for art—one which leads to all the quirky and unstable things Bataille revels in (such as pornography, delirium, and excrement).[20] And, of course, art had always been about excess (surplus), often excess in service of stepping outside the pragmatic world. In this way Bataille, for all his alarming oddity, is typical.

Finally, and related to Bataille, a fourth version of excess reaches its paradigmatic expressions in postmodernism and consumer culture. Its central theorist is Fredric Jameson, who presents not so much a theory nor an apologia for excess as an analysis of its function in late capitalist, postmodern culture. His mordant critique sees postmodern excess, a kind of "strange new hallucinatory exhilaration," as either a value-free aesthetic (with its own dangers) or a celebration of consumerism.[21] Jameson's paradigmatic example is the Westin Bonaventure in Los Angeles. Of it he writes that it was a "bewildering immersion" in which "You are in this hyperspace up to your eyes and your body."[22] Postmodern excess, for Jameson, reached well beyond architecture. Excess was a feature of late capitalism, and would also be seen in cyberpunk, which "determines an orgy of language and representation, an excess of representational consumption."[23] In its manifestations in art, this excess of postmodernism in the arts can be either celebrative or more judgmental, and, at times, as in Jeff Koons's work, it is difficult to tell which way it wants to lean.[24]

These four theories of excess begin to reveal how excess works when it appears in art—but they provide only a partial revelation. On one hand, all four theorists recognize that excess instigates a redirected and involuntary attention and an uncontrolled affect. All four claim that excess is inextricable from feelings of euphoria, of confusion, of being overwhelmed.

Excess overtakes the perceiver's mind and body, with unpredictable consequences. Partly for these reasons (with the exception of some postmodern cultural models), excess is typically seen to be entwined with danger, and it is selective—uninterested or unable to deal with the more banal forms of excess, such as the decorative.

But, on the other hand, the standard approaches to excess, while making large claims for human experience in general, don't begin with art—if they address it at all—and, if they do address art, see it as an undifferentiated mass. Kant, for example, uses nature as his focus in his discussion of the sublime. He doesn't attach the excesses of sublimity to art (and instead sees art as the realm of the beautiful) and has only a glancing reference to the pyramids and St. Peter's—which are sublime for him because they are both really big things. When it does appear in theories of excess, art is treated as an undifferentiated mass. For example, Bataille's is a version of a dominant tradition of understanding art as supplemental, beyond the ordinary—his is a melodramatic version of such concepts as defamiliarization and aesthetic contemplation. *All* art from Bataille's perspective is the same version of excess, beyond the pragmatic. However, this doesn't separate out particular works of art that are in excess of culturally understood norms for art at the time. The consequence is that, with the exception of camp, art excess is implied to be an unmodified extension of these more comprehensive excess theories, theories that do not or cannot address artworks that seem, in comparison to other artworks, excessive. Two consequences follow. First, with the limited exception of Bataille and theories of consumerism, theories of excess don't see excess as cultural, and therefore they don't see excess as partaking in a discourse of the natural and unnatural. Second, they don't believe that the experience of excess can be an occasion for analysis. In short, while large claims of dominant theories of excess give excess conceptual heft and ambition, they miss nuance, and the complexities and varieties of aesthetic experience.

***

An analysis that begins with art achieves both a more nuanced understanding of excess and delineates more clearly the larger expressive possibilities of excess. Most important, unlike the abject or the sublime, art excess arises from a made thing, a thing that is a product of an intent—a distinction missing in the theoretical principles of both the abject and the sublime. We understand products of intents in ways different from other things in the world; they mean in different ways. To give a banal example, a poem means in a different way than does a mountain—while art is understood to be purposive, for most people a mountain is not. Second, because the excess I am discussing is *art* excess it is an excess that steps on and is entangled with semiotics and representation. Even with abject art, even art made of bodily fluids and excretions—art which consequently gives rise to some of the affects Kristeva describes—the origin of the excessive experience is still seen as an artwork, a work produced by a person, and we wonder why is *this* art? How should I look at it? What does it mean? The work of art is always bound up with representation (it either is a representation itself, or it uses the tools of representation, or it addresses questions of representation), and its excesses are entangled with that. Excess becomes semiotic in the artwork, making it accessible to analysis. And here, then, Kant's exclusion of art from the sublime makes some sense—art can represent the sublime, but that is not the same as *being* sublime.

Further, when placed in the context of art, excess is relational, an exponential exaggeration of a culturally understood norm for an object or experience. Going beyond a norm, a norm explicitly or implicitly understood, the excessive artwork subverts our expectations of the "normal," or the "adequate." That relational quality is important because it makes the excessive moment an *argument*. Excess, violating a *culturally expected* norm, is a judgment about a property, not simply an objective property itself.

Excess in art is achieved through three overlapping features, all understood to be handled "inappropriately" by the excessive work. The first is number: through repetition, or through what we might think of as multiplicity and abundance, such as in *Gesamtkunstwerken*, where the stimuli come through multiple senses, or the many quotations in *The Waste Land*. Second, excess and its effects are also created around issues of size, such as largeness or disproportion of scale, as in Joyce's *Ulysses*, where inappropriate magnification of detail explodes the realist novel: recall the famous list of Bloom's attraction to water. And finally, excess is made manifest through issues of focus, of what we might think of as the exaggeration of non-quantifiable properties—properties that are exaggerated, but that aren't understood in terms of quantity or size—things like a stressed register, or overly complicated rhyme, or narrative coincidence, or heightened vocabulary. Edith Sitwell's work, for example:

> That hobnailed goblin, the bob-tailed Hob,
> Said, "It is time I began to rob."
> For strawberries bob, hob-nob with the pearls
> Of cream (like the curls of the dairy girls),
> And flushed with the heat and fruitish-ripe
> Are the gowns of the maids who dance to the pipe.
> Chase a maid?
> She's afraid![25]

This kind of imbalance, less garish but more portentous, is also seen in Eliot's "Sweeney Erect":

> Paint me a cavernous waste shore
>   Cast in the unstilled Cyclades,
> Paint me the bold anfractuous rocks
>   Faced by the snarled and yelping seas.
>
> Display me Aeolus above
>   Reviewing the insurgent gales
> Which tangle Ariadne's hair
>   And swell with haste the perjured sails.[26]

In Eliot's quatrain poems, momentary eruptions of an oddly heightened diction (arising from different kinds of semantic fields), a diction in excess of both pragmatic and poetic norms, throw standard interpretive practices off kilter. The shifts in tone are disruptive, jostling one's attention to a different kind of mental activity, and creating an odd discontinuity in reading.

When it appears at moments in a text, as moments of rupture, excess creates an odd aesthetic experience. Excess in such texts has the effect of a sudden and awkward shift, with a startling lack of balance among parts. Excess feels startling—the shift to a new register seems more exponential than incremental—unearned, tangential. It shifts attention, and *kinds* of attention. Startling, the excessive work redirects focus to something where the focus should not be so detailed, or should include other things, or should be more general. In art, excess-induced instability encourages not so much terror or ecstasy, as distraction, creating problems for the aesthetic unity that the later New Critics valued so highly. Excess leads to an instability of affect, sometimes heightened, and sometimes just an affect that has not been clearly settled into. One is *not* led to a kind of quiet contemplation, or even, in the conservative aesthetic terms of the day, of being "moved." While that instability doesn't always lead to a spectacular affect such as the sublime, there is always, at least, a mild anxiety, or a kind of vertigo, even with the excesses of camp—the bad taste that is flaunted, the good taste that is flouted.

The excessive artwork, while presenting an inappropriate and overwhelming foreground, and leading to a short-circuiting of normative interpretation—the excessive work overwhelms by putting to the side directed comprehension and interpretive closure. Excess creates an interpretive instability in which one isn't sure where to focus, or what protocols to use when one *is* focusing. Excessive artworks (and excessive experiences) have what Peter Rabinowitz has termed unclear "rules of notice"[27]—one is unclear where to look, what to highlight, and what interpretive procedures to use. For example, excess creates problems of register: there is no clear center, no principle of hierarchies anymore. Harold Monro, recall, complained of *The Waste Land* that the poem "may appear like a drawing that is so crowded with apparently unrelated details that the design or meaning (if there be one) cannot be grasped until those details have been [...] assembled and related to each other."[28] This may account for the interpretive problems of works like *The Waste Land*—its excesses don't allow interpretation to rest, or readers to achieve any kind of mastery. Similarly, the closer one looks at a work like Picasso's *Portrait of Daniel-Henry Kahnweiler*, the more it refuses to simplify: the smaller become its constituent parts, the more they refuse to cohere representationally or semiotically, and the more they overwhelm you.[29] These vacillations forestall both generalization *and* differentiation, the central activities of meaning-making.

The complicated experience that excessive works encourage is not the same as the traditional values of richness or inexhaustibility. While richness confirms or complicates rather than startles, excess is more centrifugal. Excessive works of art make both noticeable *and* awkward the properties that they exaggerate. In its exaggeration of some primal basic characteristics of Kahnweiler, the portrait's mimetic features work like caricature (as Adam Gopnik suggested years ago).[30] Indeed, all excess, when it deals with representing the human character, or the human figure, is essentially a matter of caricature—and is therefore also tied up with simplification of its source norm, an unstable movement which suggests why caricature is so central to modernism.

This movement leads to those excessive properties standing out—not just from the world more generally, but from how these properties work in most other art. Joyce's epic catalogues in the Cyclops episode of *Ulysses* are perhaps modernism's most spectacular instance. At times distractibility becomes so noticeable that the resulting interpretive stuttering becomes the excessive work's subject—think, for example of Hope Mirrlees's poem *Paris*.

>Great bunches of lilac among syphons, vermouth,
>Bocks, tobacco.
>>*Messieursetdames*
>>NE FERMEZ PAS LA PORTE
>>S. V. P
>>LE PRIMUS S'EN CHARGERA
>
>At marble tables sit ouvriers in blue linen suits discuss-
>ing:
>>La journée de huit heures,
>>Whether Landru is a Sadist,
>>The learned seal at the Nouveau Cirque
>>>Cottin. . . .
>
>Echoes of Bossuet chanting dead queens.
>>*méticuleux*
>>*bélligerants*
>>*hebdomadaire*
>>*immonde*[31]

Indeed, excess is a kind of defamiliarization, instigated by exaggeration, whether of the materials of art, or, reaching beyond, to a defamiliarization of signification itself. In modernism it tends to point in specific directions, addressing ideas of representation, making the structures of representation visible.

***

Excessive art raises two unique interpretive problems. First, Eliot's excesses trouble the singleness of the lyric voice, introducing imbalance, struggle, and discord into what would typically be the unity of a lyric poem. Because of its stepping outside of a norm and highlighting conventions of representation, excess destabilizes and mutes personal expression. Picasso's portrait of Kahnweiler, in its fracturing of surface, limits psychological depth and so presents a kind of reductionist chilliness; similarly, Eliot's *Waste Land* becomes less about voice and more about text. By destabilizing the poem's register and by muting personal expression, excess is seen to be insincere, mannered. As John Middleton Murry wrote of *Ulysses*, "the curse of nimiety, of too-muchness, hangs over it as a whole" (197). Excess is commonly understood to be diseased and perverse, unnatural. F. L. Lucas, reviewing *The Waste Land*, let fly with

> Among the maggots that breed in the corruption of poetry one of the commonest is the bookworm. When Athens had decayed and Alexandria sprawled, the new giant-city, across the Egyptian sands; when the Greek world was filling with libraries and emptying of poets, growing in erudition as its genius expired, the first appeared, as pompous as Herod and as worm-eaten, that *Professorenpoesie* which finds in literature the inspiration that life gives no more, which replaces depth by muddiness, beauty by echoes, passion by necrophily. [...] Disconnected and ill-knit, loaded with echo and allusion, fantastic and crude, obscure and obscurantist—such is the typical style of Alexandrianism.[32]

Lucas was not alone. *The Waste Land* was often seen by early detractors as unnatural, sterile, dry bones—a reaction prompted to some extent by the poem's excessiveness. No surprise here: the culturally agreed-upon is frequently seen as "natural," outside of a specific historical moment rather than culturally determined.

A second interpretive problem: one can't distort the typical functions of important things without attracting attention to them. Excess always makes the thing it is *in excess of* its subject matter. Excess is always an excess *of*—and therefore a reference to and analysis of—*something*. All works of art refer, of course, but the central reference of excess is to a violated norm. The basic structure of excess's reference, then, is always relational, in an overtly disproportionate manner, to something within the same system. As a result of that reference, excess, perhaps counter-intuitively, leads to analysis: Eliot's work both overwhelms and refers to language's pragmatic representational character and the intertextual nature of poetry.

Excess is surplus—but it is also the normative world left behind. And in its simultaneous reference to and violation of a norm, the self-consciousness of excess is always, in itself, semiotic, perhaps even *about* semiotics. Thus, Eliot's excesses—while their instabilities are not those of celebrity or consumer culture—all have a semiotic function, as do the excesses of other corners of modernism, as does art excess in general. And in all these contexts the excesses are examinations of the semiotic systems which they both violate and participate in, which is why excessive works can seem so *knowing*. They would be a lot less interesting without such self-consciousness.

That it is meta in such an imbalanced, disruptive way makes the knowingness of excess both *clear* in its presence and *opaque* in its meaning. Its doubleness implies that, while excess is always an analytic look backward, it looks back from a position of instability. These two things in conjunction—analysis and instability—have a particular consequence and function. In its meta-position of reference to a norm, but also because of its instability within this position, excess always questions ideology, dramatizing the uncertainty of perception and its categorizing, critiquing earlier certainties. Excess's analysis is *by definition* always anti-ideological, and never commonsensical. That position of instability radically shapes its critique—not so much arguing against the violated norm as caricaturing it, having the norm collapse under its own weight. So, while excess always creates a moment of bafflement, of euphoria, perhaps even of threat, cognition isn't completely short-circuited. One then might ask the question: as a semiotic system can art really achieve the self-forgetfulness of the sublime? Is art ever truly sublime? Or is art an instance in which the excesses of the sublime are represented, tamed?

***

Far from being a detriment, Eliot's excesses, I believe, make him a richer poet, and for some unexpected reasons. First, the excessive is always understood to be unnatural—and Eliot, one vest too many in his suit, was commonly seen as having difficulty being natural. Indeed, skeptics among Eliot's first readers believed that his poetic excesses (particularly his massive allusions) were part of a single package: that Eliot's awkward relationship to British or Western high culture was forced, not natural. But this forced and awkwardly deliberate relationship is a large part of what makes Eliot such an interesting poet.

Second, Eliot's excesses weren't idiosyncratic. The reach of modernist excess is long, and wide.[33] Eliot's excessive work continues and develops (on chilly modernist terms) a kind of affect seen also in the culture at large, as well as in isolated moments earlier in history, in the gothic and the carnivalesque. Within modernism, Eliot's poetry participates in modernism's larger discourse of excess, a discourse that also takes in the celebrative side of modernism, and includes Dada, futurism, Wallace Stevens's *Harmonium*, Satie's *Parade*, and Edith Sitwell's *Façade*. J. C. Squire, editor of the *London Mercury*, was typical of traditionalist skeptics inveighing against modernist excess:

> We have had in the last few years art, so called, […] "styles" which were mere protests and revulsions against other styles; "styles" which were no more than flamboyant attempts at advertisement akin to the shifting lights of the electric night signs; authors who have forgotten their true selves in the desperate search for remarkable selves; artists who have refused to keep their eyes upon the object because it has been seen before; musicians who have made,

for novelty's sake, noises, and painters who have made, for effect's sake, spectacles, which invited the attention of those who make it their business to suppress public nuisances.[34]

While Eliot was not really a central aspect of modernist "movements"— Pound asserted that Eliot had "actually trained himself *and* modernized himself *on his own*"[35]—excess forms a somewhat odd common ground between these otherwise disparate figures of modernism. Excess is essential to understanding a moment in Eliot's career and to modernism's shape: among other things, modernism was an awkwardly shared conversation about—and self-conscious exploration of—excess as a system of signification, and as an attack on the ideologically "natural" as an assumed category.

Finally, despite the instincts of our profession (particularly in our teaching) to domesticate art through interpretive control, we need to keep Eliot's strangeness. By losing the strangeness of his excesses we lose the pleasures, the disorientation. Eliot's excessive moments accentuate the time-based experience of reading, which differs from an overall interpretation of a poem like *The Waste Land*. One is left with an inability to remain in control of an interpretive teleology, an inability which can be either mourned or celebrated. It is better to celebrate.

Notes

1 "How Pleasant to Meet Mr Eliot," *T. S. Eliot: A Symposium*, ed. Richard March and Tambimuttu (Editions Poetry, 1948), 16.
2 Thomas Kelly, *First Nights: Five Musical Premieres* (Yale University Press, 200), 279.
3 Quoted in Kelly, *First Nights*, 289.
4 Kelly, *First Nights*, 295.
5 Florent Schmitt, "Les Sacre du Printemps, de M. Igor Strawinsky, au Théâtre des Champs-Elysses," *La France*, June 4, 1913. Quoted in Kelly, *First Nights*, 313.
6 "London Letter," September 1921, *Complete Prose* 2:369–70.
7 Review of *Poesies* by Jean Cocteau, *The Dial*, January 1921, 110. Modern culture's excesses were not always understood positively, of course, and modern art was not exempt from its entanglements with its surround culture. Modernism had too much advertising, publicity, celebrity

culture—as well as too much poetry, too many anthologies. It mimicked the excesses of the culture at large.
8   "Metaphysical Poets," *Complete Prose* 2:375–76.
9   *Poems* 1:49.
10 "Recent Verse," *Literary World* (1917), in *T. S. Eliot: The Contemporary Reviews*, ed. Jewel Spears Brooker (Cambridge University Press, 2004), 6.
11 *Poems* 1:25.
12 Adam Gopnik argues for the presence of caricature in Picasso's portraits around the time of his painting of Kahnweiler, and as well notes the relationship of it to Picasso's use of West African and Iberian tropes in his transformation to cubism around the time of *Les Demoiselles d'Avignon*. "High and Low: Caricature, Primitivism, and the Cubist Portrait," *Art Journal* (Winter 1983): 374.
13 "The Esotericism of T. S. Eliot," *1924*, no. 1 (July 1, 1924): 3–10. Reprinted in *T. S. Eliot: The Critical Heritage*, ed. Michael Grant, 2 vols. (Routledge, 1982), 1:206.
14 *Poems* 1:71.
15 Monro, "Notes for a Study of *The Waste Land*," *Chapbook* 34 (1923), in Brooker, *Contemporary Reviews*, 97.
16 Ransom, "Waste Lands," *New York Evening Post Literary Review* 3 (1923), in Brooker, *Contemporary Reviews*, 106.
17 *Critique of the Power of Judgment*, translated by Paul Guyer and Eric Matthews, *The Cambridge Edition of the Works of Immanuel Kant*, ed. Paul Guyer (Cambridge University Press, 2000), 134, 140–41. In his *Philosophical Inquiry into the Origin of Our Ideas of the Sublime and Beautiful* (Blackwell, 1987), Edmund Burke asserts that instability and displeasure, "the passions which belong to self-preservation, turn on pain and danger; they are simply painful when their causes immediately affect us; they are delightful when we have an idea of pain and danger, without being actually in such circumstances; this delight I have not called pleasure, because it turns on pain, and because it is different enough from any idea of positive pleasure. Whatever excites this delight, I call sublime" (51).
18 Julia Kristeva, *Powers of Horror: An Essay on Abjection*, translated by Leon S. Roudiez (Columbia University Press, 1982), 3.
19 Georges Bataille, *The Bataille Reader*, ed. Fred Botting and Scott Wilson (Blackwell, 1997), 169.
20 Bataille argues, "The wasteful excesses of luxury are analogous to sacrifice insofar as they, like a gift, 'give up' or 'give away' the use-value and exchange-value of some precious commodity and transmute it into a form of useless expenditure, not unlike excremental waste." *Bataille Reader*, 108–9.
21 Fredric Jameson, *Postmodernism, or, the Cultural Logic of Late Capitalism* (Duke University Press 1991), 33.

22 Jameson, *Postmodernism*, 43.
23 Jameson, *Postmodernism*, 321.
24 Jameson asserted that this aspect of postmodernism radically separated it from modernism: "Let us reemphasize the enormity of a transition which leaves behind it the desolation of Hopper's buildings or the stark Midwest syntax of Sheeler's forms, replacing them with the extraordinary surfaces of the photorealist cityscape, where even the automobile wrecks gleam with some new hallucinatory splendor." *Postmodernism*, 32–33.
25 "Country Dance," from Edith Sitwell, *Bucolic Comedies* (Duckworth and Co., 1923), 33.
26 *Poems* 1:36.
27 Peter Rabinowitz, *Before Reading: Narrative Conventions and the Politics of Interpretation* (Cornell University Press, 1987), 47–75.
28 Monro, in Brooker, *Contemporary Reviews*, 97.
29 See www.artic.edu/artworks/111060/daniel-henry-kahnweiler.
30 "High and Low: Caricature, Primitivism, and the Cubist Portrait," *Art Journal* (Winter 1983): 371–76.
31 Hope Mirrlees, *Paris* (Hogarth Press, 1919), 10.
32 Lucas, "The Waste Land," *New Statesman* 22 (1923), in Brooker, *Contemporary Reviews*, 115–16.
33 As many have argued, modernist claims for austerity were not only a self-serving attempt to clear some ground away from decadence and the late nineteenth century. But modernist artworks themselves only partially exemplify those sketchy claims. While that stripped-down narrative once had significant explanatory power, the 1990s recognizing of it as an interpretive straitjacket went hand in hand with the expansion of the modern canon, eventually to bad modernisms, to the middlebrow, celebrity culture, and, camp, among other things—shading over to ideas of modernism not as a repudiation but as *an expression of* excess. But even in a limited field—the canon of, say, the 1950s—the austere modernist narrative does a disservice, particularly in the face of works discussed here.
34 "Editorial Notes," *London Mercury*, November 1919, 3.
35 Letter to Harriet Monroe, September 30, 1914. Ezra Pound, *Selected Letters 1907–1941*, ed. D. D. Paige (New Directions, 1950), 40.

Special Forum: Teaching *The Waste Land*

Introduction

Megan Quigley and John Whittier-Ferguson

In a letter to Emily Hale, Eliot shared some sentiments that many of us might feel about our daily lives. He wrote:

> Teaching is very hard work—I was a failure at it myself, but that was when I first tried to make a living here, and I was nervously completely shattered anyway.[1]

We don't believe Eliot was a failure at it, but we do think teaching is very hard work and nothing to be undertaken in a vacuum. Recent scholarship, particularly Laura Heffernan and Rachel Sagner Buurma's prize-winning new book *The Teaching Archive*, has placed teaching firmly back at the center of the work we do as scholars, not only in our mission as educators, but also as a driving force and source for much of our research.[2] Our sense that the humanities classroom itself is not a place of preparation for writing or assessment, but is the site itself of knowledge production, drove our desire to share the pedagogical practices that bring such joy, creativity, and intellectual energy to our students.

We believe it is a fascinating time to be reading and teaching T. S. Eliot—we have new editions, materials, archives, and exciting new scholarship. It is also a time for reflection as we make our way through a pandemic, transformative historical and social movements, and seismic shifts in institutions and academic practices (hello Zoom!). Teaching has never seemed so important; and yet how do we do it best?

The idea for this forum originated in a conference roundtable on teaching *The Waste Land*, held at the annual meeting of the T. S. Eliot Society in September of 2021. We asked our panelists to frame their remarks by considering several different questions about their pedagogical theories and practices.[3] We preserve the original prompts here not simply in the interests of history but also because these queries continue to be of importance to us. They are also useful tools for those teachers reading this forum who may pose the same questions to themselves as a way of deepening and stretching their own practice.

Creative Assignments: Given Eliot's difficulty, erudition, and historical distance, what kinds of assignments do you create to bring Eliot alive in the classroom?

Teaching Eliot in the Antiracist Classroom: What texts and resources do you pair with teaching Eliot? As we decolonize the literary curriculum, why teach Eliot now?

Digital Eliot: What on-line resources (*The Complete Prose*, the Eliot foundation website, our Society's own website, *The Waste Land* app, Graphic Novel versions) have you effectively used (or can you imagine using) in the classroom and with what kinds of assignments?[4]

Editions: Which editions of Eliot's works do you assign to your students and why?

New Voices/New Views (current students, recent graduate students, and contingent faculty): How do you think we should teach Eliot in 2021? In what contexts and classes?

That inaugural roundtable inspired the creation of this forum in the *Annual* and the inclusion of new voices, from first-year composition instructors and their pupils to college students in Japan and India. The essays collected here invite us to think about Eliot outside the Anglophone classroom and beyond the traditional seminar or lecture hall. They think about the challenges and excitement of the new editions of Eliot's poems, prose, and letters, and the revelations of the Hale archive. After reading them we hope you will never approach teaching some of Eliot's key words— *impersonality, difficulty, Shantih*—in quite the same way.

Each of the essays here is brief, and they are all usefully focused on actual classroom practices. These are not hypothetical lesson-plans; they are reports from the field. Their authors display an essential virtue common to all great teachers: they demonstrate a capacity for imagining their subject—this compelling and forbidding poem—from the points of view of their students. Some of these pieces make direct reference to memories of their authors' own first encounters with Eliot's poem. All of them emphasize beginning to teach newcomers how to read "April is the cruellest month" not with all we now know and can lecture endlessly about, but by imagining where our students will be when they encounter this line (having already had to navigate the epigraph, the gnomic dedication, and three languages other than English). These teachers advise that, as we begin to help our students learn to care enough about the poem that they consider its further elucidation worth the trouble, we make only minimal use of the copious annotations, cribs, apps, and websites now dedicated to explication of the poem or to providing information about everything that might be connected to Eliot's masterpiece.

If we're not in the business of elucidating every possible reference to literary and cultural history in *The Waste Land*, what exactly is our task as teachers? The classrooms sketched in these essays have students formulating essential questions of their own (that it will then be the business of the class to answer); considering whatever it is in their own rich cultural inheritances that allows them to connect with even the smallest part of this polyvocal work; bringing their own voices into performances that riff on aspects of Eliot's assembly of speaking subjects, or perhaps playing the parts of Eliot's critics (using the selections gathered in Michael North's Norton Critical Edition of the poem).[5] For a number of these teachers' units on the poem, students become their own editors—annotating portions of the poem in ways that *they* find helpful; or they play Pound's part—cutting away lines from the first draft of, say, "Death by Water" and then comparing their choices with those of *il miglior fabbro*. Valerie Eliot's edition of the edited *Waste Land* manuscript proves important to a number of these teachers, not only for what it shows us about the poem's origins and its evolution under the joint labors of Tom and Vivien Eliot and Ezra Pound, but also for how the drama of the poem's evolution provides a powerful example of the importance of revision, of crafting multiple drafts, and of finding astute and scrupulous readers for one's work.[6] Early reviews help some of these teachers validate the confusion and the dismay that still attend initial encounters with the difficulty and obscurity of *The Waste Land*; those reviews also demonstrate what Eliot's first readers found immediately relevant and compelling about his unprecedented poem. And at the most recent point on the spectrum of scholarship, the very latest collection of Eliot-related materials—the 1,131 letters Eliot wrote to Emily Hale—provides students with a way into the intensely personal aspects of this richly emotional text. Virginia Woolf, in a diary entry for June 23, 1922, referencing Mary Hutchinson, famously refers to the poem as "Tom's autobiography—a melancholy one."[7] The Hale archive can serve to bring the poet's memory and desire dramatically to the heart of our own experiences of the poem.

The teaching roundtable at our annual meeting left all of us excited about the prospect of introducing Eliot's great poem to students. We feel that excitement again as we read these contributions, and we trust that you, too, will come away from this assembly eager to bring *The Waste Land* into the twenty-first century—finding new readers for its next hundred years.

Notes

1 Letter of January 20, 1931, Emily Hale Letters from T. S. Eliot, C0686, Manuscripts Division, Department of Special Collections, Princeton University Library. Published by the Estate of T. S. Eliot at https://tseliot.com/the-eliot-hale-letters.

2 Rachel Sagner Buurma and Laura Heffernan, *The Teaching Archive* (University of Chicago Press, 2020).

3 The roundtable participants were: Ria Banerjee, Guttman Community College, CUNY; Josh Epstein, Portland State University; Patrick Query, West Point; Johanna Winant, West Virginia University.
4 *The Complete Prose of T. S. Eliot: The Critical Edition, Vols. 1–8*. The T. S. Eliot Foundation: https://tseliot.com; The International T. S. Eliot Society: tseliotsociety.org; *The Waste Land* app: https://apps.apple.com/us/app/the-waste-land/id427434046; Julian Peters, graphic T. S. Eliot: julianpeterscomics.com.
5 T. S. Eliot, *The Waste Land*, ed. Michael North (Norton Critical Editions, 2001).
6 A corrected edition has been published: *The Waste Land: A Facsimile and Transcript of the Original Drafts*, centenary edition in full colour, ed. Valerie Eliot (Faber & Faber, 2022) ISBN 978-0-571-37085-6.
7 *The Diary of Virginia Woolf, Vol. 2: 1920–1924*, ed. Anne Olivier Bell and Andrew McNeillie (Harcourt, Brace, Jovanovich, 1980), 178.

Students-as-Pound
Creative Assignment on *The Waste Land*

Brian Kennedy

We all know that without Ezra Pound *The Waste Land* would not have been what it is—would possibly not have been, period. As I open my unit on Eliot's work, and particularly *The Waste Land*, I make this point by talking to my students about the interwoven experience of Pound and Eliot through the time of production of that poem. The revelation that the poem's original title was "He Do the Police in Different Voices" always seems to light a spark of recognition in them. They get the idea of the mash-up of voices. It gives them a way to wrangle what looks like total chaos otherwise. "Oh, so *that* is what's going on here," their faces say. But, as we all know, students learn by what they do more than what they hear, so I add the exercise described below to my teaching of *The Waste Land*, and students really enjoy it.

***

I first reiterate the Pound influence, with the emphasis on the fact that his vision was to cut narrative bits so that the fragments that were left sit next to each other without connective tissue. I show students some pages of the facsimile manuscript copy of the poem, from the volume edited by Valerie Eliot and first published in 1971. This has manuscript in handwriting, manuscript in typescript, and handwriting-on-typescript, everything from word changes to slashes through entire sections. I often look at "The

Fire Sermon," where Pound axes about fifteen lines prior to the "At the violet hour" section (*c.* line 215+), and directly following, where Pound chop-chop-chops words and phrases to get to the final version of lines 222+.

Then I play the recording of Eliot reading *The Waste Land*, made about thirty years after the poem's 1922 publication, and I welcome students to follow along in their texts. As Eliot finishes, I tell them to shut their books, and I give out the full, four-page, ninety-two-line, original version of the fourth section, "Death by Water." I then tell them that we're going to play Pound, and I put them in small groups with the instruction to take the original and make it into what Pound would have done.

You would think that, having just heard Eliot read the poem and having followed along in their texts, they would immediately cut to the quick and spoil the fun by saying something like, "I know he just took the last couple of stanzas." That never happens. Instead, they puzzle over the task, editing words and lines. Sometimes, someone takes out a big section. Nobody ever ends up even close to the ten lines, themselves untouched from the original version, that Eliot/Pound chose. We then do our big reveal by opening our texts and seeing the final form.

Students are always surprised at just how much Pound cut, but they also sometimes make remarkably good arguments for their own versions, showing how they have taken out narrative tissue and kept what was in line with the themes and motifs of the poem as they are now starting to understand them. As an aside, the exercise would work, it seems to me, just as well if one chose one short stanza (maybe twenty lines) from somewhere else in the poem and had students "Pound" that. Something with a fair number of emendations, like the sections mentioned above (lines 215+, 222+).

In any case, students enjoy this exercise, and they remain engaged in it. Each group wants to know why members of the other groups did what they did, so after the reveal of their cuts and Pound/Eliot's final version, we discuss and debate some more: Who makes the best Pound?

Aside from being a hands-on exercise, this activity gives students an inside feel of the process Eliot and Pound shared, and it demystifies the text. Students seem to enjoy the feeling of power that they gain by becoming co-creators of the poem. Suddenly, it's not this monster monolith that they have to decipher, but a text that they can come alongside of and be in charge of. The realization sticks with them that *The Waste Land* is not part of some mythical, untouchable canonical pantheon of verse, but a document that two humans co-created, perhaps argued over, and worked on word by word to get into final form. As students realize that this poem may well have ended up differently in its final form, the barriers between literary London and their classroom in Pasadena, California, are broken down.

Duets and Deadness

Josh Epstein

> Someone said: "The dead writers are remote from us because we *know* so much more than they did." Precisely, and they are that which we know.
> —T. S. Eliot, "Tradition and the Individual Talent"

> When I count, there are only you and I together.
> —T. S. Eliot, *The Waste Land* (1922)

Like many who regularly teach *The Waste Land*, I find myself struggling to formulate classes that not only encourage collaboration but thematize it, by working through the various kinds of interactivity performed by the text itself. It is a deeply collaborative poem in every respect, down to its very composition. And the interactive quality of the poem—its intertextual borrowings across both time and space, theatrical exchanges of voices in public houses, operatic interjections of Thames-Sisters—saturates its language and form. All of these lively exchanges notwithstanding, I often find it a struggle to talk about the multiple aural presences of the poem without watching them land with "dead sound" right in front of me.

In a seminar on modernism and media, I tried again. The class focused especially (though not exclusively) on technologies of sound recording. So, after some preliminary setup, I showed students a 1991 duet between Natalie Cole and her late father Nat King Cole, singing "Unforgettable." The use of this video was prompted by the work of two musicologists, Jason Stanyek and Benjamin Piekut, who have written about the cultural politics of recorded "collaborations" between the living and the dead, including "Unforgettable" as well as duets between the Hank Williamses Jr. and Sr., and tribute albums to Notorious B.I.G. and Bob Marley.[1] In an essay called "Deadness," Stanyek and Piekut argue that in collaborations the dead body and voice meet with live ones in what they call an "intermundane" realm, neither living nor dead. Stanyek and Piekut coin the neologism "corpaural" to think about the ways that embodied sounds escape from one body and cling to others. If any poem is intermundane, we'd have to include *The Waste Land*—the "Unforgettable" duet, in this context, resonates not only with the poem but with Eliot's poetic theories, and echoes the uncanny dislocation of reading a century-old poem as if it were part of a timeless order. It also precipitates questions central to media history and theory about the status of, say, a gramophone—something that freezes the live voice into wax, or that preserves the voices of one's deceased relatives in a semipermanent un-dead state. In its way, the intermundane "involves a perception, not only of the pastness of the past, but of its presence" ("Tradition and the Individual Talent").

For our class, then, my hope was that we might dust off Eliot's magisterial claim that the living artist gains meaning only in relation to the dead, as something that decenters the poem's cultural prestige, and reconceive how the poem treats music and text as collaborative and "corpaural," not just in the uncannily nostalgic ways seen in the Cole/Cole performance, but in more challenging forms. Collaboration in *The Waste Land* is hardly innocent, and can rarely be isolated from violence, a problem to which our class discussion cycled frequently. Still, as an entry point, I asked students to reconceive of one portion of the poem as a duet, informed by whatever contexts they wished so long as it reckoned closely with the "Deadness" essay and the poem's aesthetic choices. ("Deadness" is pitched a bit high for some undergraduates, but asking them to work through passages in groups allowed them to work through much of what they needed.)

In response to this task, students devised a few live performances of some of the dialogues/duets in the poem itself: between characters or figures, between living figures and deceased ones, between texts, between different time scales. A "live" student presenter led us through a collective performance of sections of the poem in concert with Eliot's own recorded voice (his face on the YouTube page looming over the classroom, like the Wizard of Oz). This duet with Eliot focused our attention on the formal properties of meter and rhythm, particularly in those passages of the poem that feel like duets between spoken voices and interior ones. One pair of students used the manuscripts to perform a duet between Eliot and Pound, coupling a not-bad imitation of Eliot's voice with occasional interruptions of "PERHAPS BE DAMNED!" There was an animated chess game, in homage to the title of "A Game of Chess," and though none of the students tackled it, the famous love-duet of Wagner's *Tristan* would have been low-hanging fruit (in principle—not in execution!). I had not, alas, yet learned about the Twitter bot that remixes lines from Eliot with lines from Taylor Swift.

Using the "Unforgettable" video as an initial thought-experiment, our class was able to trace several paths through *The Waste Land*, and our own critical dispositions toward it. Eliot's claim that the living artist gains meaning only in relation to the dead seemed to lose a little bit of its mustiness. This video in which liveness and deadness were made to seem entirely provisional categories, bound to proliferating media and marketable forms of sentimental nostalgia, reanimated some of Eliot's ambivalence toward the potentially enlivening effects of live music and deadening effects of mass media. One student noted the "dead sound at the stroke of nine"—the idea that sound itself was marked as both "dead" and unpredictably resonant and "unpredictably durative" in its effects, "indirect, delayed, unintended, and even unmarked."[2] She also suggested that Eliot's perplexing footnote to this line, "a phenomenon that I have often noted," might not be a singularly unhelpful gloss on the poem, so much as a register of the intermundane, the mediated cultural labor that exceeds individual agency. I found my own pedagogical resistance to Eliot's footnotes met with promising questions about the text's allusiveness as a form of intermundanity, rather than as a one-directional effort to establish the poem's authority.

The exercise found some productive resistance, as well. We found ourselves increasingly conscious of the risks of sentimentalizing this "intermundane" as a playful trope, or papering over the gendered violence that accompanies the poem's many voices. We were pressed to think about how the poem's "corpaural" effects produced not the gauzy nostalgia of "Unforgettable," but trauma, rage, and destabilizing ellipsis. As Ria Banerjee has astutely written, this poem urges us to reexamine our "readerly fear and disgust [...] recently resensitized by national political events" such as #MeToo, and to "rehear," in the poem's exhausted and indifferent voices, "injury that demands a corrective."[3] We talked, too, about questions of disability; the students' inclusion of captions and subtitles in whatever media they used, an inclusive gesture in its own right, reinscribed what the poem itself does as a written text (anyone who has seen the ululating Rhinemaidens captioned in an opera hall has wondered, on some level, about the bare matter of consonants and vowels). As we moved through the course to texts by Woolf, Forster, Rhys, and Selvon, we were also called to confront the conflicted imperial politics of sound across modernist texts, including Eliot's. A host of unresolved questions surfaced, both in the students' experiments and in their writing.

Though this discussion dated before the emergence of COVID-19, could it stir some new life into remote teaching, exhausting as it is in its new extractions of mental work, but perhaps usefully estranging in terms of how and why we value "live teaching" in relation to voices from the past? I have not had the chance to repeat this experiment, but given our unsettled (and unequally distributed) work as teachers, this may be just the time to rethink our relation to, well, time: to the "liveness" of a text or a sound medium, a text's afterlives in the classroom, and the classroom itself as a space of mediated exchange. My feelings about the proliferation of online classes, Zoom sessions, and the like are mixed (to put it mildly), but these media offer plenty of new paths. Never in my life did I think that words like "asynchronous" would be common currency for undergraduate students. I am not the first to note that *The Waste Land* is, in its way, an asynchronous learning environment—one that flattens out multiple literary and historical time scales and reanimates surprising forms of teamwork. Might those of us who find online teaching tiring (and depressingly neoliberal) in its ongoing demands for "adaptive instructional best practice assessment" want to be just as careful about fetishizing the live classroom or, at least, to be less antiquated about the needs of working students to grapple with these texts on their own timelines rather than on mine? To duet well is both to listen and to make noise; why should that reciprocal generosity have to be synchronous? *The Waste Land* offers a call for some introspection about our own pedagogical commitments, not only intellectually but in the practical work of listening to the text, and to other listeners.

Notes

1 Jason Stanyek and Benjamin Piekut, "Deadness: Technologies of the Intermundane," *TDR: The Drama Review* 54, no. 1 (2010): 14–38.
2 Stanyek and Piekut, "Deadness," 18.
3 Ria Banerjee. "Time," "Reading 'The Waste Land' with the #MeToo Generation," ed. Megan Quigley. *Modernism/modernity* (March 4, 2019), https://doi.org/10.26597/mod.0100.

Teaching Difficulty

Johanna Winant

Eliot wrote that modern art "must be difficult," and readers of *The Waste Land* have agreed that his poem fits that description.[1] While his early critics disputed whether it was nonsensical—"unable to make head or tail of it"[2]—or brilliant—"The music of ideas"[3]—there was consensus on its difficulty. *The Waste Land* has exemplified modernist difficulty for a century. As teachers, how should we handle its difficulty in our classrooms? I'll suggest in this brief essay a few ways that we can encourage students to describe the poem's difficulty—or its multiple difficulties—as precisely as possible. The goal is not to make the poem itself easy to understand, but to clarify how we can and should read *The Waste Land*. The difficulty never goes away but can, itself, be better understood.

First, it is worth noting that *The Waste Land*'s difficulty today is not exactly the same as it was one hundred years ago. In 1922, the most common accounts of the poem's difficulty attribute it to fragmentation. "It seems at first sight remarkably disconnected and confused [...] [however] a closer view of the poem does more than illuminate the difficulties; it reveals the hidden form of the work, [and] indicates how each thing falls into place."[4] I suspect that students in the twenty-first century are less jolted by quick jump cuts and multiple voices, and probably less challenged by the poem's much-vaunted disillusionment. Eliot protested this description—"When I wrote a poem called *The Waste Land* some of the more approving critics said that I had expressed the 'disillusionment of a generation,' which is nonsense. I may have expressed for them their own illusion of being disillusioned, but that did not form part of my intention"—but still, students today might find in the poem their own sense of disillusionment as they contend with intersecting crises in politics, the economy, public health, and climate.[5] *The Waste Land* has become harder in some ways too: with the defunding of the humanities limiting the number of courses that are taught combined with the crucial broadening of literary texts that are taught, students—even senior English majors—are less likely to be familiar with Dante, Webster, and even Shakespeare than their counterparts a hundred years ago were.

Teaching the poem often means offering students some decoding of it—either by contextualizing it in history, or by glossing its allusions—and while this may make some aspects of the poem easier, *The Waste Land* remains difficult. First, though, we can help students develop a vocabulary for that difficulty. In class discussion, this could take the form of asking students to develop their own categories (for example: "words I don't know," "images I don't understand," "tones I can't describe clearly"). Admitting to confusion can take some courage and requires a classroom with a lot of existing mutual respect, but it can also cement that trust further. Or we can give students George Steiner's four "classes" of difficulty from his well-known essay "On Difficulty."[6] (One could assign the essay itself for upper-level students, or use the very good summary of its categories in the introduction to *Another Order of Difficulty* by Karen Zumhagen-Yekplé for a broader range of students, or provide the paraphrase below for lower-level students.)[7]

The first of Steiner's classes is *contingent* difficulties, which can be resolved with more information. These are "the most visible, they stick like burrs to the fabric of the text," but, "Theoretically, there is somewhere a lexicon, a concordance, a manual of stars, a florilegium, a pandect of medicine, which will resolve that difficulty."[8] Eliot appears here in Steiner's essay, though the reference is not to *The Waste Land* but to his poem "Whispers of Immortality"; "it might not be immediately apparent to the reader just what 'bliss' the poet promises when he qualifies it as *pneumatic* (the finesse lies in the Attic and theological antecedents to the epithet)."[9] But while the information that would resolve contingent difficulties might not be immediately apparent, it can be traced, and the difficulty can be erased. Many of *The Waste Land*'s difficulties are contingent, but one can look up the quotations from, say, *The Tempest*.

Steiner's next class of difficulty is *modal*, when "we cannot coerce our own sensibility into the relevant frame of perception," when "Large, sometimes radiant, bodies of literature have receded from our present-day grasp."[10] Are *The Waste Land*'s difficulties also modal? Is the poem growing "remote from our own time and place" in a way that makes it hard? This would be a good question to ask students: When is *The Waste Land* difficult modally? It is not evenly so. Can its modal difficulty be eased with more information, though it lies within you rather than purely within the text? Earlier, when I wrote that *The Waste Land* has grown both easier and harder in the hundred years since its publication, I was writing about modal difficulties.

Steiner's third category of difficulty is *tactical*: when "the poet may choose to be obscure in order to achieve certain specific stylistic effects."[11] This kind of "encoding" may demand decoding, but—as we could ask students—what's the strategy behind tactical difficulty?[12] How would one argue in favor of it as enriching the reader's experience of the text? (Arguing that it damages the reader's experience is just as important but easier!) If supplemental reading would be useful here, I could imagine assigning Ronald Bush's essay "'Intensity by association': T. S. Eliot's Passionate Allusions."[13]

The final class of difficulty, according to Steiner, is *ontological*, which "confront[s] us with blank questions about the nature of human speech, about the status of significance, about the necessity and purpose of the construct which we have, with more or less ready consensus, come to perceive as a poem."[14] If students want to read more about what can be described as ontological difficulty, Zumhagen-Yekplé's book focuses on ontological difficulty in modernist novels, and in Ted Hughes's poem "Six Young Men," philosopher Cora Diamond finds "a difficulty that pushes us beyond what we can think. To attempt to think it is to feel one's thinking come unhinged. Our concepts, our ordinary life with our concepts, pass by this difficulty as if it were not there; the difficulty, if we try to see it, shoulders us out of life, is deadly chilling."[15]

Much of my pedagogy aims to help students organize and label what they can observe and already know, and so although I encourage teachers of *The Waste Land* to help students clarify their understanding of the poem's difficulty by understanding the relationship of difficulty to modernism—a hundred years ago and now—I think it is more important not to pretend that all of the poem's difficulties are contingent or modal. By offering students better vocabulary for difficulty, they can more fully describe the way the poem works and makes meaning, and also learn to trust themselves more fully as readers and thinkers.

Finally, teachers can use a slightly silly but thought-provoking activity: What would it require for modal, tactical, or even ontological difficulties to be recategorized as contingent? Could any information—even imagined information—help? How much can it help, and when? Tell students about the opening of the Emily Hale archive in 2020. Show students some examples of Frances Dickey's "Reports from the Emily Hale Archive," sponsored by the International T. S. Eliot Society. For example, we learned from her descriptions of letters that *The Waste Land*'s "Marie" was "Marie von Moritz [...] a middle-aged woman who lived in [Eliot's] *pension* in Munich, and he has transcribed her conversation exactly in the poem."[16] Ask students to compile a list of difficult moments in the text; you may have done this already if you came up with their own categories in which to sort difficulty, but if you used Steiner's, identify specific moments that fit each of his classes. Next, choose one or a few difficult moments that do not seem to be contingent— maybe "images I don't understand" or "tones I can't describe clearly"—and invent information that Eliot might have written to Hale that would resolve their difficulty. Share them—this should be fun and funny, like the icebreaker game "two truths and a lie," but *all lies*. But, in addition, this exercise should reveal that the difficulty of the poem lies beyond—maybe just beyond, but still, beyond—any withheld information. Ask students to reflect on which lies were easier to imagine and to believe. Ask them which were satisfying, which enriched the poem, and which impoverished it. There might be multiple ways of being satisfying, enriching, and impoverishing. A lie that enriches in one way might impoverish in another; for example, concocting a story that Eliot had his fortune told would recast Madame Sosostris's strangeness as a contingent or tactical difficulty, satisfying in one way, perhaps, but—and students will realize this—deflating the poem by remaking it as a code to break. It might not be possible to become entirely comfortable with difficulty, but it is possible to learn to value the discomfort of not knowing.

Notes

1 "The Metaphysical Poets" (1921), *Complete Prose* 2:381.
2 J. C. Squire, "Review of *The Waste Land*," *London Mercury* (October 1923): 655.
3 I. A. Richards, *Principles of Literary Criticism* [1924] (Routledge, 2017), 277.
4 Gilbert Seldes, "T. S. Eliot." *Nation* (December 6, 1922): 614–16.
5 "Thoughts after Lambeth" (1931), *Complete Prose* 4:226.
6 George Steiner, "On Difficulty," *Journal of Aesthetics and Art Criticism* 36, no. 3 (1978): 263–76.
7 Karen Zumhagen-Yekplé, *Another Order of Difficulty: Literature after Wittgenstein* (University of Chicago Press, 2020).
8 Steiner, "On Difficulty," 267.
9 Steiner, "On Difficulty," 264.
10 Steiner, "On Difficulty," 269.
11 Steiner, "On Difficulty," 270.
12 Steiner, "On Difficulty," 270.
13 Ron Bush, "'Intensity by association': T. S. Eliot's Passionate Allusions," *Modernism/modernity* 20, no. 4 (2013): 709–27.
14 Steiner, "On Difficulty," 273.
15 Cora Diamond, "The Difficulty of Reality and the Difficulty of Philosophy," *Partial Answers: Journal of Literature and the History of Ideas* 1 no. 2 (2003): 1–26. Both Zumhagen-Yekplé and Diamond write in the light of the philosophical work of Ludwig Wittgenstein, Eliot's nearly exact contemporary in age and also contributing to the *annus mirabilis* of 1922, and both were sometimes in the orbit of Bertrand Russell as well. Zumhagen-Yekplé also discusses Diamond's essay.
16 Frances Dickey, "Reports from the Emily Hale Archive," https://tseliotsociety.wildapricot.org/news?pg=5.

Teaching *The Waste Land*, Teaching Composition

Joshua Logan Wall

The decision to build a first-year composition course around *The Waste Land* came out of necessity. Or at least it *felt* necessary. I wanted an opportunity to teach Eliot—and to teach Eliot with all appropriate depth and slowness—but I only rarely have the opportunity to teach upper-level literature seminars. My position, I suspect, is shared by many in my generation of modernist scholars: I teach composition, off the tenure-track.

Thinking about how to teach modernists—especially poets, especially the *difficult* ones—outside their traditional classroom contexts will, I believe, be essential to the future of modernist studies. As tenure-track positions in English have continued to decline over the past decade, modernism as a sub-field has been hit particularly hard. Eliot's relationship to the seminar is more symbiotic than, say, Jane Austen's. That's not meant as a dig at Austen; I mean that she will continue to find her readers regardless. But the deliberate difficulty of much modernist poetry demands intellectual community with particular intensity. It's often in the conversations—and the writing—that both meaning and meaningfulness first emerge. The old labels of "alienated" and "isolated" really are misleading: modernist difficulty is, in fact, an invitation to intellectual camaraderie.

My attitude is that of a realist: if composition is going to continue to make up a growing percentage of English courses, we should face that development with confidence in the value of a slow encounter with modernist works, with Eliot's poetry. Many of us, after all, have learned much of what we know about writing by writing about modernism.

***

The goal of English 124 at the University of Michigan is not to learn to write a seminar paper. It is more foundational than that: to make an argument about a work of literature that goes beyond either one's own initial reactions—liking or disliking the work or a character—or the detailed but not quite *arguable* observations about literary devices that AP exams have trained some to produce.

Our unit on *The Waste Land* comes about a month into the semester, after paving the way with a more straightforward close reading of a single poem or essay (by Marianne Moore, C. P. Cavafy, Derek Walcott, or—especially—Muriel Rukeyser). For the first week, we just puzzle at it together, reading and re-reading, collaborating on a Google Doc annotation, teasing out the conversations Eliot creates. The next two weeks are deeper looks at these conversations: reading and analyzing individual sources and critical commentaries on the poem. All told, we spend about five weeks discussing the poem, conversations around it, and our own essays.

The assignment, in its simplest terms, is this: To engage in a written conversation with one or two other perspectives *about* Eliot's poem. Students can agree, disagree, contribute, tinker—as long as they add, even slightly, to that conversation's store of knowledge. The concept of this writing takes some time to grasp—it's categorically different from the timed, five-paragraph explication of a passage that all my students learned to write very well in high school. What I ask of them is something harder—thoughtfulness and the ability to communicate their thought clearly. But once they give themselves permission to draw on the open, provisional, and collaborative qualities of conversation, the barriers to writing about poetry, about modernism, about *anything* begin to shrink and crumble. Students don't have to understand the whole poem to write about it. They just need to understand what someone else has said about it—and *why*. Then, their own act of writing can add to their understanding and their interlocutor's.

We find these "other perspectives" in Michael North's Norton Critical Edition of *The Waste Land*, particularly its dozen "Reviews and Short Reactions." Brief and clear, they work alongside excerpts from New Critical perspectives and somewhat more difficult contemporary reconsiderations to offer students examples of what they themselves set out to do: Make sense of this strange, difficult work that's unlike anything else they've read before. The ones ready to throw up their hands find critics who did the same—and suddenly see that *this is a valid stance for effective literary criticism*. The trick is not stopping there but pushing forward to examine what, within the poem, provoked that reaction. *The Waste Land* frustrates, fails, maddens? Fantastic: Write about how the poem produces those effects on you and others.

Halfway through this unit, we bring literary analysis off the page and into life, performing a conversation among the various critics we've encountered. To prepare for this class, I assign students a single short essay from the Norton and ask them to take a careful, close look, paying attention not only to what it says about the poem, but also *how* it says this. What's the personality of the author? Would they be thoughtful, aggressive, pompous, or hesitant around those who disagree? Students take on personae based on what they find in the essays: There's Delmore Schwartz! There's Virginia Woolf! Oh God, Kenner's over in the corner holding forth *again*. . . . All of them, of course, invited to a massive, celebratory dinner party hosted by Eliot himself. (This is my role, down to my version of a Missouri-born Londoner's accent. The key to the exercise, I've found, is teacherly self-humiliation.)

The goal is to speak with every other guest, attempting to promote their own interpretations while taking copious notes to identify their allies and enemies. (Later we reflect on the performance by using these notes to transform the chalkboard into a detailed and messy map of all their interactions.) As they talk, gossip, and argue, they gain understanding of the perspective they've adopted and begin to form assessments of it: maybe he takes things too far; maybe she could argue more clearly. Stepping outside themselves, they more easily see how one critic might interact with another, including through *partial* agreement and disagreement. Putting aside the need to have their own fully formed opinion—letting them rely on the opinions of others, at least for a day—serves as an invitation to listen and to write essays that listen carefully. *The Waste Land*'s difficulty is an advantage here: To gain a foothold, they *have* to listen.

* * *

And then there are the drafts. This is a writing seminar, and we follow the structures you might expect, with multiple drafts and workshops all designed to lead students to revise their work, to never settle on the first version. The feedback can be extensive. For some, that's flattering: they've never had people spend so much energy on something they've written before. For most, however, it's intimidating: how can there be *that* much work left to do on a draft I thought was pretty good?

Here Ezra Pound becomes oddly helpful. Whatever they might think of my penciled-in feedback or what they hear during workshops, Pound could be *mean*. Here, after all, is one of those poems they have heard about—A Big, Important Poem—spread out, as it were, like a patient etherized upon a table. The facsimile drafts make their way around the classroom, a visual example of the first draft as merely a beginning. *The Waste Land* models an unhurried writing process to students who have internalized the clock-watching urgency of timed exams and the belief that end-of-draft means end-of-writing.

Revision is what we do in the class, the guiding theme of our syllabus, and a core element of much modernism. We learn to make things new by looking carefully at the ways that Eliot seeks to revise earlier myths and legends. Standard fare for teaching Eliot, it's also a way to link revision—often a tedious process for students learning to practice it—with a more active creativity. In this way writing about Eliot serves as a bridge to our next essay, an analysis of myth in the modern or contemporary world. The topics for this essay vary wildly—the rare shoe market, political themes in *Game of Thrones*, an analysis of the novel we've turned to after Eliot (last year, Richard Wright's *The Man Who Lived Underground*), discussions of Big Ten football culture, a comparative study of campus superstitions, a look at modern paintings or a deep dive into *The Hunger Games*.

Maybe those topics are a far cry from Eliot. But, as students work on them, I get to see lightbulbs flash again and again above each head: *This thing—that my favorite book or movie does, that my fellow Wolverine fans do, that Marvel movies and pop culture take for granted—it's the same thing that Eliot did!* Maybe they find Eliot more incoherent, more annoying, more difficult—or deeper, more thoughtful, and more beautiful—but, if nothing else, modernists begin to appear as artisans who prepared the new wood our culture is still carving.

What Have We Given?
Notes on *The Waste Land* from India

K. Narayana Chandran

*T*he *Waste Land* is a core text for my students at the University of Hyderabad when I teach a full four-credit course on twentieth-century English literature and thought. My method is to describe the unusually suggestive dimensions of Eliot's allusions as narrative *blocks*. In two senses, an allusion is at once a *builder* or an *obstructor*, furthering or blocking the reader's narrative progress. When we read *The Waste Land*, I can't predict what will work and will not, or how my students will draw upon their cultural memory to understand the poem.

For example, regarding the "Murmur of maternal lamentation," where Grover Smith alerts us to "The women weeping for Christ and women weeping for Tammuz"[1] and Harold Fisch hears "Rachel weeping for her children in chapter 31 of Jeremiah,"[2] some of my students hear more resonantly Gāndhārī's cries and curses in *Stree Parva* of the *Mahabharata*. (Doesn't she almost lament, looking at her slain hundred sons, "I had not thought death had undone so many"?) To what echoic parallels a reader responds, or does not respond, is contingent on cultural memory. In my contribution to this forum, I'll discuss one case in which their cultural memory enhances my students' experience of *The Waste Land*, and another case in which it does not.

Because my students and I are steeped in the Indian literature that Eliot also drew on for his poem, his hyacinth garden scene resonates for us with the Ṛishyaçriṅga legend of *Vana Parva* of the *Mahabharata*. The poet's direct source is evidently Jessie Weston's retelling of the Indian legend in *From Ritual to Romance*, in connection with the general myth of *freeing the waters*:

> [In the *Mahabharata*] we find a young Brahmin brought up by his father, Vibhāṇḍaka, in a lonely forest hermitage absolutely ignorant of the outside world, and even of the very existence of beings other than his father and himself. He has never seen a woman, and does not know that such a creature exists.
>
> A drought falls upon a neighbouring kingdom, and the inhabitants are reduced to great straits for lack of food. The King, seeking to know by what means the sufferings of his people may be relieved, learns that so long as Ṛishyaçriṅga continues chaste so long will the drought endure. An old woman, who has a fair daughter of irregular life, undertakes the seduction of the hero. The King has a ship, or raft (both versions are given), fitted out with all possible luxury, and an apparent Hermit's cell erected upon it. The old woman, her daughter and companions, embark; and the river carries them to a point not far from the young Brahmin's hermitage.
>
> Taking advantage of the absence of his father, the girl visits Ṛishyaçriṅga in his forest cell, giving him to understand that she is a Hermit, like himself, which the boy, in his innocence, believes. He is so fascinated by her appearance and caresses that, on her leaving him, he, deep in thought of the lovely visitor, forgets, for the first time, his religious duties.
>
> On his father's return he innocently relates what has happened, and the father warns him that fiends in this fair disguise strive to tempt hermits to their undoing. The next time the father is absent the temptress, watching her opportunity, returns, and persuades the boy to accompany her to her 'Hermitage' which she assures him, is far more beautiful than his own. So soon as Ṛishyaçriṅga is safely on board the ship sails, the lad is carried to the capital of the rainless land, the King gives him his daughter as wife, and so soon as marriage is consummated the spell is broken, and rain falls to abundance.[3]

While students ignore Weston's pointing up crucial details from the Percival/Grail legend for comparison, they now begin to see its immediate significance another way. For them, Weston's "Freeing of the Waters" holds the key to some of the blocked streams and rivulets of Eliot's fragments. All stagnant and frozen as puddles in large stony terrains, the narrative stream waits to be set free. The metaphors of stilled or muddied water bodies are plentiful in *The Waste Land*. As in the *Mahabharata* legend, we always sense someone lost in a dry and parched terrain, or hanging about riverine precincts. Heard or overheard music creeps by them (as in line 257). Someone longs for the rain. Another voice muses by slow-moving streams. And finally, in the opening movement of "What the Thunder Said," beginning "Here is no water but only rock," we hear a chorus's subjunctive thoughts on water and thirst: "Here is no water but only rock/Rock and no water [...]/But there is no water."[4] An overture, certainly, but the narrative stops short there or gets deflected. It is evident that the litanists long for *life* by water, some irrigational boon, and potential fertility while traversing dry, rocky ground. The songs of the Thames-daughters rhyme with those of the Rhine-daughters to which Eliot's note aligns them.[5] The integration of such narrative fragments is predicated upon the freeing of waters leading to fertility and new life, and redemption for those abandoned on the banks of canals and ditches along the city.

For most Indian students familiar with the popular legends of the *Ramayana* and the *Mahabharata*, the allusive trail of *freeing the waters* will certainly have yet another significance. Whether or not Eliot alludes to the legend of Bhagīratha, some of its crucial details nonetheless strike a chord in students when they consider the allusive blocks of the poem. Bhagīratha's yogic effort is Herculean. He lived in a waste land. By bringing down the recalcitrant Ganga ("sunken" as the poet qualifies it at line 395), he could perform the funerary rites for his Sāgara ancestral clan. Wasn't that alone, students wonder, "The awful daring of a moment's surrender/ Which an age of prudence can never retract"?

A detail often missed here is Ganga's own rather conceited thought that no force on earth would be able to withstand her massive downward rush and sweep from such celestial heights. But Śiva volunteers to receive and dam Ganga on his head. (Now the narrative turn at this point is quite revealing.) The mighty god not only withstands the immense pressure of the free-sliding Ganga but has her massive flow blocked and contained in just two locks of his matted hair. Gaṅgādhara (Śiva) now plays with this sunken river that suffers the ignominy of circulating within Śiva's matted locks, condemned to meandering in circles. Freeing the waters is now Śiva's privilege. Bhagīratha prays to the Lord to set Ganga free. The sunken Ganga is so released and the parched earth gratefully receives her. Fertility restored, Bhagīratha commences his dharmic austerities. Students find Eliot's method instructive. Allusive gifts so denied or declined at first are granted to supplicants after insistent prayer and willful effort.

Faint though his resemblance may be to the drowned sailor of Part V, Bhagīratha was indeed one like Phlebas the Phoenician, once just as worldly and materialistic. Water purifies Phlebas, who forgets "the cry of gulls and the deep sea swell/And the profit and loss." As he enters the whirlpool having "passed the stages of his age and youth," he is chastened like Bhagīratha who begins his renewed life of severe austerities.[6] The class now hardly sees "Death by Water" as elegizing a drowner's sea-change. For, in an esoteric rendering of this legend in *Vasiṣṭarāmāyaṇa*, they recall meeting the young Bhagīratha who asks his guru how he could end suffering and overcome the fear of old age and death, and how to fight worldly delusion. The guru gives him much the same Vedantic counsel. Renunciation, in short. "A condition of complete simplicity," which the poet of the *Four Quartets* would qualify parenthetically as "(Costing not less than everything)."[7] Bhagīratha duly practices renunciation by even giving up his kingdom to enjoy peace (*ātmaśāntiḥ*). Consider, then, Bhagīratha, who was once handsome and tall as you.

The Waste Land holds back more than it gives, or gives away, but it still preaches *dāna* (what is given, obligation-free) as a prime, supreme virtue in life. But what, indeed, has *Eliot* given? And what do I, who teach his poem, give? (Too polite to ask this, my class might have wondered at least as much.)

Sometimes the young readers in my sessions do not respond. I have seen a whole group of students remain totally untouched by any *rasa* the fragments of *The Waste Land* evoke in them—*rasa* in the exalted sense of aesthetic *enjoyment* or *pleasure*. Students love to relate to texts that embody and convey a dominant *rasa* they project through the action and suffering of its characters. *The Waste Land*, alas, is no such poem. William Empson writes:

> I was rather pleased one year in China when I had a course on modern poetry, *The Waste Land* and all that, and at the end a student wrote in the most friendly way to explain why he wasn't taking the exam. It wasn't that he couldn't understand *The Waste Land*, he said, in fact after my lectures the poem was perfectly clear: but it had turned out to be disgusting nonsense, and he had decided to join the engineering department. Now there a teacher is bound to feel solid satisfaction; he is getting definite results.[8]

It is not always easy for Indian students of English to adopt and comply with the protocols of *grim reading* to which their Western counterparts have become accustomed through the modernist classics. An Indian teacher's pedagogic options or resources may still evoke no *rasa* in their students. When students *do not* respond to Eliot's polyphonic and wide-ranging allusions, however, I still sense a confused and confusing *rasa-dhwani* at work. They discover perhaps that *bībhatsa* (caused by extreme revulsion, physical and emotional discomfort) works well with aborted narratives and tantalizing glimpses of inhumane abuse. The "abject" and the uncanny evoke extreme loathing in young minds, such as "White bodies naked on the low damp ground," "So rudely forc'd/Tereu," and the clerk-typist episode.[9] Quite puzzlingly for them, the *"shāntih"* that ends *The Waste Land* lacks the customary *Om* that should precede it, mocking the putative *śānta rasa*.[10] Eliot would seem to suggest, perhaps ironically, that even the antithesis of *rasa* is not to be dismissed. Is he not perhaps saying that only those who have *rasa* of some kind know what it is to want to get away from it? I have since then called it *virasa* (in my feeble translation, a blend of *acedia* and existential *boredom*) that poems like *The Waste Land*, some parts of fiction like Joyce's or Woolf's, or Gertrude Stein's, or drama like Beckett's or Pinter's, evoke. The unrelieved boredom of having to test students on lists and comments on Western civilization and its discontents is among the worst professional experience of Indian teachers. *Virasa* is a *rasa*. We all know it when we suffer it, although it cannot be explained by aesthetic theories that privilege enjoyment and exaltation through art. *Virasa* counteracts soothing comfort and lasting pleasure. And that realized, we shall now see why "Shantih" repeated thrice in the last line of *The Waste Land* sounds rather *virasa* to an Indian ear, pretty much like the Lord's rebuke to the wise men of Judah for having "healed the hurt of the daughter of my people slightly, saying, Peace, peace; when there is no peace" (Jeremiah 8:11).

Notes

1 *Poems* 1:69. Grover Smith, *T. S. Eliot's Poetry and Plays: A Study in Sources and Meaning* (University of Chicago Press, 1950), 94.
2 Harold Fisch, *A Remembered Future: A Study in Literary Mythology* (Indiana University Press, 1984), 139.
3 Jessie L. Weston, *From Ritual to Romance* (Doubleday Anchor, 1957), 30–31.
4 *Poems* 1:68–69.
5 *Poems* 1:75.
6 *Poems* 1:67.
7 "Little Gidding," line 256, *Poems* 1:209.
8 John Harwood, *Eliot to Derrida: The Poverty of Interpretation* (Palgrave Macmillan, 1995), 86.
9 *Poems* 1:62–63.
10 I have commented on this oddity in my "*Shantih* in *The Waste Land*," *American Literature* 61, no. 4 (1989): 681–83.

Teaching *The Waste Land* to Japanese Students

Junichi Saito

As we go about our daily lives, we may have a sudden moment of illumination when we catch a glimpse of a reality beyond our material existence. In such cases, some of us believe that we have experienced a hidden, supernatural message that comes to us from another world, from beyond our limited perspective. What I propose to explain here is how Eliot's Western Christianity might be experienced and appreciated even in a non-Christian society such as Japan.

Some Japanese scholars of English literature ask a question that goes straight to the heart of this matter of religious belief: "Can our students, or even we ourselves, really appreciate Eliot's poems and essays without any belief in, or even understanding of, Christianity?" For us Japanese, the answer will vary depending on the context. If, for example, a classroom teacher has a clear reason for choosing Eliot's works for discussion, they may be able to teach students something about their own lives by using Eliot's alien cultural context. As we Japanese run a rat race in society, we tend to think of human life from the viewpoint of economic practicality such as making money or acquiring a reputation. Eliot points us to another sphere of human life by seeking the still point of the turning world, which for Japanese students looks like the stage of nothingness of Zen Buddhism. In this way Japanese students might be able to find a new horizon of interpretation in Eliot's poems outside a Judeo-Christian culture.

However, university students seek some practical skills or knowledge in order to be competitive with others in society. As a result, many Japanese educators have given up on the idea of character-building owing to the spread of globalization. The practical effect of globalization on our culture is that many Japanese have turned their attention to profit in the global market and to cooperating with Big Business. In other words, Japanese students are not encouraged to ask themselves why they exist on the earth, what their place is in society, or what their deepest values are. Many of them try to avoid thinking about the profound topics their Japanese and Western predecessors have explored in literature, philosophy, and art.

Aside from this resistance to thinking philosophically about beliefs and ethics, Japanese students face two other hurdles in dealing with Eliot's poems: the difficulty lies in his idea of Christianity and the complex web of allusions to various literary sources, especially Western classics and the Bible. You can imagine what an uphill battle it is to take Japanese undergraduates through *The Waste Land*. Many university students in Japan have studied little of modern history, so they would not be able to grasp the relevance of Eliot's twentieth-century American "spiritual malady" for themselves. Instead, I advise students to compare the poetic line to the matters of their everyday life, which sound more significant and relevant to them, even if they have no academic knowledge of the poem's contexts and sources.

Japanese teachers of English literature have to let their students develop their own approach to Eliot's poems. It is a challenge for them to formulate an argument from a new perspective beyond their own cultural boundaries. Many scholars in Japan accept what Eliot as an English and Christian poet wrote as the truth without leaving room for further interpretation. I have found some cases in which Japanese students, intimidated by Western authority and the hidden power of the English language, will not respond to the questioning of Western professors. I would draw a parallel between Japanese silence in the face of Western powers and the way in which students and even scholars can seem paralyzed, unable to think in the presence of the Western canon. How can the Japanese eliminate our inferiority complex towards Western value standards and English? One might say that not only specialists but also average readers should play with Eliot's poems in a relaxed atmosphere, ignoring their Christian values and not worrying about English as a linguistic barrier.

If Japanese teachers of English literature ask their students to comment on the passage beginning with "A crowd flowed over London Bridge, so many," they do not know how to explain the passage. Japanese students cannot grasp its significance unless teachers explain sufficiently the conditions of society at that time, in which people were losing their belief in Christianity.

One way to instruct Japanese students on the role of Christianity in Europe is to have them read Eliot's *The Idea of a Christian Society*. Japanese teachers might reframe Eliot's own question for their students: "If it were not for Buddhism and Shintoism, what would become of our own nation?" Eliot's concern in his book then becomes not a historical question, but a personal one for Japanese students.

Japanese students will notice Eliot's sincere feelings about Christianity from the book. I ask them to consider why it would be appropriate or inappropriate to say that education should be conducted according to a Shintoistic way of life. Because of globalization and secularism, it has never occurred to my students to ask themselves: "Do our native religious traditions have something to offer in the educational reform of Japan?" Eliot argues for the place of religious principles in education and emphasizes the importance of a common fund of knowledge. Literacy can be improved not by increasing the amount of knowledge covered, he argues, but rather by ensuring a shared core of knowledge, constituted by the Greek and Latin classics and the Bible.[1] He also stresses the importance of maintaining a common spiritual tradition as Westerners in a Christian culture. An Eliotic recommendation to those reforming Japanese education might be to require students to read *Records of Ancient Matters* and *Chronicles of Japan* to help create a common cultural experience.

The passage beginning with "Unreal City" in *The Waste Land* reflects a scene in which people look like automatons after having turned away from Christian belief in Europe. For my own students, the passage reminds them of unemployed ex-salary men who looked like sleepwalkers after what Americans call "the financial crisis of 2008," but what we call the "Lehman Shock." The atmosphere of Japanese society at that time was very similar to that of the poem. This might be because many people do not have much to rely on spiritually when they experience life's suffering. As more people become alienated from each other in a "rat race" society, the poem's critique can be applied to non-Western societies, as a universal vision of hard times unmoored from spiritual meaning.

Since the undergraduates I teach do not read many reference books, even during the school year, they have to explicate the poem based on their own experience, without much knowledge of Christian culture. My solution is a simple one: I suggest that students find something in the poem that they can claim as their own. It does not matter if the poem seems to exist behind a cultural fence. I encourage them to cross the border boldly and come back with something they can make sense of with their own experience.

Even without the contexts of Western culture, Japanese students can still appreciate Eliot's poems to some extent if they try to examine the passages logically and concretely. They may need to approach Eliot's poems as an outsider, observing instead what is going on in their own lives and culture. Teachers can provide their students with background materials and help them engage their interest in and expand their appreciation of Eliot's poetry. But they also can help students find new and different meanings in Eliot's poems that are common to all human beings beyond cultural borders. One might say that students can also enjoy playing with the poems from their everyday viewpoint while maintaining their native culture.

Note

1   "The Idea of a Christian Society" (1939), *Complete Prose* 5:704–5.

Teaching Past *The Waste Land*'s Annotation Problem

Martin Lockerd

Annotated editions of *The Waste Land* hinder new readers more than they help. As is true for most of the contributors to this forum, I first encountered *The Waste Land* without the immediate aid, or hindrance, of scholarly annotation. The experience lived up to all the clichés about first readings of that daunting poem. Lacking German, Sanskrit, and Italian, I quickly concluded that I had better at least get translations of those bits before going any further. Also lacking easy access to the early internet, I turned to B. C. Southam's *Guide to the Selected Poems of T. S. Eliot*. Most of the information I found there struck me, a freshman neophyte, as totally superfluous.

My instinctive primary concern as a motivated but novice reader was to solve the most immediate sources of perplexity on the literal level. I needed to know what the words meant: the lines of foreign language, the obscure words (how many of us came into *The Waste Land* knowing what "laquearia" meant?), the place names. Luckily, Southam did provide this vital information, and I easily ignored what did not contribute to my understanding. My first copy of Eliot's poems still contains amateurish annotations drawn from Southam's book in its margins.

Like me, my students have had to wrestle first with the literal level of Eliot's poem, but their first readings of the poem are even more heavily weighted with annotations that make the process more, not less, difficult. The publication of *T. S. Eliot: The Poems, Volume 1* (2015), edited by

Christopher Ricks and Jim McCue, inspired me to teach my first single author course on Eliot as a graduate instructor. It took me several class periods to realize that my students—mostly bright English majors in their third or fourth years of school—were making almost no use of the editors' elaborate and (to my mind) fascinating notes. I scolded my students and encouraged them to engage seriously with the notes. At the time we were discussing "The Burial of the Dead," and one of my more outspoken students drew my attention to the essential problem: the notes were too copious and obscure to be of any real help to novice readers of Eliot. As evidence, she presented the notes on the title of *The Waste Land*, which did not seem to refer to the poem we read whatsoever. Only then did I realize that the student had become lost in the *fifty* pages of commentary that precede the annotations to the published version of *The Waste Land*. Once we made it to the actual annotations, things did not improve. The annotations for the famous opening clause "April is the cruellest month" went on for two pages. This, for my students, was truly a wilderness of mirrors.

In his 2016 review of the *Poems* for *Time Present*, A. David Moody captured the emerging consensus in an unsparing critique:

> Some notes, perhaps most, offer connections so tenuous as to leave one speculating about the possible workings of Eliot's subconscious. [...] There is much here to interest the psychologist and the psychoanalyst. There is also much here of value to those interested in the poetry, but they will have to be intensely *critical* in order to refine out what does elucidate.[1]

For students attempting to engage with Eliot's poetry for the first time, the psychological angle, and every other, must wait on the apprehension of the literal level. Not only did the Ricks/McCue annotations not help with this apprehension, but they positively frustrated it.

In fairness, I should point out that the otherwise admirable Norton Critical Edition of *The Waste Land* (2001) likewise threatens to bury novice readers in obscure references when what they most need is greater clarity. Let us take this well-known line from "The Burial of the Dead" as an example: "Madame Sosostris, famous clairvoyante,/Had a bad cold."

Norton editor Michael North renders the line with a footnote on the word "clairvoyante," informing the reader that "The name is taken from Aldous Huxley's novel *Crome Yellow* (1921). See pp. 40–42."[2] Students diligent enough to travel to page 40 will find a two-page excerpt from the novel and little immediate edification. The Norton edition is a good example of its genre, the critical edition; however, it is not the text most novice readers need. In early readings of the poem, we can allow Mme. Sosostris to be what she is, a personage in the poem, a part of its weird, disjointed quasi-epic. But we must make sure that our students know what a clairvoyante is or claims to be.

I turned to the internet for help. Tseliot.com, the official site of the Eliot estate, provides some great resources, including a "Life in Pictures" section, but isn't terribly helpful when it comes to the poetry itself. Its slickly annotated version of TWL falls into the same excesses as other annotated texts. The website Genius.com, originally designed and most notable for its crowd-sourced annotations of rap songs, also provides a crowd-sourced annotated version of *TWL*. Not surprisingly, the editing is of very dubious quality. Also, almost every line is highlighted and annotated. No reader could fail to drown in this sea. The internet proved just as disappointing as the approved scholarly editions of Eliot's poem.

The problem is obvious: novice readers are more likely to be hindered than helped by existing annotated editions of *The Waste Land*. The solution is less clear, but I would like to briefly propose one possible approach that emerged from my own semi-abortive attempt to make Eliot more accessible to my students. Attempting to work around the annotation issue, I taught a class called "T. S. Eliot in the Digital Age." We spent the first half of the semester studying all of Eliot's public domain poetry (at that time, everything published prior to 1923), and the second half of the semester creating a web-based annotated text called Accessible Eliot. The philosophy was simple. I asked my students to annotate only those things that left them confused on their first readings of a poem, that prevented comprehension of the literal level. The results were mixed but promising.

In constructing Accessible Eliot, I learned that: (1) students are good at identifying their immediate needs in terms of annotation (e.g., What's the Starnbergersee? What does clairvoyante mean? Who is Tiresias?); (2) students struggle to construct accurate annotations without guidance because they are unfamiliar with the long tradition on which Eliot draws and must, therefore, sift through the detritus on the internet—a daunting task. I quickly found that most students justifiably don't care about shadowy allusions, no matter how much I do. None really cares that the opening lines allude to Chaucer, let alone a 1914 letter by Rupert Brooke or the migratory patterns of nightingales (all things cited by Ricks and McCue), because none has a meaningful attachment to Chaucer or Brooke or ornithology. My own pet theory is that Eliot drew ironically on the opening lines of Robert Browning's "Home-thoughts, from Abroad"—"Oh, to be in England/Now that April's there"—but my students genuinely don't care to hear about another poem when trying to make an initial foray into the overwhelming one in front of them. What they do care about is the apparent contradiction in that opening line between suffering and the start of spring. At least one level of meaning emerges without the myriad allusions.

Accessible Eliot failed, ultimately, because its value lay in the process, not the product. It led me to a simpler, student-centered approach that I have used since this experience:

1   Have the students read the poem on their own and underline things that make no sense on the literal level, assuring them that deeper analysis will come later. They don't need to look up anything at this point.

2   Read through the poem together in class and work collaboratively, with the assistance of the internet, to clarify those parts of the poem that are literally incomprehensible on the first reading. Here, you, the instructor, have a chance to use your knowledge of the poem to answer students' most pressing questions and help them sift through the bad information they find online. In the process of finding answers to these questions, you will invariably end up in a series of short lecture-discussion sessions. Expect this to take two class periods moving at a good clip.

3   That done, circle back around on day three and move from the literal to a more analytical level of discussion, asking not "What do these words mean?" but "What is this poem doing?"

This approach is neither novel nor high-tech, but it may help liberate us from an annotation crisis of our own creation.

Notes

1   A. David Moody, "*The Poems of T. S. Eliot, Volume I: Collected & Uncollected Poems; Volume II: Practical Cats & Further Verses*, ed. Christopher Ricks and Jim McCue," *Time Present* 88 (Spring 2016): 11.
2   T. S. Eliot, *The Waste Land*, ed. Michael North (Norton Critical Editions, 2001), 6n4.

Teaching *The Waste Land* with the Hale Archive

Frances Dickey

The opening of the "Hale archive"—Eliot's 1,131 letters to Emily Hale, his American muse—presents valuable and even essential opportunities for renewing how we teach Eliot's poetry, including *The Waste Land*.[1] With the digital publication of this archive, everyone in the world now has access to Eliot's private correspondence with the woman whom he told "I shall always write primarily for you." These letters contain much information about his poetry, both retrospective commentary on poems written before 1930 ("A Cooking Egg," "Gerontion," *The Waste Land*, "Animula," *Ash-Wednesday*, and others) and passages of narration and reflection that he transposed into later poems, especially "Landscapes" and *Four Quartets*. While by no means overriding the scholarship that has shaped our understanding of Eliot's oeuvre, such an extensive body of self-commentary will inevitably change our interpretations. The humanizing revelations in these letters have the potential to cut across the cultural differences and knowledge gaps that make *The Waste Land* so challenging to teach.

Extensive knowledge of Eliot's biography is not necessary to appreciate the role that Hale played in his life and understand how important she was to his creativity. They knew each other as early as 1905 when both were teenagers studying in the Boston area, and his feelings for her developed in 1912–13 during amateur theatricals at the house of his cousin, Eleanor Hinkley. He later told Hale that he came to realize that he was in love with her after they attended Wagner's *Tristan und Isolde* together in December 1913. On the eve of his departure for Europe in 1914, he awkwardly told her something of his feelings, but did not ask her to wait for him, still less propose marriage. He went on to marry Vivien Haigh-Wood in 1915. After this point, Hale loomed large in his imagination as the might-have-been of a different life. After long separation, they met up again in 1930 and began a correspondence that would last until 1956—the eve of his marriage to another woman, Valerie Fletcher.[2] The rise and fall of their epistolary romance during this quarter century form the shadowy but vital background of *Four Quartets*, many of whose "moments" are rooted in experiences that Eliot recorded in his letters to her. For teaching *The Waste Land*, however, the most pertinent information appears in the second letter of his collected correspondence to Hale, written November 3, 1930:

> I want to convince you that my love for you has been the one great thing all through my life. [...] please [...] re-read the hyacinth lines in <Part I.> The Waste Land, and the lines toward the very end beginning "friend, blood shaking my heart" (where we means privately of course I) and compare them with Pipit on the one hand and Ash Wednesday on the other, and see if they do not convince you that my love for you has steadily grown into something finer and finer. And I shall always write primarily for you.

Eliot astonishingly tells Hale that his poetry, written for her, traces the refinement of his feelings from the disappointment of "A Cooking Egg," through *The Waste Land*'s excruciating memories of his failure to connect with her at the crucial moment, to the sublimation of earthly into divine love in *Ash-Wednesday*. No doubt, Eliot's primary objective in this letter was literally to convince Hale of his love, a goal that he simultaneously pursued and undermined throughout much of their relationship.

Yet in writing to Hale, Eliot also intended to create a record whose posthumous opening would reveal the full meaning of his poetry. In December 1930, he asked her permission to archive her letters at the Bodleian Library (ultimately, he burned them). He wanted their letters to counteract a misunderstanding of his poetry that he himself had promoted. As he wrote to her in 1932:

> There will be so much in existence to give a very false impression of me, and so few clues to the truth. [...] I have again and again seen the impression I have made, and have longed to be able to cry "no you all are wrong about me, it isn't like that at all; the truth is perfectly simple and intelligible, and here it is in a few words." (February 19, 1932)

As Eliot well knew, these declarations ran counter to the common reading of his poem as a lamentation for the decline of Western civilization and other "impersonal" readings that his own statements in "Tradition and the Individual Talent" had encouraged. While those readings are still valid, Eliot's letters suggest that the personal sources of his poem were more conscious and deliberate than most critics (apart from Lyndall Gordon and Ronald Schuchard) previously appreciated.[3]

How, then, should we incorporate this information into our classroom explorations of *The Waste Land*? The poem's literary sources are still just as central. Repeated allusions to Dante, Shakespeare, and Wagner remain a bedrock that any reader who wishes to look beneath the surface must explore. But we now can better explain Eliot's specific choices: for example, his revelation that Hale was the Hyacinth girl with whom he fell in love at a performance of *Tristan und Isolde* illuminates his personal reasons for placing quotations from that opera before and after the "Hyacinth garden" scene in Part I. Further, the speaker's ambiguous silence in her presence, whatever other meanings it may suggest, has its roots in the chagrin he felt at his failure to speak to the girl he loved ("the heart of light, the silence"). Further, in Part V, the Sanskrit commands *Datta, Dayadhvam, Damyata* relieve the grief and despair of previous sections and point towards spiritual enlightenment, regardless of Eliot's reasons for including this surprising intertext. Yet we now understand that these injunctions resonated personally for Eliot because he studied the *Upanishads* at the time that he was courting Hale in Cambridge.[4] If he had followed Prajapati's advice then, his life might have turned out differently; the gift of self and trust he withheld from Hale, he instead gave to Vivien

Haigh-Wood, leading to the unhappy marriage sketched in "A Game of Chess." Explaining these contexts to students and including the relevant passages from Eliot's letters—just those I provide in this essay are probably enough—make the poem more comprehensible on a human level. Unhappiness in love is an experience that anyone can relate to. Including "cryptic love poem" among *The Waste Land*'s genres diminishes some of the alienation and intimidation that students feel as they approach what seems to them a wall of erudition.

Students often respond to the poem's dense intertextuality, at least initially, by questioning whether it is a deliberate attempt to confuse them. The Hale letters also reveal that this intuition is not entirely wrong. As Eliot wrote to Hale when he was finishing "Burnt Norton," "I can't tell whether this will be a good poem or a bad one; at any rate, it is I think a new kind of love poem, and it is written for you, and it is fearfully obscure," explaining that its obscurity will allow her to deny any knowledge of its personal contents and adding that he chose an epigraph of "two quotations from Heraclitus (in Greek) which make the poem more difficult to understand than it would be without them" (January 14, 1936). The same is probably true of *The Waste Land*, which replays scenes from the "mess" that Eliot felt he had made of his life: his failure to propose to Hale, his disastrous marriage with Vivien, her substance abuse, the shame he felt about his act of adultery with Nancy Cunard (in the deleted "Fresca" episode), and his grief for his father's death, which runs like a subterranean river through the poem.[5] These experiences by themselves hardly make for great poetry; indeed, his devices for self-concealment give the poem its distinctive texture and elevate it above a "personal and wholly insignificant grouse against life."[6] Yet, after all the accretions of scholarship and exegesis, the fresh perspective of Eliot's letters to Hale have the potential to validate new readers' intuitions about Eliot's difficulty and ground his poem "in the foul rag and bone shop of the heart."[7]

Notes

1. Emily Hale Letters from T. S. Eliot, C0686, Manuscripts Division, Department of Special Collections, Princeton University Library. Digital publication, edited by John Haffenden, at https://tseliot.com/the-eliot-hale-letters.
2. For the full story, see Lyndall Gordon, *The Hyacinth Girl: T. S. Eliot's Hidden Muse* (W. W. Norton & Co., 2022), which I have reviewed in this volume of the *Annual*. More information about Hale can be found in several other pieces published in the *T. S. Eliot Studies Annual*: Dickey and Sara Fitzgerald, "In Her Own Words: Emily Hale's Introduction to T. S. Eliot's Letters," 3 (2021): 1–9; Fitzgerald, "Emily Hale: The Beginning of our Exploring," 3 (2021): 161–69; Fitzgerald, "The Love of Her Life: Emily Hale's Theatrical Career," 4 (2022): 161–96; and Fitzgerald, "Religion, Rites, and Emily Hale," in this volume.
3. Appreciated, that is, before the opening of the Hale archive. Lyndall Gordon, *Eliot's New Life*, 2nd ed. (Oxford University Press, 1988) and *T. S. Eliot: An Imperfect Life* (Norton, 1999); Ronald Schuchard, *Eliot's Dark Angel: Intersections of Life and Art* (Oxford University Press, 1999).
4. For more on Eliot's study of Sanskrit texts, see Manju Jain's comprehensive examination in this volume of the *T. S. Eliot Studies Annual*, "Through the Looking Glass: T. S. Eliot and Indian Philosophy."
5. Eliot told James Joyce on January 4, 1932, that Henry Ware Eliot "died still believing, I am sure, that I had made a complete mess of my life—which from his point of view, and possibly quite rightly, I had done" (*Letters* 6:13). For Vivien's substance abuse, see Ann Pasternak Slater, *The Fall of a Sparrow: Vivien Eliot's Life and Writings* (Faber & Faber, 2021). For Nancy Cunard, see Gordon, *The Hyacinth Girl*, 96–97.
6. *Waste Land Facsimile*, 1.
7. W. B. Yeats, "The Circus Animals' Desertion," *Collected Poems*, ed. Richard J. Finneran (Macmillan, 1989), 348.

The Wrong Way to Teach *The Waste Land*

Anthony Cuda

I've been teaching *The Waste Land* the wrong way for nearly two decades now. To steal (not borrow) what Eliot wrote about Shakespeare in 1927: "it is probable that we can never be right; and if we can never be right, it is better that we should from time to time change our way of being wrong."[1] Before I completely undermine the chutzpah of my title, though, I'll hazard the assertion that, yes, I do believe there are wrong ways to teach the poem, or at least ways that blunt its sharp edges or, to change the metaphor, ground its electric current. For instance, I recoil at the thought of teaching it as Eliot's real-life version of Dante's *Inferno*—inevitably followed by his purgatorial *Ash-Wednesday*, etc.—a method that artificially calms its anxieties by giving them relief in a future that the poet couldn't have imagined in 1921. Likewise, approaches that encourage students to gauge the poem's moral "failures" against orthodox Christian values that he would only embrace years later, that focus solely upon the a "quest" toward the chapel perilous, or that inexplicably discern a celebration of past glories contrasted with modernity's squalor. Half-acknowledged anachronism, teleology, or nostalgia is usually to blame. But if it's churlish to call them "wrong," okay: let's simply say that they don't help me to access the poem's most compelling energies in class.

Not that the history of my own errors has been without contradiction and embarrassment. As a graduate student in a heady and one-sided love affair with deconstruction, I taught poor college freshmen about the slippages and failures of language that caused the poem's crisis, and we explored how its resignations and torments coincide with failures of communication. Later, I insisted to my first undergraduates that the "bogus" notes were useless, and I offered to sell them real estate in Wisconsin if they truly believed that legends of the holy grail would solve the poem's riddles.[2] Instead, we lingered with its emotional surfaces—anxieties, panic, relief, longing—and with the dazzling patterns that appear when you let your eyes focus on the glass rather than trying to peer through it. Alas, not long afterwards, I dove headlong into those same notes with my doctoral students, convinced that even the poem's simplest emotions were blocked without the subterranean energies of its sources in anthropology, classical studies, and the Cambridge Ritualists.

One year, I began at the end and worked backwards. "Discuss and provide evidence, for or against: All of *The Waste Land*'s disappointments result from failures of its personae to follow the edicts of the Thunder." Another, I backstitched the entire poem through the loop of the epigraph, slowly threading a patch labeled Nietzsche to the inner pocket. "Discuss and provide evidence, for or against: The poem's most memorable personae are all versions of the Sibyl, seers who have peered into the darkness (like Kurtz!) and now find themselves tragically paralyzed, having lost their will to live." I even spent one three-hour graduate seminar assembling a catalogue, as I've done here, of ways that I *might* begin a graduate seminar on *The Waste Land*. I find it remarkably hard to let go of such things!

So it's fitting that my most recent way of being wrong involves precisely that problem: what it means, for Eliot, to hold on and to let go. It's inspired by two of my favorite scenes in the poem, which have held lasting sway over my imagination through years of error: Marie's memory at the beginning, and Eliot's first comment on the Thunder, near the end.

> And when we were children, staying at the archduke's,
> My cousin's, he took me out on a sled,
> And I was frightened. He said, Marie,
> Marie, hold on tight. And down we went.
> In the mountains, there you feel free.
> [...]
> Datta: what have we given?

> My friend, blood shaking my heart
> The awful daring of a moment's surrender
> Which an age of prudence can never retract[3]

I believe these verses articulate the feeling towards which the poem most fervently strains: the exhilaration and release of a moment's surrender, of acquiescing and letting go in the face of struggle, uncertainty, and fearfulness. But poems are always compelled by conflicting desires, and so I suggest that this governing desire is locked in a struggle against the opposing forces of holding on: protectiveness, contraction, tensed withdrawal, or sometimes just the refusal to forget.

Only after this introduction do we begin to talk about the poem's shifting voices, its allusions and music hall ditties, its biographical, religious, and anthropological substructures. Because for my students, as for Eliot, these topics and methods become compelling only under the intense light of strong feelings. And for all its disillusionment and despair, *The Waste Land* brims with incredibly strong feelings. When we return to the tensions of those originary desires—which I sometimes describe as Thomas Mann does in *Death in Venice*, by opening and closing my fist—we talk about their immediate appearance in the first stanza.[4] First, a vision of protective, isolated safety: covered in snow, underground, contracted into itself. The initial seven lines are also rhythmically and sonically cramped, butting themselves up against those insistent participles, strung with velar nasal phonemes that actually trap airflow behind an upcurled tongue: the voice holding itself back. This is the poem's closed fist: numbed, defended, solitary—but safe!—the world of Prufrock's "Love Song." But then, summer's dramatic entrance: lines lengthen, phonemes open into rounded vowels, and Eliot introduces a "we" that emerges into sunlight and surprise: caught in the rain, talking, sharing coffee. A fantasy nearly unbearable, were it not so vividly presented. Surrender, he implies, involves someone else, and it precipitates the unexpected, both atmospheric and aural. This is the poem's open hand: extended, relaxed, undefended—a little risky. I nearly sing these lines in class, with breathless and ringing voice, which makes the transition unmistakable. I do the same with the line, "And down we went./In the mountains, there you feel free," with its blissful release.[5] Students feel how the poem momentarily entertains a glimpse of self-abandon, before quickly clamping down: "I read much of the night."

I ask them to search *The Waste Land* for words and phrases that seem clustered around one end of the spectrum or the other, toward the frightened, contracted fist or toward the risky, open hand of surrender. Roots and leafy fingers "clutch" desperately; eyes are "fixed" downward; Philomel is "forced"; the carbuncular clerk assaults and "gropes"; rooms, carriages, dressing chambers are all claustrophobically "closed" off.[6] In these metaphors they encounter, over and again, sources of the poem's agonies—coiled, isolated, violent, or stymied. And, alternately, students sense the unsettling liberations of Philomel's inviolable voice, shattering the room's enclosure, filling the desert; a speaker's sudden eruption into ragtime lyrics, breaking his silent panic; the sweet Thames running softly; the repetitive, open-vowel clusters interrupting the tightly compacted river song ("Weialala leia/Wallala leialala"); even the ironically soothing "goonight" wishes at the bar scene's end.[7] And of course, tuned to this frequency, they can properly regard Phlebas himself, self-forgotten and abandoned to the sea's floor, given over to submarine whims and to the necessity of the rising and the falling tide: not a *memento mori*, as he first seems, but an icon of self-surrender.

I admit, though, that even this approach has recently come to seem wrong. Not least because it wholly idealizes surrender, standing safely back in judgment, hiding behind an implicit hierarchy of feeling that the poem doesn't bear out. In fact, in *The Waste Land*, "holding on" and "letting go" are always entangled emotional impulses—like desire and repulsion, or love and loathing. Among the poem's affective achievements is dramatizing that entanglement so relentlessly. For instance, Marie is the first embodiment of surrender we encounter, and yet the very condition for her freedom is that she "hold on tight," because to let go would bring disaster. Her exhilarating reminiscence sustains and preserves both impulses in a single scene, in breathless suspension. Why is the "handful of dust," which appears a few lines later, so unexpectedly frightening? It's an emblem of mortality of course—ashes to ashes—but for me, more importantly, it's the very paradigm of trying to hold on to something that slips through the fingers; the harder you try, the more you'll leave behind, finally looking down at only "the broken fingernails of dirty hands."[8] It bespeaks an embarrassed futility, ashamed of its own clinging. An inverted scenario occurs in Lower Thames Street, "where the walls/Of Magnus Martyr hold/ Inexplicable splendour of Ionian white and gold."[9] Despite that abrupt line end—as if the poem were trying to tighten its rhythmic grip—those stone walls can't possibly "hold" the beauty that Eliot envisions spilling over and beyond them. "Ionian white and gold" describes the church's columns, but an equally radiant splendor floods the scene from within and without, in an uncontainable moment of illumination and relief. It must be held, he implies, but it cannot be held in or held back. It's a photographic negative of the "empty chapel" in the poem's last part, which is likewise both enclosed and open, a hand grasping at the wind, with "no windows, and the door swings."[10] Even the gorgeous, moving phrase that began my reflections— "the awful daring of a moment's surrender"—carries its own internal stopwatch, the sealed, inaccessible enclosure of "a moment" rather than a month, a year, a lifetime. How ambivalent it is, too, in its ghostly echoes of the poem's cancelled epigraph, "Did he live his life again in every detail of desire, temptation, and surrender during that supreme moment?"[11] And following close on its heels is a series of words like "draped," "seals," "rooms," and "retract"—framed in the negative but echoing with threats of enclosure, as if the poem's diction were intent on keeping the two impulses bound together, despite its syntax.[12] When I return to this, the Thunder's first pronouncement, I find that the "blood shaking my heart" isn't merely the adrenaline, the shudder of risk and release. It's also the terrible knowledge that sometimes I can only hope to hold on to something meaningful by letting it go, and vice versa, that I cannot abandon something without finding a way to hold on to it. Sometimes doing either seems unthinkable; at others, I can't discern where one stops and the other begins.

    I admit that this approach is particularly poignant to me because it aligns with how Eliot viewed his most intimate personal relationships. Almost immediately after they were married, he could neither wholly embrace nor abandon Vivien, and her equally ambivalent push and pull produced a marriage filled with tension, creativity, dependence, and ultimately much misery for them both. And of course he held tightly to his shimmering memories of Emily Hale in Boston, even while he relinquished hope and married abroad. As they grew intimate in reunion after 1930, he professed to surrender desire but wrote time and again of his ardor and enduring love. And the desperation of his attempt to keep her at a safe distance was ultimately matched only by the intensity of their collapse into overwhelming closeness when they came together in Chipping Campden in 1935 and after. In the letters, in fact, sometimes "surrender" itself means both letting go and its opposite. In one letter, he resigns himself to living alone forever, to growing old alone, writing "the completeness of surrender is what counts." In another, after perhaps their most intimate encounter, he begs her to describe exactly what she remembers, so that he can "surrender my memory to its perfection," that is, ensure that he carves out a place for it more permanent and enduring than his own reminiscence.[13]

Will I abandon this approach next semester? You know, from wrong to wrong the exasperated critic proceeds. But maybe I am less exasperated and more like the Rum Tum Tugger, "a terrible bore": "always on the wrong side of every door."[14] The fact that this way of teaching *The Waste Land* reveals continuities between the poem's parts; brings emotional urgency to the fore; and aligns so remarkably with such intimate personal aspects of Eliot's life doesn't necessarily make it right. But for now I'll hold on tight to this way of being wrong.

Notes

1 *Complete Prose* 3:245.
2 *Complete Prose* 8:127.
3 *Poems* 1:55, 70.
4 Of the protagonist, Mann's narrator remarks: "one sharp observer said of him in company, 'You see, Aschenbach has always lived like this,' and the speaker contracted the fingers of his left hand into a fist; 'never like this,' and he let his open hand droop comfortably from the arm of his chair. That hit the mark." "Death in Venice," translated by Kenneth Burke, *The Dial* 76 (March 1924): 219.
5 *Poems* 1:55.
6 *Poems* 1:55, 57, 58, 64, 59.
7 *Poems* 1:65, 61.
8 *Poems* 1:66.
9 *Poems* 1:64.
10 *Poems* 1:70.
11 *Poems* 1:323.
12 *Poems* 1:70.

13 Letters of April 19, 1933 and October 3, 1935. Emily Hale Letters from T. S. Eliot, C0686, Manuscripts Division, Department of Special Collections, Princeton University Library.
14 *Poems* 2:10.

Reading Eliot Aloud

Isabelle Stuart

Winner of the 2022 *T. S. Eliot Studies Annual* Peer Seminar Prize

It has become a critical commonplace that Eliot is a poet of the page. F. R. Leavis thought of his voice as "disconcertingly lacking in body," even to the extent that it made him an "unintelligent" reader of his own work, while Christopher Ricks picks up on this vocal "flatness," finding that his poetry is written "consciously at a remove from the directly speakable," to cite two influential accounts.[1] This understanding of Eliot as a non-performative poet has obscured the verse performance contexts he engaged with throughout his life, from his early days in St. Louis to the main body of his poetic career in London. Growing up, he was subject to the entwining of literature and recitation that persisted in late Victorian education, while also encountering the influential Delsarte method of dramatic expression at his dance classes.[2] His move to Boston coincided with the glory years of Samuel Silas Curry's Boston School of Expression, and Eliot's relationship with Emily Hale, a teacher of elocution and drama with a gift for speaking verse, brought these early American recitation contexts forward into his later life. Primed by his American experiences, in 1914 Eliot arrived in a city where a popular movement for verse speaking reform was taking place alongside and loosely entwined with the emergence of poetic modernism, a coincidence which has never been fully explored.

Early twentieth-century British society was experiencing its own verse speaking revival. Mark Morrisson describes how by the late Victorian period elocution had left behind its roots in public oratory and legal training to become a "fine art," intrinsically "connected to the experience of literature" throughout the United Kingdom, a relationship cemented by W. B. Yeats and Florence Farr's immensely popular psaltery tours in the early years of the twentieth century.[3] The Poetry Society, founded in 1909 as the Poetry Recital Society, positioned itself at the helm of this movement for the reform of verse speaking by holding examinations, competitions, and training courses around the country. Despite the Society's own conservative tastes in poetry, it intersected with poetic modernism in unexpected ways, as is visible in Harold Monro's editorship of *The Poetry Review* in 1912. For the year of his editorship, *The Poetry Review* featured poems and criticism from poets like Ezra Pound and Richard Aldington alongside the Society's journal *The Poetical Gazette*, which made up the publication's back pages. This unlikely partnership was fostered by a shared belief in the importance of reading poetry aloud, both to expand poetry's audience and from a mutual conviction of the aesthetic superiority of poetry written for the voice. In January 1913, Monro opened the Poetry Bookshop to continue furthering the cause of poetry recitation. The staff there, Monro declared, "regard the books on sale in the shop merely as printed scores" for performance; the bookshop would host biweekly readings of and by many of the leading modernist and Georgian poets for the next two decades.[4] Already by September 1914, only months after his arrival in England, Eliot was familiar enough with Poetry Bookshop readings to satirize their conditions in a letter to Conrad Aiken, imagining giving "a few lectures, at 5 p. m., with wax candles" to become a "sentimental Tommy."[5] Next month, he recommended Aiken ask the Poetry Bookshop to stock his new book of verse, implying he already appreciated it as a center of modern poetic London.

This appreciation was reciprocated: while Monro is often remembered as the publisher who refused to print "Prufrock," by December 14, 1915, he was reading it himself as part of a programme of "Free Verse Poems" to an audience of thirty-four.[6] Eliot's attendance at Yeats's sold-out 1916 performance at Clifford's Inn Hall is well recorded, and it is likely that he also attended other readings, possibly with Pound, another frequent visitor and reader. By 1919, Eliot and Monro were personal friends, visiting and corresponding with one another regularly. Time spent at the Poetry Bookshop may have laid the groundwork for Eliot's other key verse speaking engagement, his work with Elsie Fogerty, founder of the Central School of Speech and Drama, on the choruses for his verse plays in the 1930s. Fogerty is listed as an "Occasional + plays" reader in a post-war list of Poetry Bookshop readers, and seems to have been a relatively frequent performer there from the shop's early days.[7] Fogerty's testimonial for Monro's widow, Alida Klemantaski, in 1934, attests to their felt community in furthering the cause of modern verse speaking. She writes of Klemantaski, "I have known her for many years [...] I consider her to be one of the greatest influences in promoting the modern movement for true poetry speaking."[8]

Tracing Eliot's engagement with this extensive web of recitation cultures can shed light on distinctive yet opaque features of his poetic development, such as his ambiguous syntax and enigmatic sense of poetic voice. At the time, as Carrie Preston has observed, these oral practices were so prominent that "Eliot could respond to them without identifying them by name," yet contemporary understandings of modernism as a literary movement centered on the printed page have left such oral contexts out of earshot.[9] This article seeks to outline those contexts and indicate their influence on Eliot's verse during the period from his arrival in England to the publication of "Gerontion" in *Ara Vos Prec* (1920). Charles Bernstein and Jerome McGann have productively illuminated how the material "visual coding" of the modernist poem shapes its meaning, but equivalent attention has not been paid to the oral materiality of these works, perhaps due to the comparative challenge of bringing the oral into focus.[10] Denis Donoghue, for example, employs Marshall McLuhan, then a rising star of media studies, to stress the obsolescence of Yeats's oral paradigm to what he sees as a visual–Symbolist–modernist poetic tradition, writing that today (or in 1966) "our minds work by seeing meanings as we see black marks on a white page without hearing the sounds for which they stand."[11] Recent developments in sound studies have disproven this serene assumption: both scientific and literary studies stress that even completely silent reading references sound, activating areas of the brain associated with hearing, so that we can never fully escape the traces of orality.[12] This paradigm recalls Yeats's own fervent belief in the innate orality of poetry, a belief which Ronald Schuchard's meticulous 2008 study of Yeats's and Farr's poetry speaking brought back into view after decades of neglect. Schuchard's study is exemplary in its careful attention to the rich seam of material relating to the performance and oral dissemination of Yeats's poetry, and his work delineates fertile ground for further research, as Robert Volpicelli's MSA prize-winning study of the modernist lecture tour in the United States has demonstrated.[13]

Haun Saussy's recent cultural history of orality has emphasized the degree to which McLuhan's arguments, while momentous, were also exaggerated due to the need for his emergent field to gain visibility, "to block the light given off by more brilliant and familiar objects."[14] It follows that we can today more clearly appreciate that "the gestures of differentiation between orality and literacy belong to the rituals of argumentative sociality."[15] Here, Saussy's argument for breaking down inviolable divisions between oral and literate texts dovetails with Chris Mustazza's call in 2018 for a "methodology that accounts for both sight and sound by further complicating the distinction and making use of the wealth of poetic sound recordings available to us."[16] Such an approach can take into account the ways we really do experience literature, and especially poetry, as oscillating between the oral and the visual, a mutuality which was clear to poets like Eliot who were active participants in the oral poetic contexts of the 1910s and 20s. Reading "Gerontion" alongside these recorded texts and historical verse speaking contexts can shed new light on familiar features of Eliot's poetics. In this essay, I focus on two aspects of this relationship. First, I explore how a contemporary emphasis on the impersonal in poetry performance provided an important model for Eliot's disembodied sense of poetic voice. Second, I indicate the complex relationship between punctuation and performance, inflected by careful attention to breath and physicality, that structures Eliot's own poetry performance practices. This sense of an oral syntax can recontextualize the recordings that Eliot saw as crucial to understanding his poetics, but which have been more frequently dismissed than appreciated since. Beyond these individual realignments, attention to the oral materiality of Eliot's poetics entails a shift from reader to listener which emphasizes the immediacy and performativity of a poetic corpus too often confined by its professorial textual trappings.

I. Performing Impersonality in the Modernist Monologue

The essays which appear in *The Sacred Wood*, published the same year as *Ara Vos Prec*, are a striking witness to the overlap that had developed between Eliot's poetic theory and that of the verse speaking movement. In "The Possibility of a Poetic Drama," as in contemporary verse speaking discourse, performance and personality emerge as interconnected concerns: "The performer is interested not in form but in opportunities for virtuosity or in the communication of his 'personality.'"[17] Eliot acknowledges the suppression of personality to be a crucial element of the performer's craft, condemning the modern actor for his attempt to elude this obligation. In a 1919 review of *The Duchess of Malfi*, he refines this understanding of the role of the reciter, writing that, rather than improved or interpreted, "poetry can only be transmitted," positioning the performer as an utterly transparent medium for the conveyance of the work.[18] In Eliot's eyes, then, the performer's personality must be absolutely subjugated to the work of art they are performing—a relationship which replicates the dynamic between poet and poem he outlines in "Tradition and the Individual Talent," the essay placed immediately before "The Possibility of a Poetic Drama" in the collection.

These ideas about performative impersonality were a commonplace in the verse speaking reform movement that arose in the early 1900s. A new preference for performative impersonality developed in reaction to the Victorian tendency towards overacting and artificial use of gesture in poetic performance, a tendency cultivated by the immensely popular Penny Reading movements of the later nineteenth century.[19] The verse speaking movement of the early twentieth century, especially as represented by the aristocratic Poetry Society, sought to distance itself from these working-class styles by advocating minimal gesture and warning against readers who saw the readings as opportunities to display their own personalities rather than relay the poem. This current is made clear in

Lady Margaret Sackville's inaugural speech on the founding of the Poetry Society in 1909, where she proclaims that poetry recitation requires "an attitude of surrender on the part of the speaker" so that "for the moment he is identified with the words he utters": the ability to do so is predicated on his possession of "a power of emotion equal to that contained in the poem itself."[20]

The same ideas took root in mainstream poetic modernism, as can be seen in Monro's endorsement of Yeats's psaltery method, which makes up the frontispiece to the same September 1912 issue of the *Poetry Review* in which Sackville's 1909 speech was reprinted. There, his language harmonizes with Sackville's own to memorialize Yeats's and Farr's verse speaking efforts on the occasion of Farr's departure to Sri Lanka:

> We can but regret our loss of so fine an artist, and hope that there are others who [...] have sufficient restraint and self-surrender to submit themselves, after her manner, to the cadence and rhythms of poetry, becoming, for the time being, a sensitive medium for their conveyance to the audience, rhapsodist rather than exponent, instrument rather than representative.[21]

Monro reiterates the ambivalent sense of impersonality preached by proponents of the new verse speaking, placing behind it the authority of an already established literary pedigree by linking it back to Yeats's and Farr's project. What today seems like the eccentricities of the Poetry Bookshop's performance conditions were driven by the same logic of performative impersonality: heavy curtains and dim candlelight were intended to focus attention on the sounds of the reader's work rather than the sight of their person. In the 1920s, a curtain was occasionally introduced to cover the speakers entirely, especially in performances of multiple voices, a technique which the Poetry Society also endorsed. The command to "surrender" to the poem echoes through each of these accounts of performative impersonality; it is telling that Eliot reaches for the same word twice in "Tradition and the Individual Talent," first when he demands a "continual surrender of himself as he is at the moment to something which is more valuable," then in his resounding penultimate pronouncement that "the poet cannot reach this impersonality without surrendering himself wholly to the work to be done."[22]

This emphasis on performative impersonality came hand in hand with a preference for dramatic monologues across the different strands of the verse speaking revival. While the Poetry Society usually recommended Victorian monologues, with a particular fondness for Robert Browning, the Poetry Bookshop championed radical new versions, like Charlotte Mew's "The Farmer's Bride," which Monro also published. The result was a different sense of the dramatic monologue in performance: alienated from the body of the speaker, personality had to be expressed vocally, and was no longer visibly rooted within the single speaker. The influence of these experimental monologue contexts can be felt in the distinctive poetic voice Eliot begins to develop in "Gerontion." Eliot's understanding of "Gerontion" as a "kind of preliminary stage" to *The Waste Land* is especially pertinent to his treatment of poetic voice in the poem, which offers a marked departure from the distinctive monologue speaker of "Prufrock," but has not yet launched into the polyvocality of *The Waste Land*.[23] The textual voice of "Gerontion," though conceivably the utterances of a single speaker, the "little old man" of the title, energetically strain this premise. The opening of the poem shows this vocal tension particularly well:

> Here I am, an old man in a dry month,
> Being read to by a boy, waiting for rain.
> I was neither at the hot gates
> Nor fought in the warm rain
> Nor knee deep in the salt marsh, heaving a cutlass,
> Bitten by flies, fought.[24]

These lines stage a scene of recitation. The boy's voice reading aloud a text about the battle of Thermopylae is interspersed with the old man's concurrent denial of his involvement; his own past is thus framed in the negative, eroding the speaker's presence inside the poem. The "neither ... nor ... nor" demarcates the old man's voice from the recited tale, which has its own distinctive spondaic pulse ("at the hot gates," "fought in the warm rain," "knee deep in the salt marsh") that is disrupted by the old man's off-beat negatives. The composition of the passage implies we are hearing two voices: the historical narrative read aloud by the boy alongside the voice of the ill-defined old man, complicating the operation of the poem as a straightforward dramatic monologue. As the poem progresses, the two voices implied by the poem's opening precipitate an improbably various lexis and dramatic shifts in tone, consciously testing our belief in this poem as the vocal emanations of a single speaker.

Critical responses to the poem often rely on its operation as a straightforward act of ventriloquism, despite these oddities. For Vincent Sherry, Eliot ventriloquizes the anachronistic liberal project in the form of one of its aging spokesmen, whereas Anthony Julius imagines the poem's voice as a thin disguise for Eliot's own: in his reading the poem only "purports" to be a dramatic monologue as part of its "deception."[25] While Julius's recognition of the poem's discomfort with the monologue form is perceptive, his eagerness to locate Eliot's own voice jars with contemporary monologue performance practices. Rather, these critical understandings of the poem adhere to the definition of the dramatic monologue that Eric Griffiths identifies at its Victorian origin, that "the imagined speaker is 'simply speaking' while the poet arranges that his words happen to fall into verse."[26] As "Gerontion" was written, the disembodied dramatic monologues performed at the Poetry Bookshop deliberately complicated this "simple" act of speaking, alienating it from the personality of the speaker at all. Eliot's later definition (itself delivered orally) of the dramatic monologue form as "when [the poet] is saying [...] only what he can say within the limits of one imaginary character addressing another imaginary character" diverges from Griffiths's in its peculiar sensitivity to the "limits" of the monologue form: it is these limits that "Gerontion," informed by contemporary poetry recitation contexts, consciously pulls at, and which *The Waste Land* would explode.[27]

II. Eliot's Spoken Syntax

Eliot's idiosyncratic punctuation has raised questions and hackles since his early years as a poet. In September 1920, John Quinn questioned his "avoidance of punctuation," suggesting that a comma might aid both grammar and rhythm.[28] Eliot's reply was confident: "I see reason in your objection to my punctuation; but I hold that the line itself punctuates [...]

That is because I always pause at the end of a line in reading verse, which perhaps you do not."[29] He not only assumes that Quinn will be reading the poems aloud to judge their punctuation, but also that there is a right and a wrong way of doing so, at least for his own verse. This sense of a precise spoken form for his syntax resurfaces remarkably intact fifteen years later, in Fogerty's anecdote from her work with Eliot on the choruses for *Murder in the Cathedral* (1935), as relayed by E. Martin Browne: "'On one occasion he came up to me during rehearsal and murmured very confidentially "That should be a colon, not a semi-colon." I think this was the only spontaneous remark he ever made in rehearsals.'"[30] The anecdote is comical; it shows Eliot playing to his public persona of the bookish poet–professor, ironizing a pedantic difference in juncture between a colon and a semicolon, but it also reinforces Eliot's assertion that he understood his syntactical rhythms not only to directly reference the oral but to operate according to a strict set of oral assumptions.

Given the opportunity to record his poems in the 1930s and 40s, Eliot's orally located understanding of rhythm becomes even more explicit. Ricks's suspicion that it was "mildly perverse" for Eliot to record poems like *The Waste Land*, given that they are "created for the printed page," itself gains a degree of perversity beside the direction that Eliot makes in the sleeve notes to his 1947 recording of *Four Quartets*:[31]

> A recording of a poem read by its author is no more definitive an "interpretation" than a recording of a symphony conducted by the composer. [...] What the recording of a poem by its author can and should preserve, is the way that poem sounded to the author when he had finished it. The disposition of lines on the page, and the punctuation [...] can never give an exact notation of the author's metric.[32]

Eliot adheres to the same multi-dimensional oral understanding of "metric" that he alludes to when explaining his punctuation choices above, the logic of which understands a recording to be the most comprehensive guide to a poem's rhythms. The anxieties Griffiths sees as endemic to the Victorian grappling with print and voice are recast: instead of the "transcriber's plight," Eliot, writing in a post-gramophone era, sees the performer's possibilities, especially when it comes to evolving a more complex and subtle oral understanding of "metric."[33] Although these notes date from 1947, the same possibilities of a multi-dimensional orally located understanding of metric resound through both verse speaking and free verse discourse of the 1910s and 20s, motivating, for example, Pound and Amy Lowell's separate attempts to define an orally located understanding of rhythm through experimental phonology.[34] Fogerty similarly stresses this link between free verse prosody and verse speaking. Her 1923 primer devotes long sections to prosody, prescribing "a study of prosody on modern lines" as the best cure for sing-song recitation.[35] She writes that "the more we are persuaded [...] that the poet is not fettered by the thousand rules of the metrist," the more she has become convinced that the "eternal laws" to which the poet must conform are laws conditioned by the nature of their medium, "And that medium is speech."[36] For Fogerty, as for Eliot, no verse is free; Fogerty supplies the refinement that these residual laws are located in the oral form of the poem.

If we follow Eliot's own direction towards oral form as a means of understanding his poetics, we can see that his syntactic patterns, ambivalent on the page, allow him to exploit the expanded phonetic possibilities perceived in non-metrical verse when read aloud. Perhaps the most distinctively Eliotian sentence structure to emerge from "Gerontion" is the repeated combination of enjambment with an unbalanced medial caesura, which enables Eliot to make use of line and sentence end pauses independently of one another in constructing the rhythm of the passage. This structure characterizes some of his most memorable later lines, from the opening of *The Waste Land*:

> April is the cruellest month, breeding
> Lilacs out of the dead land, mixing
> Memory and desire, stirring[37]

To "Burnt Norton":

> Words move, music moves
> Only in time; but that which is only living
> Can only die. Words, after speech, reach[38]

READING ELIOT ALOUD   225

With the help of recording analysis programs such as those Marit MacArthur and Mustazza have pioneered, we can let oral performance clarify the "author's metric" here.[39] Eliot's 1933 recording of "Gerontion" makes use of remarkably regular and symmetrical pitch curves, often returning to the same high and low pitch points in successive cadences. While this pattern is evident throughout the recording, it appears especially regular in the fifth stanza, where the syntactical pattern outlined above also emerges most fully:

> After such knowledge, what forgiveness? Think now
> History has many cunning passages, contrived corridors
> And issues, deceives with whispering ambitions,
> Guides us by vanities. // Think now
> She gives when our attention is distracted
> And what she gives, gives with such supple confusions
> That the giving famishes the craving. // Gives too late
> What's not believed in, or if still believed,
> In memory only, reconsidered passion.[40]

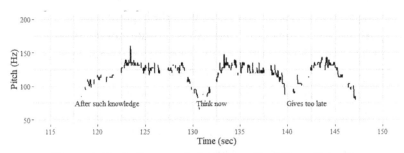

Figure 1. Pitch-time graph for "Gerontion", lines 33 to 41.

Figure 1 is the pitch-time graph of these lines. The moments marked with a "//" above represent the pauses between the end of one pitch curve and the beginning of the next in the graph, also labelled with the first few words of each curve on the graph. We can see here not only how clearly and symmetrically these pitch curves rise and fall, but also that they align exactly with the mid-line caesuras created by the new sentences in these lines, rather than coinciding with the line endings, which manifest instead as briefer pauses within the pitch curve of a breath. Such an effect would suggest Eliot was working with pitch and breath patterns independent from the line in this stanza to orally reinforce the emphasis on these midline sentence breaks.

Fogerty's expanded oral understanding of metric championed the careful cultivation of breathwork, a subtle effect which could take center stage in the modern recitation movement given the shift away from overacting and gestural recitative methods. She writes that the "successive pulse-beats of verse are, physiologically, breath-pressures," reorienting conventional metric into a movement which takes breath as its measure, rather than the metronome.[41] Her primer follows other verse speaking manuals in drawing attention to the physical process of breathing, aiming to make the verse speaker conscious of these processes in order to isolate and regulate them. Such a process suggestively underlies the structure of these recorded lines from "Gerontion," where the line endings operate a sonic syntax that generates meaning in relation to the overarching structure of the breath. Allowing breath to generate its own phrasings in this way, we can hear that "After such knowledge, what forgiveness?" is delivered as a rhetorical question. Giving no pause for answer, it forms part of a pitch-bound phrase which immediately continues to the end of the following sentence. Positioned as they are at the beginning of each successive pitch phrase, "Think now" and "Gives too late" sound like echoes of the original "Think now." The structure of these repetitions translates the aural logic of the echo into a principle of time: the first two sentences form the longest pitch curve, followed by the medium pitch curve of the next sentence, with the shortest falling at the end. Ricks's designation of Eliot's reading voice as "flat" misses the complex, multi-faceted oral structures that emerge from considering these performance contexts. Instead, these contexts point to the subtle, orally located understandings of rhythm that circulated in modernist poetic and verse speaking communities during the period that saw the rise of free verse, understandings which can bring us closer to the "symphony" Eliot finds in his own recordings.

Notes

1. F. R. Leavis, "The Poet as Executant," *Scrutiny* 15 (1947): 80; Christopher Ricks, *T. S. Eliot and Prejudice* (University of California Press, 1988), 181, 189.
2. Robert Crawford, *Young Eliot: From St. Louis to The Waste Land* (Vintage, 2016), 52.
3. Mark S. Morrisson, "Performing the Pure Voice: Elocution, Verse Recitation, and Modernist Poetry in Prewar London," *Modernism/modernity* 3 (1996): 30.
4. Harold Monro, "The Bookshop," *Poetry and Drama* 1 (1913): 387.
5. *Letters* 4:64.
6. Notebook, Harold Monro Papers, London, British Library, Add. MS 57756 A, 47r.
7. Notebook, British Library, Add. MS 57762 A, 68r.
8. Preserved in British Library, Add. MS 57765, 2r.
9. Carrie J. Preston, *Modernism's Mythic Pose: Gender, Genre, Solo Performance* (Oxford University Press, 2011), 125.
10. Charles Bornstein, *Material Modernism* (Cambridge University Press, 2001), 2.
11. Denis Donoghue, "Yeats and the Living Voice," *Studies: An Irish Quarterly Review* 55, no. 218 (1966): 147.
12. See, for example, Christopher I. Petkov and Pascal Belin, "Silent Reading: Does the Brain 'Hear' Both Speech and Voices?," *Current Biology* 23, no. 4 (2013): 155–56; Garett Stewart, *Reading Voices* (University of California Press, 1990).
13. Ronald Schuchard, *The Last Minstrels: Yeats and the Revival of the Bardic Arts* (Oxford University Press, 2008); Robert Volpicelli, *Transatlantic Modernism and the US Lecture Tour* (Oxford University Press, 2021).
14. Haun Saussy, *The Ethnography of Rhythm: Orality and Its Technologies* (Fordham University Press, 2016), 4.
15. Saussy, *The Ethnography of Rhythm*, 4.
16. Chris Mustazza, "Machine-Aided Close Listening: Prosthetic Synaesthesia and the 3D Phonotext," *Digital Humanities Quarterly* 12, no. 3 (2018).
17. *Complete Prose* 2:283.
18. *Complete Prose* 2:173.
19. For the phenomenon of Penny Readings, see Evelyn M. Sivier, "Penny Readings: Popular Elocution in Late Nineteenth-Century England," in *Performance of Literature in Historical Perspectives*, ed. David W. Thompson (University Press of America, 1983), 223–31.
20. Reprinted as Lady Margaret Sackville, "Presidential Address," *Poetry Review* 1 (1912): 454.

21 Harold Monro, "Notes and Comments," *Poetry Review* 1 (1912): 424.
22 *Complete Prose* 2:108, 112.
23 Cited in *Poems* 1:558.
24 *Poems* 1:31.
25 Anthony Julius, *T. S. Eliot, Anti-Semitism, and Literary Form*, revised ed. (Thames & Hudson, 2003), 41; Vincent B. Sherry, *The Great War and the Language of Modernism* (Oxford University Press, 2003), chap. 3.
26 Eric Griffiths, *The Printed Voice of Victorian Poetry* (Clarendon Press, 1989), 75.
27 *Complete Prose* 7:817.
28 *Letters* 1:557.
29 *Letters* 1:557.
30 As relayed in E. Martin Browne, *The Making of T. S. Eliot's Plays* (Cambridge University Press, 1969) 84.
31 Ricks, *T. S. Eliot and Prejudice*, 180.
32 *Complete Prose* 7:8.
33 Griffiths, *The Printed Voice of Victorian Poetry*, 24.
34 Pound largely in his dealings with the Abbé Rousselot in Paris in 1911; Amy Lowell undertook her own experiments with Dr. Patterson at Columbia from 1916.
35 Elsie Fogerty, *The Speaking of English Verse* (J. M. Dent, 1923), 145.
36 Fogerty, *The Speaking of English Verse*, 106, 107.
37 *Poems* 1:55.
38 *Poems* 1:183.
39 For an introduction to their work, see Marit MacArthur and Lee Miller, "After Scansion: Visualizing, Deforming, and Listening to Poetic Prosody," *Arcade: A Digital Salon*, arcade.stanford.edu/content/after-scansion-visualizing-deforming-and-listening-poetic-prosody.
40 *Poems* 1:32.
41 Fogerty, *The Speaking of English Verse*, xvi.

What the Thunder Said
Environmental Agency in *The Waste Land*

Caylin Capra-Thomas

The working title of *The Waste Land*, "He Do the Police in Different Voices," has pointed critics towards voice as a central entry point to Eliot's poem. Leonard Diepeveen explores the nuances of quotation and allusion,[1] John Xiros Cooper considers the poem's socio-verbal context and its transformative action on sociolinguistic codes,[2] Michael Levenson argues for considering scene instead of image as the context for the poem's voices,[3] and Alireza Farahbakhsh, among others, observes the fractured, elusive selfhood created by the poem's lack of a central speaker.[4] A new avenue which we might carve into the already well-lined critical map of voice in *The Waste Land*, however, is to move on, as Eliot did, from *voice* to *land*. That Eliot ultimately decided to name the poem *The Waste Land* after having nearly called it "He Do the Police in Different Voices" signals that his text is concerned with voice and land in nearly equal measure. That is, however, not to abandon entirely the poem's perennially compelling questions of voice; those interested in voices in *The Waste Land* will find their readings enriched by considering them in connection with the poem's equally compelling questions of land, which ecocritics have begun to take up in recent years.

Scholars endeavoring to read *The Waste Land* ecocritically tend to gravitate to the idea of "waste." Gabrielle McIntire uses Eliot's representation of pollution to classify the poem as a "fallen post pastoral," where nature has been compromised and thus cannot offer renewal, respite, or

229

refreshment.[5] Andrew Kalaidjian fits *The Waste Land* into a modernist tradition of "dark pastoral" where the poem's human speakers are no longer interested in cultivating wasted lands, but rather in languishing among them.[6] Spencer Morrison examines Eliot's overlaying of the desert onto the cityscape, which he also sees as preoccupied with ruin.[7] And in the 2022 *T. S. Eliot Studies Annual*, Jahan Ramazani argues for *The Waste Land* as a precursor and source for the "world elegy," a poem of mourning for the world in a time of human-made climate change, actively resisting the traditional elegy's now impossible and irresponsible promise of consolation and redemption.[8] These and other critics have put Eliot's poem in the center of ecomodernist studies, their focus on the poem's devastated landscapes likely reflecting our own ever-growing environmental crisis. Already underway at the turn of the nineteenth century, the environmental degradation caused by the industrial revolution certainly drew Eliot's eye, as the smoky air and desertified landscapes of his poetry attest. Still, it seems unlikely that Eliot would have been writing about a monolithic "environment" in the kind of totalizing crisis we experience today. It becomes then important to also look beyond the pollution, ruin, and waste of *The Waste Land* and consider how else land might function in this poem. What do Eliot's environments *do* besides vex their inhabitants? One thing the poem's land does is interact with the voices that sound within and from its environments. Reading these voices together with the land offers the ecocritic an additional means of understanding the poem.

If ecology is the relationship between nature and culture, there is no ecocritical reading of *The Waste Land* that can eschew the role of the human in the environment.[9] Human voices sound within, react to, and interpret the poem's environmental elements, but to read at this intersection our notion of voice must also include speakers and language beyond the human. While the throng of human voices can muffle them, there are numerous non-human entities producing a range of meaningful utterances in this poem. In "The Burial of the Dead," the cricket gives "no relief," which is to say, chirps nonstop, and the poem's final section is also named for an environmental utterance: "What the Thunder **Said**."[10] In this section, we hear the thunder, the cicada, the dry grass singing, the sounds of the hermit thrush, the murmur of some airborne entity, the whistle of bats, wells and cisterns singing, the rooster's call, and nightfall's rumors.[11]

Plants, animals, land formations, and weather are all features of the environment, so the moments when they sing or speak are moments where land and voice intersect directly.

In his foundational essay, "Some Principles of Ecocriticism," William Howarth establishes links between ecology and human expression, noting that many words used in geology come from human domains, like "shelf," "basin," and "belt," and that literary studies in turn borrows words from geographical ideas: we work in a particular "field," "map" disciplines, and consider texts that traverse "boundaries."[12] Thus, Howarth shows us that land and language have had a fertile exchange outside of poetry's traditional pastoral modes long before *The Waste Land*, but he also gives us tools to excavate that connection in any literary text:

> Ecocriticism, instead of taxing science for its use of language to represent (mimesis), examines its ability to point (deixis). [...]
> In learning to read land, one can't just name objects but point to what they do: pines live in sandy soil, oaks in clay, and thus their rates of water absorption differ.[13]

Howarth's way of reading instructs us to consider the world within and beyond the poem to make meaning. Barry Commoner wrote that the first law of ecology is that everything is connected to everything else.[14] We can perform a "close reading" of the elements of the environment in *The Waste Land* to understand that its land interacts with and impacts both the poem itself—its movement, structure, and fragmentary ending—and what the poem contains—its speakers, creatures, and what they say.

In *The Waste Land*'s second verse paragraph, nature's audible vocalizations arrive in the form of cricket chirps: "... for you know only/A heap of broken images, where the sun beats,/And the dead tree gives no shelter, the cricket no relief,/And the dry stone no sound of water..."[15] In this moment, land and voice intersect directly in the cricket, both an insect and thus a feature of the land as well as an entity producing meaningful utterances. The cricket giving "no relief" can be read as chirping ceaselessly—a familiar sound to anyone who has kept their window open on a hot summer night while trying to sleep—and these cricket chirps are full of ecological information. To begin, the chirping itself communicates to other crickets the desire to attract a mate to reproduce or to sound the alarm over danger.[16] The chirping communicates to humans the heat of the environment; according to Dolbear's Law, the external temperature can be determined accurately using a mathematical formula based on the rate at which crickets chirp.[17] The higher the rate of chirping, the hotter the environment. Eliot has already described this stanza's environment as one "where the sun beats," and so we can assume its heat, but since crickets are also nocturnal singers, we can understand it as one where that heat persists well into the night, when the temperature should be cooling off.[18] Understanding the crickets' ecological message can alter our perception of subsequent lines. For example, the invitation that follows "(Come in under the shadow of this red rock)" becomes more seductive than one might initially perceive—an invitation into shady respite from the intense heat.[19]

We can also understand this heat as quite dry, as this stanza's trees are dead, its stones dry, and there is no water to be *heard*. (Note Eliot's choice to remark the absence of water by the absence of its voice!) Ecocritical readings of the poem have made much of this dryness, especially in its final movement, "What the Thunder Said." McIntire, for example, has said that in this section Eliot may have been anticipating the threat of fresh water scarcity associated with our current climate crisis.[20] Terblanche argues that this section sees Eliot concerned over soil erosion and presaging desertification.[21] Although the dry conditions of "What the Thunder Said" impact the poem's voices, the altitude of the landscape depicted plays an equal but hereto unexplored role. While there are many moments of land–voice interaction in *The Waste Land*, in this short research note I'll focus on how Eliot develops this interaction in Part V.

In this section's first stanza, the mountains are part of the landscape as "distant" sites of seasonal change, but they get closer as the poem moves forward. "Here," the speaker says in the beginning of the second stanza, "is no water but only rock/Rock and no water and the sandy road/The road winding above the mountains[.]"[22] The mountains are now close enough to see that our road winds up and into them, and the speaker follows this road, continuing to lament an environment that gets dryer and more uncomfortable the further they ascend:

> Here one can neither stand nor lie nor sit
> There is not even silence in the mountains
> But dry sterile thunder without rain
> There is not even solitude in the mountains
> But red sullen faces that sneer and snarl
> From doors of mudcracked houses[23]

Thus far, the only voice sounding in the mountains is the thunder. Like the cricket, the thunder is an entity in which voice and environment intersect—an element of the environment that produces meaningful sound—and which gives us important ecological information. We know we are going further up into the mountain not only because of the shifting meaning of the word "here," which moves from the road to the mountains, but also because of the "dry sterile thunder without rain."[24] Dry thunderstorms occur at very high altitudes, where, due to the elevation of the cloud base, rain has further to fall and thus can evaporate before it hits the ground.[25] A high altitude might be why one can "neither stand nor lie nor sit," as humans need time to acclimate to and become comfortable in higher elevations, and the poem shows us that the I is only just ascending.[26] The altitude might also explain why the human life that we do meet seems hostile and emits only hostile utterances, sneering and snarling, as the lack of oxygen at higher elevations (hypoxia) has been linked to higher rates of depression, anger, low mood, and anxiety over time, although the initial effect is euphoric.[27] High altitudes also dull feelings of thirst, leading to dehydration, which, in combination with the dry climate, can partially account for the speaker's obsession with water.[28] This environment's impact on the brain can also give us new ways to read the conclusion of the second stanza, as well as the mysterious stanza that follows it.

The third stanza develops with short lines in half-formed second conditional statements that gradually grow longer as they move from a dry environmental reality into a place of almost hallucinatory reverie:

> If there were the sound of water only
> Not the cicada
> And dry grass singing
> But sound of water over a rock

> Where the hermit-thrush sings in the pine trees
> Drip drop drip drop drop drop drop
> But there is no water[29]

High altitudes can cause confusion and disorientation, and hallucinations at extreme heights. This speaker's disorientation could be amplified by the auditory oversaturation of the cicada, as cicadas can sound at a level of 100 decibels.[30] Like the cricket, the cicada sings to attract a mate, but they do not need 100 decibels worth of sound for this purpose; rather, an oversaturated soundscape would make it difficult for predators to locate them.[31] Because of the arid climate, which allows the land to "sing" as air moves through its dried grasses, as well as the high altitude, we can also appreciate that "the sound of water over a rock/Where the hermit-thrush sings in the pine trees" is not a reality of the speaker's present environment, as the hermit thrush, a North American bird, resides in middle altitudes.[32] And so, the song of the dry grass, the sonic overwhelm of the cicada, and the altitude-related confusion and dehydration create disorientation that manifests as impossible environmental utterance: the "Drip drop drip drop drop drop drop" of imagined water.

This disorientation gives way to hallucinations of a "third who always walks beside you" in the fourth stanza.[33] Eliot's notes to these lines say that he was influenced by an account of the Shackleton Antarctic expedition, wherein it was reported that crew kept counting one more person than was actually in their party.[34] It is well documented that people tend to hallucinate spectral figures when operating within extremities, oxygen deprivation and thirst among them, and since these conditions have been met in "What the Thunder Said" we can read the question of "the third who always walks beside you" as the result of an environmentally induced hallucinatory state.[35] Eliot may also have been influenced in his thinking by the place where he composed "What the Thunder Said": Lausanne, Switzerland, itself 1,023 feet above sea level, and, more importantly, with a view of the French Alps across Lake Geneva. Talk of mountains and the effects of elevation may have been common among the other residents of the *pension* where Eliot stayed during his treatment by Dr. Vittoz.[36]

The poem proceeds from this hallucinatory state to make land and voice unfamiliar—or to travel to unfamiliar lands and speak in foreign tongues. The stanzas that follow the appearance of the mysterious "third" meld human with environmental qualities to delirious effect. Something that is capable of flying high in the air is heard making a "murmur of maternal lamentation," "hordes" of unnamed beings swarm like insects, bats are given baby faces, and a once domesticated rooster has taken over a deserted chapel and stands atop it, crowing in French ("Co co rico co co rico").[37] Also facilitated by the environmentally induced delirium is the poem's movement into distant lands and languages, with Eliot twice using languages spoken by or relevant to the people on those lands to describe their features, as when he uses the Hindi "Ganga" for the Ganges or the Sanskrit "Himavant" for the (also Sanskrit) Himalayas.[38] At the end of all this roaming through land and language, the thunder speaks in a human tongue: "DA/*Datta*: what have we given?"[39] All three of the interpretations of this divine syllable—*give, sympathize, control*—can be heard in the voice of god and the thunder as it rolls out, "Da Da Da."[40]

The thunder's utterance sets in motion the poem's final lines, which offer spiritual meaning at the intersection of land and voice:

London Bridge is falling down falling down falling down

Poi s'ascose nel foco che gli affina
Quando fiam uti chelidon—O swallow swallow
Le Prince d'Aquitaine à la tour abolie
These fragments I have shored against my ruins
Why then Ile fit you. Hieronymo's mad againe.
Datta. Dayadhvam. Damyata.

Shantih shantih shantih[41]

Here, the section's languages—and thus the lands from which they arise—meld and mix: English, Italian, French, Sanskrit. Although each of these lines alludes to an earlier literary work, here at the end of *The Waste Land* we do not know who or what is giving voice to them. Delirium melts utterance, dissolving notions of a human self completely into their linguistic environment, which is born of their physical environment, in the form of a mantra recited at the end of ritual: "Shantih   shantih   shantih[.]"[42] The environment might be negatively impacted by human activity. It might be hot, cold, dry, or otherwise uncomfortable. But the voices of *The Waste Land* are deeply enmeshed with these environments, sometimes in ways that bring them into alignment with the knowledge and experiences of their non-human elements or inhabitants, sometimes in ways that utterly disorient their resident humans. An ecological reading of its land and voices reveals a poem that is not only observing environmental degradation, but also engaging with that environment in ways that have meaning for and beyond its degradation.

Notes

1. Leonard Diepeveen, *Changing Voices: The Modern Quoting Poem* (University of Michigan Press, 1993).
2. John Xiros Cooper, *T. S. Eliot and the Politics of Voice: The Argument of The Waste Land* (UMI Research Press, 1987).
3. Michael Levenson, "Form, Voice, and the Avant-Garde," in *The Cambridge Companion to The Waste Land*, ed. Gabrielle McIntire (Cambridge University Press, 2015), 87–101.
4. Alireza Farahbakhsh, "Eliot and Postmodern Selfhood," *Journal of Language, Literature and Culture* 2009, no. 111 (May 1, 2009): 69–86.
5. Gabrielle McIntire, "*The Waste Land* as Ecocritique," *Cambridge Companion to The Waste Land*, 178–93.
6. Andrew Kalaidjian, *Exhausted Ecologies: Modernism and Environmental Recovery* (Cambridge University Press, 2020).
7. Spencer Morrison, "Geographies of Space: Mapping and Reading the Cityscape," *Cambridge Companion to The Waste Land*, 24–38.
8. Jahan Ramazani, "Burying the Dead: *The Waste Land*, Ecocritique, and World Elegy," *T. S. Eliot Studies Annual* 4: 7–23.
9. William Howarth, "Some Principles of Ecocriticism," in *The Ecocriticism Reader: Landmarks in Literary Ecology*, ed. Cheryll Glotfelty and Harold Fromm (University of Georgia Press, 1995), 71.
10. *Poems* 1:10, line 23.
11. *Poems* 1:68–71, lines 327, 342, 353–56, 366–68, 379, 384, 392, and 415.
12. Howarth, "Some Principles of Ecocriticism," 75, 77.
13. Howarth, "Some Principles of Ecocriticism," 80.
14. Barry Commoner, *The Closing Circle: Nature, Man, and Technology* (Dover, 1971), 29.
15. *Poems* 1:55, lines 21–24.

16 "Can You Tell the Temperature by Listening to the Chirping of a Cricket?" Library of Congress, November 2019, www.loc.gov/everyday-mysteries/meteorology-climatology/item/can-you-tell-the-temperature-by-listening-to-the-chirping-of-a-cricket/.
17 A. E. Dolbear, "The Cricket as Thermometer," *American Naturalist* 31 (1897): 970–71.
18 "Field Crickets," Missouri Department of Conservation, https://mdc.mo.gov/discover-nature/field-guide/field-crickets.
19 *Poems* 1:55, line 26.
20 McIntire, "*The Waste Land* as Ecocritique," 186.
21 Etienne Terblanche, *T. S. Eliot, Poetry, and Earth: The Name of the Lotos Rose* (Lexington Books, 2016).
22 *Poems* 1:68, lines 331–33.
23 *Poems* 1:68, lines 340–44.
24 *Poems* 1:68, line 342.
25 Paulina Firozi, "Here's what to know about dry thunderstorms and how they increase wildfire risk," *Washington Post*, July 20, 2021.
26 *Poems* 1:68, line 340.
27 E. C. Heinrich et al., "Cognitive Function and Mood at High Altitude Following Acclimatization and Use of Supplemental Oxygen and Adaptive Servoventilation Sleep Treatments," *PLOS One* (June 2019); Barbara Shukitt-Hale and Harris R. Lieberman, "Nutritional Needs in Cold and High-Altitude Environments: Applications for Military Personnel in Field Operations," ed. B. M. Marriott and S. J. Carlson, Institute of Medicine Committee on Military Nutrition Research (National Academies Press, 1996), www.ncbi.nlm.nih.gov/books/NBK232882/.
28 Sonam Chawla and Shweta Saxena, "Physiology of High-Altitude Acclimatization," *Resonance: Journal of Science Education* 19, no. 6 (2014): 545.
29 *Poems* 1:69, lines 352–58.
30 Henry C. Bennet-Clark, "How Cicadas Make Their Noise," *Scientific American* 278, no. 5 (1998): 58.
31 Bennet-Clark, "How Cicadas Make Their Noise," 59.
32 Cornell Lab of Ornithology, "Hermit Thrush Overview," *All About Birds*, 2019, www.allaboutbirds.org/guide/Hermit_Thrush/overview.
33 *Poems* 1:69, line 359.
34 *Poems* 1:76.
35 Michael Shermer, "The Sensed-Presence Effect," *Scientific American* 302, no. 4 (2010), 34–35.
36 Eliot called the place "dull," but seemed to enjoy talking French with other travelers and patients. See *Letters* 1:614, 617.
37 *Poems* 1:69–70, lines 366–68, 379, and 385–92.

38 *Poems* 1:70, lines 395, 397.
39 *Poems* 1:70, lines 400–401.
40 *Poems* 1:699.
41 *Poems* 1:71, lines 426–33.
42 *Poems* 1:71, line 433.

Towards a Reparative Reading of "Portrait of a Lady"

Huiming Liu

Controversy over Eliot's representation of women and his treatment of them in life has only increased over time and will likely continue with the publication of his letters to Emily Hale. Many critics have examined Eliot's misogynistic portrayal of women. Lyndall Gordon draws upon biographical materials to illustrate the stereotypes of femininity in Eliot's writing: "Eliot chose to write about women as a baffling and alien creature, frozen in an image."[1] She summarizes the feminine stereotypes in Eliot's Bostonian early poems as "the gushy romantic, the dangerous enchantress, the languid socialite."[2] The lady in "Portrait of a Lady" seems to fit into such gender stereotypes—a Bostonian socialite who goes to concerts and expresses gushy romantic views about music. The speaker in the poem despises her and tries to detach from her. Like Gordon, Rachel Potter also points out that Eliot associates bourgeois femininity with romantic egotism and that he also mocks "the cadences and sentiments of pretentious Boston drawing rooms."[3] Eliot's portrayal of the lady appears offensive and misogynistic to many readers.

However, Cyrena Pondrom approaches the gender issue in "Portrait" from another perspective and comes to a different conclusion. She argues that critics like Gordon have assumed that the portrayal of the lady in this poem is completely reliable while the lady's sentimental and pretentious image is constructed simply by the male persona in quotation marks.[4] Pondrom further argues that Eliot "refuses to ally with either figure in

'Portrait' but instead offers a critique of the gender roles that each acts to the fullest."[5] Pondrom points to the fact that the gender roles of the lady and the man in this poem are artificially performed to the fullest from a single perspective of the masculine poetic persona.

Building on Pondrom's analysis, I interpret the exaggerated and unreliable performativity of gender roles as the speaker's defense mechanism of shame in the poem. The following scene reveals the dramatic urgency to find words in order to cover his humiliation: "And I must borrow every changing shape/To find expression ... dance, dance/Like a dancing bear,/Cry like a parrot, chatter like an ape."[6] He feels humiliated because she directly exposes to his face that he is not prepared for their relationship. As both Gordon and Pondrom have pointed out, humiliation is the key affect in "Portrait."[7] Eve Sedgwick's frameworks of "reparative reading" and "paranoid reading" provide a subtle explanation of gender politics through the affects of shame and humiliation.

Sedgwick proposes that cultural critique tends to take the form of paranoid reading that places its faith in exposing systematic oppressions and developing strong theories to anticipate similar oppressions in the future.[8] For Sedgwick, paranoia is only one of the many forms of knowledge and there should be spaces to practice other forms of knowing. In *Touching Feeling*, where she proposes forms of reparative reading, shame is the central focus in critical evaluation of gender dynamics in literature. For Sedgwick, paranoia suggests a "dogged, defensive narrative stiffness" of temporality "that's characterized by a distinctly Oedipal regularity and repetitiveness: it happened to my father's father, it happened to my father, it is happening to me, it will happen to my son."[9] Yet reparative reading, such as through analyzing shame or hope, allows the readers to transcend the paranoid circle for a while and ruminate about the possibility that "the past could have happened differently" or "the future may be different."[10] Hence reparative reading can lead to more "specific train of epistemological or narrative consequences" that paranoid reading, despite exposing the unmystified view of systematic oppression, does not *necessarily or intrinsically* do.[11] Meanwhile, it is important to point out that Sedgwick's reparative reading does not mean a denial of the oppressive system but instead it is often founded upon the conclusions of paranoid reading. After knowing the oppressive mechanism, we can then know where and how to repair: "It is sometimes the most paranoid-tending people who are able to, and need to, develop and disseminate the richest reparative practices."[12] In the case of Eliot and gender, the exposure of gender oppression by feminist critics such as Potter and Gordon has made room for the discussion of shame and reparative reading of the poem.

Having established the rough framework of paranoid and reparative reading, it is worthwhile now to first analyze the specific gender issues in "Portrait" that have triggered paranoia among critics—the gender role expectation that humiliates the speaker of the poem. Returning to Pondrom's argument on the artificial performance of gender roles in "Portrait," in my view the division between femininity and masculinity is mainly articulated through the detachment/sentimentalism stereotype. The lady's sentimentalism is highlighted through her overflowing responses to music and her dramatic style of speeches:

> "So intimate, this Chopin, that I think his soul
> Should be resurrected only among friends
> Some two or three, who will not touch the bloom
> That is rubbed and questioned in the concert room."[13]

And, " *how, how* rare and strange it is, to find/In a life composed *so much, so much* of odds and ends."[14] Contrary to her overt sentimentalism, the speaker constructs his masculinity through deliberate detachment from the lady's musical taste and ignoring her words: "Inside my brain a dull tom-tom begins/Absurdly hammering a prelude of its own/Capricious monotone."[15] Her sentimentality is portrayed through music that makes her seem like a stereotypically dangerous enchantress for the male speaker. From the perspective of paranoid reading, the speaker is paranoid about femininity and confines the lady into her gender role expectation in his description. Furthermore, shame plays a huge role in the poem, entailing both a paranoid reading and a reparative attempt. Given that the lady is portrayed only in the words of the humiliated speaker, it is sensible to doubt that the overt sentimentality is less reliable than it seems; her "enchantress" image serves as an excuse for the male speaker's wounded masculinity. The final moment of humiliation comes when the lady exposes that he isn't prepared to give what she expects from him. His scornful and detached attitude comes from the expectation of masculinity which makes their communication difficult and leads to the final shame. Further, shame plays a huge role in the poem, entailing both a paranoid reading and a reparative attempt.

The turning point comes at the end of the poem, which shifts the affective mechanism of shame from the recurring memory of paranoia to a space for reparative reading. As he looks back on his experience with the lady, the speaker attempts to repair his wound by dissolving the gender division at the end of the poem when he shifts the tone, perspective, and temporality. Eliot shows the disintegration of the gender politics of emotion by writing in the lady's style. He laments the passing time just as the lady used to. He almost renounces himself as a detached masculine artist by adopting the sentimental style of the lady's speech, as in "'You let it flow from you, you let it flow'" and "'Yet with these April sunsets/ that somehow recall/My buried life.'"[16] The speaker laments in a similar way at the end: "Well! and what if she should die some afternoon,/Afternoon grey and smoky, evening yellow and rose;/Should die and leave me sitting pen in hand[.]"[17] The similar color and image of twilight recur in the speaker's internal monologue at the end to show that he shares the same concern for temporality. The speaker then returns temporarily to the vocabularies of paranoia and re-thinks who has the advantage in the relationship after all. Yet, unlike the scornful buffing of his masculinity in the earlier parts of the poem, he shores up such paranoia against his ruins and gives the advantage to her:

> Doubtful, for a while
> Not knowing what to feel or if I understand
> Or whether wise or foolish, tardy or too soon ...
> Would she not have the advantage, after all?[18]

His hesitation shows his regretful wish for a possibly different result. It may be too soon but the passing of her youth pushed him to the final encounter with her. It may be tardy because their relationship was much less intimate than he thought. Out of the wish for reparation, he seems to finally reconcile that he should have acknowledged his failure. He not only failed to communicate his own sentiments towards her but also failed to see through the gender stereotype of sentimental femininity. We can see here that writing shame not only entails the paranoia of defensive gestures towards past events (as in the unnatural gender performance in the early parts of the poem), but also the reparative wish to really transcend the gender prejudices in time.

Eliot's writing of shame in this poem is also consistent with his poetics in "Tradition and the Individual Talent," including both paranoia and reparation in Sedgwick's sense. Eliot famously remarks: "Poetry is not a turning loose of emotion, but an escape from emotion; it is not the expression of personality, but an escape from personality. But, of course, only those who have personality and emotions know what it means to want to escape from these things."[19] The Eliotic "escape from emotion" in "Portrait" is the seemingly detached masculinity that attempts to cover up his shameful feeling. His poetics of catalyst aims at arriving at a new emotional state that includes acknowledging emotions, understanding them, writing through them, and creating something new in the poem: "A number of floating feelings, having an affinity to this emotion by no means superficially evident, have combined with it to give us a new art emotion."[20] In the same way, Eliot writes about the experience of shame in "Portrait" and at the end the poem arrives at a new emotional state in which the gendered division is temporarily repaired.

The new emotional state is conveyed in the ambivalent tone. "Well! and what if she should die some afternoon,/Afternoon grey and smoky,/evening yellow and rose/Should die and leave me sitting pen in hand[.]"[21] He confesses his sentiments towards her in her style of lamentation about the timing when he met her at last before he left. At this point the poem transcends gender division. The poetic speaker is no longer paranoid about his humiliation by gender role expectations. Instead, what matters to him is recollecting his own sentiments towards the lady and accepting and confessing his own sentiments. He returns to musical terms that used to be an exaggeration of her sentimentalism and further relates it to Orsino's experience in *Twelfth Night*: "This music is successful with a 'dying fall'/Now that we talk of dying—/And should I have the right to smile?"[22] The smile is a positive gesture of reconciling with the past shame. Yet the thought of death reminds him of the lady's lamentation of her past prime, so he hesitates to smile at the end. At the end the poem reaches an emotional state which includes regret about the shameful encounter, recollection of his interrupted sentiments, delight in reconciliation with his own sentiments, and melancholy in the past and loss. The poem not only exposes misogynistic stereotypes but also reveals their potential psychological harm inflicted upon both sides. Meanwhile, the focus of shame can lead readers to interpret in a more reparative aspect and see the psychological changes in his gradual overcoming of the gender division.

At this point, it is important to emphasize that reparative reading does not mean denying the presence of gender prejudices in the poem. Even if the speaker attempts to reconcile the gender division by adopting the lady's sentimental style at the end, the poem still repeats the trauma of gender division and recalls the misogynistic paranoia in many readers' minds. But we can also choose to stop the paranoid cycle for a moment and offer a different reading that could possibly construct a space for reconciliation, even if such a space may seem to be too personal or utopian. As Sedgwick points out: "The vocabulary for articulating any reader's reparative motive toward a text or a culture has long been so sappy, aestheticizing, defensive, anti-intellectual, or reactionary that it's no wonder few critics are willing to describe [it]."[23] My reading of the final reconciliation in the poem also risks over-aestheticizing. But it is still worth exploring a different mode of affect when we practice cultural critiques such as gender analysis and trying to reach out of the cycle of paranoid reading that can only repeat the well-established and sometimes reductive knowledge of oppression.

To speak more specifically about the limitations of paranoid reading in "Portrait," the dead-end cycle is manifest in the narrative structure of the poem. The poem tells the humiliating experience of a failed relationship, inviting readers to ruminate about the causes for such a shame at the end. The poem naturally leads the reader to think in a paranoid way about what is to blame for his humiliation. Feminist critics would accuse the poetic persona as an egotistic male-centered person who deliberately ignores the lady's feeling and confines her into flat stereotypes instead of giving real voices to her. But given that the poem is spoken only from the male's perspective, it allows the reader to wonder how much of the lady's quoted passages are reliable, to what extent is the poetic persona biased, and which aspects of the story are covered up. Since unreliability underlies shame as the structuring affect of the poem, the speaker's ostensible paranoia points to the more subtle psychological activities that can possibly open to a temporary literary space for reconciliation over gender dispute. Meanwhile, at the end, his shift into a style of lamentation, his struggle over temporality, and his regretful wonder further suggest that he is also seeking a different result with her that could possibly repair his wound. The masculine shame in "Portrait" can be regarded as a form of reparative writing that hopes to overcome gender stereotypes. Following Sedgwick's reparative model, the ending of "Portrait" allows us to envision reconciliation.

Sedgwick's concept of reparative reading has successfully explained "the limitations of present theoretical vocabularies" and envisions a more diverse and subtle discussion of the affects in critical writing. Despite the demand for more reparative reading, however, there may be a limit to its application to Eliot's works; for example, the anti-Semitism in his poetry is not amenable to reparative reading.

Notes

1. Lyndall Gordon, *The Imperfect Life of T. S. Eliot* (Oxford University Press, 2012), 36.
2. Gordon, *Imperfect Life*, 36.
3. Rachel Potter, "T. S. Eliot, Women and Democracy,"*Gender, Desire and Sexuality in T. S. Eliot*, ed. Cassandra Laity and Nancy K. Gish (Cambridge University Press, 2009), 224.
4. Cyrena Pondrom, "Conflict and Concealment: Eliot's Approach to Women and Gender,"*A Companion to T. S. Eliot*, ed. David E. Chinitz (Blackwell, 2009), 327–28.
5. Pondrom, "Conflict and Concealment," 328–29.
6. *Poems* 1:13, lines 26–29.
7. Gordon, *The Imperfect Life*, 65; Pondrom, "Conflict and Concealment," 328.
8. Eve Sedgwick, *Touching Feeling: Affect, Pedagogy, Performativity* (Duke University Press, 2003), 130.
9. Sedgwick, *Touching Feeling*, 147.
10. Sedgwick, *Touching Feeling*, 146.
11. Sedgwick, *Touching Feeling*, 127.
12. Sedgwick, *Touching Feeling*, 150.
13. *Poems* 1:10.
14. *Poems* 1:10; emphasis added.
15. *Poems* 1:11.

16 *Poems* 1:11.
17 *Poems* 1:14.
18 *Poems* 1:14.
19 "Tradition and the Individual Talent" (1919), *Complete Prose* 2:111.
20 *Complete Prose* 2:111.
21 *Poems* 1:14.
22 *Poems* 1:14.
23 Sedgwick, *Touching Feeling*, 150.

A "Companionable Guide" to T. S. Eliot
Review of Robert Crawford's *Eliot After* The Waste Land

Timothy Materer

Eliot After The Waste Land, by Robert Crawford. London: Jonathan Cape, and New York: Farrar, Strauss, and Giroux, 2022. xi + 563 pages.

After the lively narrative flow of Robert Crawford's *Young Eliot*, the deliberative pace of *Eliot After* The Waste Land may surprise the reader. Crawford's strategy is to present in detail the "complex contradictory messiness" of Eliot's life instead of finding, in the way of many critics and sometimes the poet himself, a "teleological pattern." He presents Eliot's "life and work without undue moralising, letting readers reach their own conclusions."[1] He generally achieves this goal in recounting controversial issues such as Eliot's treatment of his first wife Vivien, his strain of antisemitism, his mostly epistolary affair with his first love and muse, Emily Hale, and his marriage to a woman thirty years his junior, Valerie Fletcher.

Crawford recounts Eliot's many prejudicial remarks about Jews, which drew on "deep veins of American and English racism"; but he also describes Eliot's constructive involvement in Jewish causes, providing readers with arguments to make pro or con about the duration and degree of the poet's antisemitism.[2] His close personal and intellectual friendships with the Jewish refugees Adolf Lowe and Karl Mannheim and interest in publishing books about Judaism are cited along with the crude Jewish stereotypes in his poetry. Crawford thoroughly analyzes Eliot's notorious statement about "free-thinking Jews" in *After Strange Gods* and his "infuriatingly unconvincing" attempts to excuse his statement as innocent of racial bias.[3] Crawford's analysis of Eliot's anguish about leaving Vivien at this time, and his description of the racist atmosphere of Charlottesville, Virginia in 1933, where Eliot gave *After Strange Gods* as a lecture series, place the incident in a complex historical and psychological context. He further cites Eliot's later protests in 1941 against antisemitism in France and his statement in 1953 about Nazi and Russian antisemitism, in which Eliot discerned a "pattern of *policy* and *hysteria* [in] all anti-Semitic movements."[4] Crawford wisely offers no generalization about Eliot's antisemitism but does imply that Eliot slowly overcame his prejudices—realizing, as in "Little Gidding," "things ill done and done to others' harm."

Thanks in part to recent scholarship and John Haffenden's densely annotated editions of the letters, Crawford gives a reliable account of Eliot's marriage to Vivien Haigh-Wood. Unknown to Eliot, who married in haste, from her adolescent years she had serious health problems and addiction to drugs. Crawford begins his account in *After The Waste Land* when they had been married for seven years and several years after Vivien's adultery with Bertrand Russell. He identifies the "young society woman" of Eliot's brief affair in 1922, which partly "revenged Vivien's affair with Russell" and "left him with the taste of ashes," as the socialite Nancy Cunard and the inspiration for the character of the vulgar Fresca, who was fortunately eliminated from *The Waste Land* manuscript.[5] In 1923, Vivien was deeply disturbed by her friend Lucy Thayer's sexual obsession with her. In a letter in 1925, Eliot supposedly writes to the *Criterion*'s patron Lady Rothermere that "Lucy had been 'persecuting my wife . . . with her very obscene attentions.'"[6]

Citing Anne Pasternak Slater's *The Fall of a Sparrow: Vivien Eliot's Life and Writings* (2020), Crawford concludes that Eliot's letter to Rothermere was actually written by Vivien herself; and he cites Slater's suggestion that Vivien suffered from "Munchausen's Syndrome" in feigning or exaggerating symptoms to win sympathy. Unfortunately, Crawford does not also mention Slater's contention that a rude and angry letter to Marianne Moore at *The Dial* about the rejection of Vivien's story, "The Paralysed Woman," was written not by Eliot, who was invariably courteous to his literary correspondents, but by Vivien.[7] Soon after this crisis, a greater one occurs when the Eliots are traveling in Italy with Eliot's brother Henry and his new wife in April 1926. Volume 3 of Eliot's letters and Carole Seymour-Jones's *Painted Shadow* have only confused the account of the nature of Vivien's crisis at this time. In a letter of August 18, 1932, Eliot wrote that Vivien, "soaked" in the sedative bromidia, was convinced "the police were pursuing her from country to country."[8] After a hushed-up trip to consult a doctor in Germany, and Vivien's attempted suicide in Paris, she was placed in a French sanatorium specializing in nervous diseases.

Eliot separated from Vivien in 1933 when he returned from America. Although he attempted to avoid seeing her, her obsessive pursuit of him inspired his conception of the furies in his play *The Family Reunion*. In July 1938, her brother Maurice Haigh-Wood informed Eliot that Vivien "was found wandering in the streets at 5 o'clock this morning [...] full of the most fantastic suspicions & ideas. She asked me if it was true that you had been beheaded. She says she has been in hiding from various mysterious people, & so on."[9] Renting several different properties in London to elude her imaginary pursuers, she was deeply in debt. Crawford cites the carbon of a letter Eliot sent to his brother-in-law: "I give you my authority to apply for certification of your sister, Mrs T. S. Eliot, if Dr Bernard Hart thinks advisable."[10] Given the misinformation about Eliot's treatment of his wife's committal, Crawford goes into useful detail about the legalities of the committal and describes Dr. Hart and other physicians who examined Vivien. After she was taken to "Northumberland House Mental Hospital, whose high walls enclosed substantial grounds," Eliot never saw his wife again.[11]

Crawford gives the sharpest insights into Eliot's character in telling the story of Eliot's devotion to Emily Hale. He met her while an undergraduate at Harvard University and acted with her in amateur theatricals. Seeing her again in London in the summer of 1923 brought back intense memories that are reflected in the Hyacinth garden scene in *The Waste Land* and the rose garden of "Burnt Norton." In a letter to Hale of July 1931, he tried to explain his actions. He felt "shaken to pieces" sitting with her at *Tristan und Isolde*; how, leaving America in 1914, he had said to her on their "last evening" together, "'I can't ask anything, because I have nothing to offer'", which had been his way of signalling that his only ambition was to be able to ask her to marry him—and to which, he feared, she had made no response.[12]

Crawford describes Emily not only as a Boston patrician but also as an actress and teacher admired by her students as exciting and colorful and (like Eliot himself) "*always* acting."[13] When Emily met him again in London, she was aware of his troubled marriage and hoped to clarify their relationship. True to his suppressed nature, Eliot "maintained his sphinx-like mask of composure, however intensely he felt the pain and duty of marriage to Vivien."[14] Yet he later told Emily that, from the date of their London meeting, "My active spiritual life dates."[15]

Crawford explores Eliot's contradictory mixture of religious and erotic categories in an illuminating analysis of "Ash Wednesday." The poem draws on Eliot's amalgam of desires for Emily and spiritual advice from Eliot's accommodating spiritual adviser Father Underhill. He tells Emily that the Lady of "Ash Wednesday" is a tribute to her. He explains that loving her is not wrong but indeed "a gift of God to help me in troubles and for spiritual development" and that she fills the void left by the death of his mother.[16] Crawford asks,

> Did he want a mother, a muse, a lover, another wife, or a Blessed Virgin? Apparently, all of them. Emily's being an ocean away, coupled with his transformation of her into an "exceptional object" of devotion, helped license his lonely, needy outpourings.[17]

Emily naturally felt that he was not seeing her as she really was and "did not feel able to match his ardour, or even fully to understand him."[18] In January 1936, Eliot wrote, "I kiss your toes and the soles of your feet," and also that she should seek Christ-like joy.[19] Eliot considered "Burt Norton" a secret love poem for Emily. Crawford comments, "Burt Norton celebrated the intensity of their moment, their closeness, and sensed, with a note of disturbance, the possible presence of children; but it was and is a philosophical meditation without love's physical contact, and it possesses a heightened awareness of 'waste sad time.'"[20] According to Crawford, the poem "reveals something messily irresolvable."[21]

The Unitarian Emily could not understand Eliot's refusal even to consider a divorce from his wife, and the impasse over the issue recurs frequently at length. He claims in a letter dated Holy Saturday 1933, "if I had a divorce it would be the greatest misfortune to the Anglican Church since Newman went over to Rome."[22] They also clash over Emily's Unitarian beliefs and her temerity in taking communion in an Episcopal church. Crawford's quotations from Eliot's analysis of the sexual conflicts in D. H. Lawrence's novels help in understanding Eliot's erotic urges. Eliot's confesses to Emily in 1933:

> What I desire with you is as much Conflict as Unity. I know both the desire to dominate, to influence, to make someone else into my own image; and the desire to be ruled, to be dominated, to be influenced, to make myself into someone else's image. The desire to be a master, and to be a slave.[23]

Eliot worried that his sense of living a spiritual "inward life" within his "outward life" might, as Crawford puts it, "shade toward duplicity."[24] The death of Vivien Eliot in January 1947 revealed this duplicity when he told Emily that he could not marry again. In an eloquent letter of February 14, 1947, he tells Emily he feels like an unwrapped Egyptian mummy that "crumbles into dust in a few moments until nothing is left but the bones. [...] I meet myself face to face as a stranger whom I have got to live with, and make the best of, whether I like him or not."[25] Later he tells her that he now realizes, "I was wholly unfitted for married life."[26]

Emily receives another, culminating shock when she learns that Eliot had married his young secretary Valerie Fletcher in January 1957. Their relationship remained cordial until Eliot heard that Emily had not only turned his letters over to Princeton University Library but added some comments of her own. In November 1960, he drafted, with Valerie's knowledge, a letter to be filed with the Princeton letters, which would not be opened until fifty years after their deaths. He then wrote harshly that "Emily Hale would have killed the poet in me; Vivienne nearly was the death of *me*, but she kept the poet alive."[27] After untactfully asking Eliot if he would deposit her letters to him at Princeton, Emily learned that he had ordered them burned. In September 1963, he altered the conclusion of his 1960 letter, primarily, as Crawford emphasizes, for the audience of Valerie, the woman who has "transformed" him. He explains that after his first wife's death, "I came to see that my love for Emily was the love of a ghost for a ghost, and that the letters I had been writing to her were the letters of an hallucinated man."[28]

Eliot's romantic relationships are reflected in his later creative works. His play *The Family Reunion* reflects, in addition to the trauma of his marriage, his feelings about Emily in the character of Mary. His plays all brood on "long-concealed personal secrets."[29] His love for Valerie inspires *The Confidential Clerk* (1953). The play's theme of "the hurt of childlessness, longing for reconciliation, and [...] a guilt-ridden older man with a complicated past who has fallen for a younger woman" was typed and retyped by Valerie Fletcher, and Eliot was "conscious of his secretary's benign scrutiny."[30] The exhaustive detail of Crawford's account of Eliot's love for Emily Hale is judicious and skillfully integrated into the events of Eliot's life. But Emily is indeed a "ghost" as glimpsed in Crawford's analysis of Eliot's letters. For a more empathetic description of the relationship, as well as compelling accounts of Eliot's marriage to Vivien Eliot and other women such as Mary Hutchinson and Mary Trevelyan, Lyndall Gordon's *The Hyacinth Girl: T. S. Eliot's Hidden Muse* (2022) is the definitive source. Her account is anchored in her research in the complete Princeton archive of letters—rather than just the selection Crawford draws upon—as well as an additional twenty-five letters from Hale that Eliot preserved after 1947 and extensive research on Hale's life.[31]

As Eliot ages and his creativity declines, the description of people and events in *After* The Waste Land is increasingly dense. Crawford is finally content to imagine Eliot resembling one of the poet's cats with a "Deep and inscrutable singular name." He is right to resist the desire to "neaten" Eliot's life because the materials assembled in his research allow readers to make independent judgments. Crawford succeeds in his ambition to be "a narrator, companionable guide, critic, historian, and assembler of images."[32]

Notes

1. Robert Crawford, *Eliot After The Waste Land* (Jonathan Cape, 2022), 2.
2. Crawford, *Eliot After The Waste Land*, 278.
3. Crawford, *Eliot After The Waste Land*, 318.
4. Crawford, *Eliot After The Waste Land*, 436.
5. Crawford, *Eliot After The Waste Land*, 7.
6. Crawford, *Eliot After The Waste Land*, 55.
7. Ann Pasternak Slater, *The Fall of a Sparrow: Vivien Eliot's Life and Writings* (Faber & Faber, 2020), 231–38.
8. Crawford, *Eliot After The Waste Land*, 78.
9. Crawford, *Eliot After The Waste Land*, 278.
10. Crawford, *Eliot After The Waste Land*, 279.
11. Crawford, *Eliot After The Waste Land*, 280.
12. Crawford, *Eliot After The Waste Land*, 28.
13. Crawford, *Eliot After The Waste Land*, 30.
14. Crawford, *Eliot After The Waste Land*, 28.
15. Crawford, *Eliot After The Waste Land*, 30.
16. Crawford, *Eliot After The Waste Land*, 146.
17. Crawford, *Eliot After The Waste Land*, 147.
18. Crawford, *Eliot After The Waste Land*, 147.
19. Crawford, *Eliot After The Waste Land*, 247.
20. Crawford, *Eliot After The Waste Land*, 244.
21. Crawford, *Eliot After The Waste Land*, 248.
22. Crawford, *Eliot After The Waste Land*, 205.
23. Crawford, *Eliot After The Waste Land*, 203.
24. Crawford, *Eliot After The Waste Land*, 198.
25. Crawford, *Eliot After The Waste Land*, 394.
26. Crawford, *Eliot After The Waste Land*, 396.
27. Crawford, *Eliot After The Waste Land*, 469.
28. Crawford, *Eliot After The Waste Land*, 478.
29. Crawford, *Eliot After The Waste Land*, 439.
30. Crawford, *Eliot After The Waste Land*, 434–35.
31. Lyndall Gordon, *The Hyacinth Girl: T. S. Eliot's Hidden Muse* (W. W. Norton & Co., 2022), 341. Reviewed in this volume of the *Annual* by Frances Dickey.
32. Crawford, *Eliot After The Waste Land*, 3.

Eliot among the Women
Review of Lyndall Gordon's *The Hyacinth Girl* and Ann Pasternak Slater's *The Fall of a Sparrow*

Frances Dickey

The Hyacinth Girl: T. S. Eliot's Hidden Muse, by Lyndall Gordon. London: Virago, and New York: W. W. Norton & Co., 2022. 496 pages.

The Fall of a Sparrow: Vivien Eliot's Life and Writings, by Ann Pasternak Slater. London: Faber & Faber, 2020. xiii + 770 pages.

"Here are the only documents in my possession which cast any light on my life and work [...] and which also, if I may say so without vanity, show me in a rather favourable light!" Eliot wrote to Emily Hale in early 1931, pressing on her his desire to archive her letters as part of his literary remains; "they are too beautiful in themselves not to be preserved; [and] if I have any reputation left in two generations, I want it known how very very great is, will be and always was, my debt to you."[1] Eliot always planned to rock the literary world with the posthumous revelation of his love for Hale as the previously unknown wellspring of his poetry. What he did not plan for, of course, was his own change of heart and guilty conscience that later drove him to burn her letters. The greatest irony in Eliot's statement is that his own letters *succeeded* in preserving a record of his debt to Hale—a record that hardly shows him in a favorable light. With the opening of the Hale archive and the publication of Vivien Eliot's writings, we are now in a better position to understand Eliot "among the women" than at any other time in the last hundred years.[2] Lyndall Gordon's *The Hyacinth Girl: T. S. Eliot's Hidden Muse* and Ann Pasternak Slater's *The Fall of a Sparrow: Vivien Eliot's Life and Writings* shine the spotlight of biography on Eliot and the two women who served as his muses. The realities are painful but clarifying and essential to our understanding of the poet.

In *The Hyacinth Girl*, Gordon reveals the pattern of Eliot's ambitions for his poetic career woven into his relationships with Emily Hale, Vivienne Haigh-Wood, Mary Trevelyan, and Valerie Fletcher. Given how much Eliot cared for the opinion of posterity, he has proved lucky to receive such a fair hearing from one of our foremost literary biographers, whose integrity and record as a feminist critic give her perspective unassailable credibility. After a century of revolutionary change in women's lives and consciousness, as we look back on his unequal relationships with these women, Eliot's behavior hardly bears examination. The digital publication of his letters to Hale will inevitably create further resentment against this towering literary figure who combined insight into female subjectivity with callous selfishness and misogyny. When Lyndall Gordon first sketched the outlines of Eliot's secret muse in *Eliot's New Life*, in 1988, Frank Kermode greeted her thesis with insulting condescension, calling her account "vaguely disgusting."[3] Over thirty years later, the opening of the Hale archive bore out her interpretation at a level of detail beyond what even Gordon, perhaps, hoped for. Yet *The Hyacinth Girl* is not a victory lap. The Hale letters confront Eliot scholars with difficult realities that call into question the integrity of the poet. This correspondence, being one-sided, is also bewildering and full of gaps. Without moralizing or parading her considerable erudition, which nevertheless continually supports her narrative, Gordon skillfully guides us through Eliot's dealings with the women who enabled his achievements and down the twisting path of his quest for posthumous fame. She ultimately delivers an accolade he must have sought, calling him "a master of the private love-letter, one of the most eloquent who ever lived," but not before putting him, and us, through the honest reckoning that these letters require.[4]

Two main challenges confront anyone who reads Eliot's letters to Hale: processing what we learn about him and answering the further questions raised by this new information. His letters refer to previously undocumented events, obscure people, and, most of all, the contents of Hale's own letters, which he later destroyed. A story emerges, but it is incomplete, and, moreover, strongly biased towards himself and the image he wishes to pass on to posterity. One is swayed by his powerful eloquence while being outraged by his lack of consideration for the well-being and even the existence of his correspondent. Faced with the difficulties of telling this story fairly, Robert Crawford opts for factuality in the second volume of his biography, *Eliot After The Waste Land*, trying to withhold interpretation.[5] But the Hale letters deliberately reveal that Eliot "is telling his life through his poems, striving to devise a spiritual autobiography suited to his time," as Gordon writes, and one cannot read either his poems or letters without interpretation. John Haffenden's edition of these letters will presumably resolve many of the unanswered questions about who, what, and where. We must still find a way, however, to understand both correspondents as human beings and reconcile what we learn in the letters with Eliot's poetry and drama. Here Gordon provides the starting point for all future criticism that takes the Hale material into account—as it must.

Rather than rehearsing the narrative of Eliot and Hale's prolonged, unsatisfied romance, which readers will find engagingly told in *The Hyacinth Girl*, I will highlight a few of Gordon's interpretive insights that the correspondence archived at Princeton does not reveal on its own. We begin to see more clearly how Eliot's poetry and his life constitute a hall of mirrors: his writing may be autobiographical, but—not surprisingly—he also sought and found experiences that followed the pattern laid down by artworks. The most obvious example is Eliot's expectation that Hale would play the role of an unattainable Beatrice to his Dante. But Gordon has identified another influence running through Eliot's work and life from early to late, often connected to Hale: the ballet *Le Spectre de la rose*, performed in Paris in 1911, in which a young girl sleeps in her chair while Vaslav Nijinsky dressed as the Rose dances around her, "as a vision of love," "not seek[ing] to overpower" the innocent girl but to express "love in its divine sense."[6] Gordon finds this ballet not only behind Eliot's rose gardens but also in "Suppressed Complex," "A Cooking Egg," the scent of roses that Eliot made a leitmotif of his letters to Hale, his tender descriptions of holding the sleeping Hale on his lap, his late re-writing of his life in dedications to his second wife ("the rose garden which is ours and ours only") and his disavowal of Hale in his "love of a ghost for a ghost" letter. The ballet provided a foundational pattern for his own evocations of love and sexuality throughout his life—and perhaps an excuse, too, for it ends with Nijinsky leaping gracefully out of a window, leaving the girl behind.

At the start of their correspondence, Eliot pointed Hale to "Pipit" along with *Ash-Wednesday* and *The Waste Land* as evidence that "my love for you has steadily grown into something finer and finer. And I shall always write primarily for you."[7] With Gordon's expert assistance we can now see Hale's place in the enigmatic "A Cooking Egg." *Invitation to the Dance* is the music for *Le Spectre de la rose*, "supported on the mantelpiece" in Pipit's sitting room—obviously not a copy of the score, but a scene from the ballet, condensing Eliot's feeling towards Hale in a single image (just as "the change of Philomel" is displayed "above the antique mantel" in *The Waste Land*).[8] Reflecting Eliot's "regret for his first love and the unreality of existence without her," the poem glances towards Piccarda, the first blessed soul Dante encounters, thus intertwining Eliot's two aesthetic ideals for love.[9] Composed in 1919 after the death of his father, the poem expresses "revulsion and distrust of worldly people" as Eliot looks back to when he was in love and his future seemed bright. Gordon's reading of this and other poems pass quickly—her interpretations deftly sketching out what a less confident critic might belabor—but serve as beacons through the sad tale of Eliot's manipulative and exploitative relationships. The purpose of knowing anything about Eliot's life, after all, is to understand his poetry, as these moments remind us.

Other original insights into Eliot's intertwining of life and literature include: the presence of Nancy Cunard behind Princess Volupine in "Burbank with a Baedeker" and Fresca in *The Waste Land* (also perhaps the Cleopatra figure of "A Game of Chess"); his understanding of his life in terms of Dostoevsky's "Great Sinner," the plan of an unwritten novel published in the *Criterion*; how "Eyes that last I saw in tears" records Eliot's encounter with Hale at Eccleston Square in 1923; his dedication of *Ash-Wednesday* "to my wife" as a Dantean "screen"; the influence of Nathaniel Hawthorne on Eliot's self-conception ("pure Arthur Dimmesdale," as Gordon remarks at one point);[10] how *Murder in the Cathedral* answers Hale's demand that he divorce Vivien, which Eliot felt would constitute a betrayal of the Church; and many illuminating connections between Eliot's life and letters and *Four Quartets*, *The Family Reunion*, *The Cocktail Party*, and *The Elder Statesman*.

After Eliot and Hale came together decisively in fall 1935, leading to the composition of "Burnt Norton," Eliot made clear he still had no intention of giving her the satisfaction of public recognition or even physical consummation, ostensibly on moral grounds. Gordon refrains from judging Eliot but helps us to see how his repeated rejections led to Hale's depression and the unraveling of their union (as he becomes more cagey and manipulative in his letters, the story requires a biographer's mediation). He continued to protest his love and beg for her responses, but in practice he slowly abandoned her, for example not lifting a finger as his own relative, Samuel Eliot, ran Hale out of her job at Smith College in 1942.[11] With no college degree, property, nor immediate family, Hale existed hand to mouth, while Eliot, living rent-free as the "prize pet" in Mrs. Mirrlees's country refuge, watched his professional and financial fortunes grow.[12] Their break came in 1947 when he declined to follow through on his promises of marriage in the event of his wife's death, but even before this, as Gordon writes, "Unwarmed by bodily contact, [Hale's] physical presence appears to fade, so that while she remained full-blooded to her friends and to the girls she taught, Eliot was writing to a communicative ghost of his own creation—what it seems he had always meant her to be."[13]

Eliot moved on to other female supporters: Mary Trevelyan, one of the "daughters of the Victorian vicarage,"[14] who served as his companion and "guardian" during the 1940s and 50s, and Valerie Fletcher, his secretary whom he married in 1957. Here Gordon successfully treads a fine line, treating Valerie sympathetically but holding Eliot to account:

> When he found himself ready, marital love came as an entrancing gift and it brought a special benefit to him as poet. For this union with a woman a generation younger offered a chance to firm up a future for what he would leave. This entailed rewriting the past so as to take Emily out of his story and centre his new wife as the one and only partner and chosen carrier of his works.[15]

What emerges from the last chapter of Eliot's life is less how he finally found happiness in domesticity and physical love (the official story) than how he used these experiences and Valerie herself to put the finishing touches on his legacy plan.

Among other evidence, Gordon cites twenty-five letters from Hale that Eliot spared in the conflagration of 1963.[16] From these letters we learn how gracefully Hale took on the role of "friend" after sixteen years of being treated as a secret lover—with a humility that probably only further inflamed Eliot's bad conscience. Four of her letters from fall 1956, concerning the archiving of his correspondence at Princeton, were torn and then repaired. Gordon pointedly asks, by whom? Eliot's feelings and decisions at this time were driven by his secret engagement to Valerie, his guilt and rage towards Hale, and his desire to cover up inconvenient parts of his past. The torn letters suggest Eliot's realization that he was no longer completely in control: Hale had finally impressed on him that she was more than a blank slate for his imagination, and perhaps he recognized the irony of his early declaration that her letters would show him to posterity in a favorable light. As for ironies, perhaps the greatest is that Eliot's gift waned as he distanced himself emotionally from Hale—"from the time of bodily freeze," as Gordon says.[17] Though he found comfort in Mary Trevelyan's company, an adoring lover and devoted archivist in Valerie, and the worldly fame he had always sought, he lost the spark of poetic genius that might have transformed his drawing room dramas from embarrassing episodes of autobiography into works of art with universal meaning. As for Hale, though she lost the man, she knew she would be forever part of his poetry, which she had helped bring into being. To give Gordon the last word: "The very movement of his poetry is the glimpse of 'reality' followed by the drop into the 'waste sad time' before and after. When his wary character ventures 'among the women' the gift for vision fades. But then Emily enters to quicken the poetic moment."[18]

***

Immortalized as a neurotic wife in *The Waste Land*, skewered by Bloomsbury contemporaries ("a bag of ferrets"), and used as an interpretive tool by a parade of critics and biographers, Vivien Eliot has been the subject of gossip for the last hundred years.[19] In *The Fall of a Sparrow*, Ann Pasternak Slater attempts to tell the unhappy story of Eliot's first wife as objectively as possible. The work has three parts: the life, closely based on Vivien's archive at the Bodleian Library (her fiction, surviving diaries, account books, and scrap books); her writings, some previously published in the *Criterion* and others printed for the first time; and a digital text of her papers, including diaries, at the TSEliot.com website. Interspersed throughout Slater's text are detailed interludes ("Notes") sorting out such rumor-shrouded questions as the nature of Vivien's infidelity with Bertrand Russell, the drugs she took, and "Captain Eliot's" flat. Though Slater's rigorous investigations cannot illuminate every corner of Vivien's murky life, she does dispel many of the errors and half-truths damagingly asserted twenty years ago by Carole Seymour-Jones in *Painted Shadow*.[20]

Most biographies are premised on the significance of their subject's life, while biographies of the wives of famous men perch uneasily between the wife's importance and her husband's. If the marriage is unhappy, the husband's failings can provide a *raison d'être* for the story of the wife, like Effie Gray, wife of John Ruskin, or Zelda Fitzgerald. In this vein, Seymour-Jones depicted Eliot as an angry, alcoholic homosexual whose misogyny doomed their marriage from the start (at this distance, her hit job seems catty more than feminist, laying much blame on the mothers of both parties). One of Slater's missions, as a commissioned biographer, was to dismantle that account of the Eliots' marriage, and to her credit she avoids assassinating Vivien's character on behalf of her husband's reputation. Whether because Slater scrupulously avoids a sensationalist narrative or simply because Vivien's life was messy and incoherent, her *Life* reads as a more or less disconnected sequence of years. Beginning in 1914, the year of Vivien's earliest surviving diary and one year before the fateful "convergence of the twain" at a dance hall in London, each year has its own chapter through to her committal at Northumberland House in 1938. Information about Vivien's childhood and youth might help create a narrative with a three-dimensional protagonist, but that is not Slater's aim; she seeks to lay out the events of Vivien's life as documented by her writings and Eliot's published *Letters*, augmented by editors Valerie Eliot and John Haffenden's annotations.

One constant in Vivien's life does help explain what Virginia Woolf called her "chops and changes": substance abuse.[21] While Woolf and others noted Vivien's ether use in the 1930s, Slater is the first to tell the story of her lifelong drug addictions. According to second-hand accounts, Vivien suffered tuberculosis of the bone as a child, an illness whose symptoms can include severe back pain, and she began using pain-killers on a doctor's prescription as a teenager.[22] While it is not known how regularly she used substances in the early years of her marriage, many of her nebulous health complaints may be traced to chloral hydrate, a "hypnotic depressant" that was a Victorian "novelty narcotic of choice"— Dante Gabriel Rossetti was a famous user—leading to addiction within two weeks and causing permanent liver damage.[23] (Vivien's doctors more than once raised an alarm over her liver, which might seem like quackery from a modern perspective, but was accurate; indeed, she wrote "fearful liver" in her diary as early as 1914.)[24] Overdose symptoms include neurological and digestive impairments and skin conditions, all of which she complained of, while withdrawal can lead to "delirium and hallucinations, deep stupor," unconsciousness, and death.[25] Vivien's years-long addiction to chloral hydrate was discovered in 1925 and explains her strange behavior as described in Eliot's letters, including a period of eleven weeks in early 1925 when she did not get out of bed, sleeping almost continuously, more than once seeming near death. (The context of "The Hollow Men" becomes clearer.) After 1925, though her doctors kept her from using chloral, she seems to have had recourse to other addictive substances, including barbiturates, bromides, ether, paraldehyde, phenacetin, and Adalin.[26]

Many of Vivien's physical and psychological ailments may have originated in and interacted with her drug use. Slater diagnoses Vivien with Munchausen Syndrome, "a psychiatric disorder whose sufferers feign disease in order to draw attention, sympathy, lenience, or reassurance to themselves [...] currently redesignated as 'factitious disorder imposed on self' (FDS)."[27] Childhood illness is a risk factor for FDS. Slater believes that whenever Eliot became the center of attention, Vivien responded by pretending to be sick. Of course, she may also have induced real bodily illness by taking drugs when she felt insecure or anxious. Similarly, the eating disorder Slater identifies was probably exacerbated by chloral-induced digestive problems. None of her doctors possessed the knowledge of addiction to which we now have access, and at this distance it is difficult to tell which of her maladies were "real" and which "feigned," when she was also physically and psychologically addicted to mind-altering substances. In short, if there is any narrative that holds together her life, it may be a downward spiral that we are sadly familiar with.

An addict's life becomes focused on acquiring and using the addictive substance, no matter what the cost, depleting the family's emotional and financial resources and causing their partner to cover for them through lies and concealment. As the spouse of a substance abuser, Eliot was also not in control of his life: his letters are full of last-minute changes of plans to accommodate her wishes and the steady drumbeat of after-hours labor to pay her medical bills. The trauma experienced by spouses and families of addicts is well known, leading to financial stress, disruption of home life, anxiety, depression, guilt, anger, insomnia, substance abuse, weight gain, and illness—conditions all documented in Eliot's letters or others' accounts of him.[28] Struggling to explain and contain his wife's erratic behavior without knowledge of the underlying malady, Eliot sought the causes in himself. In 1925, he wrote: "In the last ten years—gradually, but deliberately—I have made myself into a *machine*. I have done it deliberately—in order to endure, in order not to feel—*but it has killed V*."[29] This oft-quoted statement has seemed like a confession of wrongdoing, providing circumstantial support to some of Seymour-Jones's accusations, but Eliot's constant feelings of guilt towards Vivien may instead reflect his desperate attempt to establish his agency in a situation that neither of them could control. Slater does not elaborate this dimension of their relationship, but thanks to her detailed sleuthing one can easily imagine a plausible explanation of their married life in which neither party was really to blame for the disaster.

The Fall of a Sparrow opens with Vivien's relationships with Charles Buckle and Scofield Thayer, painting a picture of a "temperamentally volatile, and tactically manipulative," sexually adventurous young woman, already using illness to gain an advantage over others.[30] Slater prints three previously unpublished, flirtatious letters that Vivien sent to Thayer in the same month as her wedding to Eliot.[31] Soon she is exercising her manipulative power over Eliot as his wife, but Slater believes there was no affair with Bertrand Russell until 1917, and even then, "a one-night stand is all we know for certain."[32] This infidelity is followed by a period of growing social experimentation, and "by 1919 it looks like an understanding was reached by both partners; Vivien was free to wander, and seems to have tried to encourage Eliot to do likewise."[33] In his letters to Emily Hale, opened just after this biography's publication, Eliot confesses to a single episode of adultery—probably with Nancy Cunard.[34] Slater suspects Vivien of sexual "adventurings" but finds no specific evidence, and the 1926 "scandal" in Rome was probably drug abuse, not an affair. Sometimes the attention paid to Vivien's possible indiscretions grows wearisome, at this late date, but the *Sparrow*'s table was set by the *Painted Shadow*, and Slater accepts the task of refuting Seymour-Jones's allegations one by one. Knowing what we do now about Eliot's long passion for Emily Hale (which may have been at its most powerful in the 1920s, *before* they reconnected), the idea of Eliot renting a flat at Burleigh Mansions for the purpose of secret liaisons with Leonid Massine, Jack Culpin, and other men is absurd. When we take account of Vivien's increasing drug use during the early twenties, it seems unlikely that either partner was up to anything besides trying to preserve appearances.

Slater also corrects the record on matters that are potentially more significant for literary scholars, particularly the re-attribution of three letters that, she claims, were written by Vivien under her husband's name. Readers of Volume 2 of Eliot's *Letters* may have noticed two odd missives dated June 18, 1925, from Eliot to Marianne Moore and Lady Rothermere, powerful women with whom he had painstakingly cultivated good relations. Both contain paranoid accusations against Lucy Thayer, Vivien's one-time friend and companion (cousin of Scofield); the letter to Moore is positively insulting. Moore had just rejected Vivien's story "The Paralysed Woman" for publication at the *Dial*. No matter how angry, Eliot rarely took such a tone with a valuable literary contact. Slater shows how easy it would have been for Vivien, suffering from a chloral-fueled psychosis, to pass off her writing as her husband's, and how Eliot discreetly "wiped up" the mess she had made with both women.[35] In January 1926, she may also have been responsible for Eliot's strangest epistolary production, a page of the *Nursing Mirror* sent to Conrad Aiken (in the hospital) with the words "blood," "mucous," "shreds of mucous," and "purulent offensive discharge" circled. This "letter" has been used to support the view that Eliot's objectionable Bolo phase continued into middle age (Jayme Stayer has argued compellingly that "the vast majority, and probably all, of the Bolo poems were composed at Harvard").[36] Pointing to Vivien's penchant for writing on newspaper clippings, her "morbid fascination" with menstruation, her access to Eliot's correspondence, and his apparent ignorance of the incident, which gravely offended Aiken, Slater makes a strong case that he had nothing to do with it.[37] We can hope that her corrections will be incorporated in any future edition of the *Letters*.

While such scholarly details may appeal only to a specialized audience, Vivien's writings collected in this volume have a permanent literary interest. And if their interest derives from Vivien's proximity to Eliot—well, the same is true of numerous other authors that most of us know only because he alluded to them (Charles-Louis Philippe, anyone?). Vivien's writing career for the *Criterion* was brief—just one year—and ended in a nearly fatal episode of substance abuse, but, while it lasted, her photographic eye captured her corner of Bloomsbury and married life with Eliot from a uniquely intimate perspective. Among the many writers to exploit the literary potential of their lives, Vivien and Eliot were the first and most knowledgeable. Enterprising readers may have dug up the productions of "F. M." (for "Fanny Marlow" and "Feiron Morris") in dusty issues of the *Criterion*, but a dozen other stories, poems, and numerous fragments are published here for the first time, showcasing Vivien's inclination towards the "subjective, instinctive, and outspoken" and her "naturally carefree rather than consciously modern" style.[38] While Jim McCue claims that Eliot drafted a majority of F. M.'s works, Slater defends the authenticity of Vivien's writing, her voice emerging fully in "Thé Dansant."[39] As Eliot stepped back to give her free rein, her stories became both more autobiographical and weirder, such as "The Paralysed Woman," a thinly veiled account of the Eliots and their helpers Jack Culpin and Pearl Fassett during a summer holiday at Eastbourne: "For two months Sibylla and Felice stayed in the high up sea-side flat, like two birds swung in a cage."[40] Immured in this claustrophobic ménage, Sibylla develops an unhealthy obsession with her wheelchair-bound neighbor.

Every story contains intriguing portraits, centered on the unhappy consciousness of a woman unsatisfied by her empty life. An anxious husband returns home from work in "Ellison and Antony," disappointed but not surprised to find his wife occupying his study ("Antony stooped & kissed Ellison rather gingerly. Ellison's smile was strained. They both seemed to wait uncomfortably. Antony's mind on these occasions was a blank").[41] In "Columbina," the writer "Cino" "thumped his typewriter" all day, and "by his side on the floor he dropped sheets of paper, one by one, as they were finished. They lay about him like an untidy snowdrift."[42] After dinner he goes to the theater and she stays behind: "Somewhere in her mind there was a fatigue, a fatigue which hurt like a physical pain if it was touched. Having to make definite plans touched it. Having to even answer a definite question touched it."[43] In another story, Sibylla's husband is absent when "Old Hart" (Sydney Schiff) and "B. R." (Bertrand Russell— "this aristocratic heretic," "desiccated and pedantic") turn up to pay her an evening visit. "'The universe is very vast,' said the philosophical mathematician. 'That means nothing,' thought Sibylla, who had heard him say it on countless occasions."[44] Her guests leave and André has not returned. She goes to bed, saying to herself, "'It is lonely,' […] 'It is very lonely. But if a ship were to pass, one would not hail it. One would not hail it.'"[45]

In "Au Revoir," Vivien unsparingly depicts her own mental instability during the departure of Eliot's family at the end of their 1924 visit:

> as she begins to explain the nightmare his delay has caused her she finds herself seized by the throat & caught up by a fit of rage & passion. Throwing all her parcels down the stairs—which are fortunately quite deserted—she hits André on the face with her umbrella. Having done it once she does it again. The whole world totters—it spins around her. She longs to destroy herself, & looks wildly about but there is no window low enough from which to cast herself, no knife or weapon presents itself for her purpose. She sits on the stairs in a silent convulsion while André collects the parcels. He then takes her arm tightly & gets her out into the street, where she walks mechanically beside him sunk in utter blackness.[46]

No biographer can capture the feeling of what it was like to be caught in that nightmarish relationship better than Vivien herself. As she wrote in the same story, "everything must be faced, & what was more, slapped in the face—to show one was not afraid of it & knew it for what it was."[47] But in the end, the satisfaction of slapping reality in the face couldn't hold back the building tide of addiction, making Vivien's reality worse while temporarily easing her awareness of it, as "Feiron Morris" plaintively attests in "Song in the Night":

> Ah dream on dreaming
> Dream dont fade away
> Pain unendurable
> To face the day
>
> Need I wake ever
> Ah let me dream, on
> Wings, flying ever—
> Ah—fading—ah—gone.[48]

Notes

1. T. S. Eliot to Emily Hale, January 12, 1931. Emily Hale Letters from T. S. Eliot, C0686, Manuscripts Division, Department of Special Collections, Princeton University Library. Published at tseliot.com. See Benjamin Franklin's *Autobiography*: "I scarce ever heard or saw the introductory words, 'Without vanity I may say,' &c., but some vain thing immediately followed."
2. "Eliot among the women" echoes, of course, "Prufrock among the women," the excised portion of "The Love Song of J. Alfred Prufrock," and was Gordon's working title for *The Hyacinth Girl*.
3. Frank Kermode, "The Feast of St. Thomas," *London Review of Books* 10, no. 17 (September 29, 1988).
4. Lyndall Gordon, *The Hyacinth Girl: T. S. Eliot's Hidden Muse* (W. W. Norton & Co., 2022), 362.
5. Robert Crawford, *Eliot After The Waste Land* (London: Jonathan Cape, 2022), reviewed in this volume of the *Annual* by Timothy Materer.
6. Gordon, *Hyacinth Girl*, 24-26.
7. T. S. Eliot to Emily Hale, letter of November 3, 1930, Emily Hale Letters from T. S. Eliot.
8. *Poems* 1:38, 58.
9. Letter of November 3, 1930, Emily Hale letters from T. S. Eliot; Gordon, *Hyacinth Girl*, 84-85.

10 Gordon, *Hyacinth Girl*, 166.
11 Gordon, *Hyacinth Girl*, 269.
12 Gordon, *Hyacinth Girl*, 279.
13 Gordon, *Hyacinth Girl*, 276.
14 Gordon, *Hyacinth Girl*, 318.
15 Gordon, *Hyacinth Girl*, 338.
16 Gordon, *Hyacinth Girl*, 299.
17 Gordon, *Hyacinth Girl*, 282.
18 Gordon, *Hyacinth Girl*, 397.
19 This review first printed in *Time Present* 105 (Winter/Spring 2022). Quote from letter of November 8, 1930, *The Diary of Virginia Woolf, Vol. 3: 1925–1930*, ed. Anne Olivier Bell and Andrew McNeillie (Harcourt, Brace, Jovanovich, 1980), 331.
20 Carole Seymour-Jones, *Painted Shadow: The Life of Vivienne Eliot, Wife of T. S. Eliot* (Knopf Doubleday, 2009).
21 *The Diary of Virginia Woolf, Vol. 4: 1931–1935*, ed. Anne Olivier Bell and Andrew McNeillie (Harcourt, Brace, Jovanovich, 1982), 123. Quoted in Preface to *Letters* 6: xv.
22 Ann Pasternak Slater, *The Fall of a Sparrow: Vivien Eliot's Life and Writings* (Faber & Faber, 2020), 115, 249.
23 Slater, *Fall of a Sparrow*, 216.
24 Slater, *Fall of a Sparrow*, 11.
25 Slater, *Fall of a Sparrow*, 217.
26 Slater, *Fall of a Sparrow*, 351–55.
27 Slater, *Fall of a Sparrow*, 115.
28 Anthony Fathman, a medical doctor, was the first to identify Eliot in this way; see his "Viv and Tom: The Eliots as Ether Addict and Co-Dependent," *Yeats Eliot Review* 11, no. 2 (1991): 33–36.
29 *Letters* 2:627.
30 Slater, *Fall of a Sparrow*, 7.
31 Slater, *Fall of a Sparrow*, 18–19.
32 Slater, *Fall of a Sparrow*, 73.
33 Slater, *Fall of a Sparrow*, 98.
34 See Gordon, *Hyacinth Girl*, 96.
35 Slater, *Fall of a Sparrow*, 231–38.
36 Jayme Stayer, *Becoming T. S. Eliot: The Rhetoric of Voice and Audience in Inventions of the March Hare* (Johns Hopkins University Press, 2021), 189. Reviewed in this volume of the *Annual* by Edward Upton.
37 Slater, *Fall of a Sparrow*, 239–43.
38 Slater, *Fall of a Sparrow*, 512.
39 Slater, *Fall of a Sparrow*, 510.
40 Slater, *Fall of a Sparrow*, 582.
41 Slater, *Fall of a Sparrow*, 598.

42 Slater, *Fall of a Sparrow*, 599.
43 Slater, *Fall of a Sparrow*, 601.
44 Slater, *Fall of a Sparrow*, 627.
45 Slater, *Fall of a Sparrow*, 628.
46 Slater, *Fall of a Sparrow*, 614.
47 Slater, *Fall of a Sparrow*, 615.
48 Slater, *Fall of a Sparrow*, 633.

From Tom Eliot to T. S. Eliot
Finding Voice and Audience in Jayme Stayer's *Becoming T. S. Eliot*

Edward Upton

Becoming T. S. Eliot: The Rhetoric of Voice and Audience in Inventions of the March Hare, by Jayme Stayer. Baltimore, MD: Johns Hopkins University Press, 2021. xiv + 360 pages.

In *Modernism* (2011), Michael Levenson argues that modernist artists, though employing a confrontational rhetoric and style, were involved in a series of complex negotiations with their audiences. "Modernism needs to be understood not as an elite craft refined in secret but as a complex exchange between artists and audiences," he writes, "a large, literate public found itself entreated and defied, encouraged and repulsed. The revulsion of many prepared the pleasure of some."[1] Resisting a too-easy opposition between artist and middle-class audience, Levenson suggests that both artists and audiences were shaping one another, that both were dynamic and changing.[2] True, many modernist writers portrayed their art as skewering the bourgeoisie, giving rise to what he calls modernism's "oppositional culture."[3] Nevertheless, though modernist artists attempted to shock and provoke, they also sought an audience willing to be shocked and provoked. Thus, he concludes, "There was no Modernism without individually audacious artifacts, but equally there was no Modernism without relationships among artists, their works, and the institutions and audiences that encircled them."[4]

Jayme Stayer's excellent new book, *Becoming T. S. Eliot: The Rhetoric of Voice and Audience in* Inventions of the March Hare (2021), shows us such a negotiation between poet and audience almost in real time. Taking the *Inventions* notebook as a privileged site to trace this negotiation, he shows in painstaking detail how Eliot conceived of a revolutionary poetic voice that had the power to bring an audience into being by giving readers the eerie perception of being intimately addressed. Stayer shows how this negotiation with audience was integral to the transformation of the poetic voice of Tom Eliot from St. Louis, Missouri, into the thoroughly modern, alienated, and utterly recognizable voice of "T. S. Eliot." He traces the development of this voice in *Inventions* poem by poem, stage by stage, watching the young Eliot first attempt to please his family and academic authority figures, and then venturing with increasing assurance to craft an audience rhetorically, both within the poems and in his actual readership.

Stayer traces this unfolding development through Wayne Booth's rhetorical concepts of the "implied author" and "authorial audience," distinguishing for each poem in *Inventions* the perspective of the speaker, the audiences (both accepting and skeptical) within the poem, and the poetic techniques on display that shape the poem's actual audience.[5] Throughout, he is constantly aware of the exquisite tension in these poems as Eliot provokes (and thus shapes) his audience to view itself in dialectic tension with the poetic speaker and the poems' shifting internal audiences. Stayer's book exemplifies the more nuanced approach to audience that Levenson called for, but ironically opposes Eliot's own insistence that poetry does not come from a consideration of audience: "Real poetry comes primarily from a pressure inside us, and not from a call from an audience."[6] To this dictum, Stayer carefully replies, "Perhaps the 'call from an audience' may not have been conscious to the poet during the writing process; nonetheless, the evidence of that rhetorical pressure is easily found in all his poems."[7] What follows is a veritable masterclass of rhetorical analysis demonstrating how each poem considers potential audiences. For each poem in the notebook, Stayer provides a sophisticated analysis of the rhetoric of voice, perspective, and audience, along with a discussion of relevant biographical and literary context. These analyses make this book an insightful resource for both students and scholars alike and will prove Stayer an important interlocutor for future commentators on these poems. Though these readings are of the highest scholarly rigor, I could also envision using this book with students as both a revealing study of the early Eliot and a series of case studies of how to perform successful rhetorical analysis of complex poetry.

The ambition of the book goes beyond rhetorical analysis, however. Invoking Mikhail Bakhtin's notion of "ideological becoming," Stayer shows that Eliot's rhetorical experimentation reflects the process of self-formation through dialogical negotiation:

> When these external, authoritative discourses (inherited or discovered) meld into an internally persuasive discourse in the notebook poems, Eliot no longer sounds like a teenager vaguely pining for freedom and romance. Instead, he sounds like a social critic, an explorer of consciousness. He sounds like T. S. Eliot, a fully rounded self, rather than a clump of adolescent contradictions. This process of assimilation—the transformation of externalized, authoritative discourses into an internally persuasive discourse—is what Bakhtin terms "ideological becoming."[8]

Eliot's rhetorical experimentation is doubly dialogical, taking place at the intersection of poet and audience, and at the intersection of authoritative external discourses. Eliot's pursuit of a voice is also, for Stayer, a dialogical negotiation of worlds, of the development of a unique poetic voice that is not monological, but inherently polyphonic, indeed internally hybrid. Stayer's characterization of Eliot's poetic becoming reflects Eliot's own observation in *Knowledge and Experience* that the task of the soul "does not consist in the contemplation of one consistent world but in the painful task of unifying (to a greater or less extent) jarring and incompatible ones, and passing, when possible, from two or more discordant viewpoints to a higher which shall somehow include and transmute them."[9] Stayer shows us this "painful task" unfolding on each page of the notebook. He presents the early notebook as an example of dialogical self-becoming enacted through a series of vocal performances, of trying on voices. Each voice is performed in relation to an audience, real and/or imagined, and to various discursive sources and traditions that have influenced the poet. The performances move from imitation to a dialogically inflected, unique poetic voice. At the same time, Eliot's self-becoming also—ironically—shaped an actual modern audience. We readers develop in dialogue with Eliot's poetic persona.

Eliot's "ideological becoming" takes off when Eliot begins, at times clumsily, to combine three crucial poetic voices: those of Laforgue, Baudelaire, and the ragtime music he heard in St. Louis and Boston. Stayer demonstrates how Eliot "tries on" the voices of Laforgue and Baudelaire in his poems of 1909, following his discovery of Arthur Symons's *The Symbolist Movement in Literature* in 1908. The Laforguean voice introduces a cutting irony and the Baudelairean voice an unswerving engagement with modern human suffering. "While Laforgue taught Eliot to explore the boring and attack the conventional," Stayer writes, "it was Baudelaire, the greater if less immediately useful poet, who demonstrated for Eliot how to inspect the ugly and the sordid. [...] Eliot's adoption of these French moves sharpens his vision; they enable him to see what he had not seen before."[10] This performance of poetic voices is never simply a mechanical matter of imitating poetic technique; in wrestling with form, Eliot is always already wrestling with the content, the worldviews embodied in the technique he is trying on.

In addition to Laforgue and Baudelaire, ragtime and jazz rhythms deeply influenced Eliot's early "voice lessons" and enabled his later triumphs, as Stayer illuminates, building on the vital work of David Chinitz's *T. S. Eliot and the Cultural Divide*.[11] He notes Eliot's 1910 formal advance of adopting short, pointed lines to provide crucial moments of poetic modulation and, at times, blunt, direct address:

> In a magical, original solution, the two previously warring elements of seriousness and sarcasm modulate, finally, into a coherent voice. The rhetorical advance that allows Baudelairean gravity to coexist with Laforguean irony is a three-in-one tool that enables Eliot to shift from one voice to another: a combination of shortened lines, tight rhymes, and snappy rhythms to mark an irony that is jaunty rather than destructive. This jazzy, tonal shift not only solves a major trouble of Eliot's notebook poetry, it is also one of the gestures that marks his mature poetry.[12]

The rhythms of American ragtime enable Eliot's formal modulations between Laforgue's irony and Baudelaire's examination of modern, urban alienation and depravity. His irony becomes "jaunty" or playful rather than "destructive," carrying the audience along musically. Stayer suspects that the original source for this formal innovation of short, rhythmic lines lies in Laforgue's poetry itself, but that this voice merged quickly with the jazz rhythms of the day.[13]

Stayer's observation that jazz rhythms moderate and transform Laforgue's sarcastic irony into something more musical and engaging becomes a crucial part of his argument later in the book. Eliot's "three-in-one" technique finds its culmination in the achievement of "Prufrock," Stayer claims, with a poetic persona who both reveals and conceals, confronting the audience with modern suffering, confiding and beckoning to that audience, and continually deflecting the audience's attentions. Eliot's initial audiences, beginning with Harriet Monroe, were perplexed by this baffling persona, especially in Prufrock's apparent lack of emotion.[14]

Eliot's understanding of suffering had developed, and the persona he showed to his audience was an agonizing one, embodying "the fragmentation of the modern mind and the suffering it endures."[15] Stayer's approach perhaps concludes in a Baudelairean vision of "Prufrock." The voice of Prufrock works, he claims, because Eliot addresses the suffering of his audience by examining his own in horrifying detail. True, Laforgue's irony has been employed in critical fashion, and Eliot's jazzy modulations have become a powerful tool of shifting voices, but in the end Prufrock's persona derives its devastating power from the dialectic of intimacy and detachment.[16] "By the end of the notebook," Stayer writes, "the relationship between artist and audience has matured into a compound of trust and distrust, an ambivalence that is artistically exploited by the author for the designs he intends in 'Prufrock': the harrowing evocation of the risks of intimacy and the dissolvent nature of identity."[17] The alienation of the poet from his audience is enacted in the rhetoric of the poem itself, a rhetoric that deflects attention, defers the engagement with overwhelming questions, and fragments the speaker. But both the poet and the reader perform this alienation, heightened by moments of attempted intimacy. "However small these interventions, their muted, defiant honesty offsets the preponderant weight of social expectation and Prufrock's own evasions. Part of what we recognize as admirable and interesting in 'Prufrock' is this balanced reserve, beneath which lies a sense of panic."[18] What "Prufrock" gives us is a rhetoric of paradox, of direct address and evasion, of trust and distrust, demonstrating its alienation by the fugitive ventures of attempted intimacy.

Stayer ultimately sees "Prufrock" opening the way for a healing, communal recognition of suffering. "[T]he rhetoric of the poem partially (and paradoxically) heals [...] alienation by the very fact of its disclosure: an audience is identified, a community found."[19] He concludes by noting how contemporary critics have repeated the initial evaluations of Eliot's poetry as devoid of sympathy, cold, and distanced. He notes Kenneth Asher's criticism of Eliot's work as lacking "empathy," or Marjorie Perloff's critique of Eliot's elitism, with "no sympathy with the lower classes."[20]

Stayer takes these criticisms seriously and offers a robust defense of the poetic achievement of *Inventions*: a voice vulnerable in its brutal honesty yet self-protecting in its constant ironic deferrals.[21] Yet the poems' own success ultimately answers these criticisms. As Stayer notes, "Prufrock" ultimately found its audience—such as the contemporary poets Carl Phillips, Mark Levine, and Jorie Graham, all inspired to become poets in part through an encounter with Prufrock's voice.[22] Eliot's voice created a reading community—such as the International T. S. Eliot Society that Stayer led as President—that discusses his poetry, criticizes it, and finds the poetry's diagnosis of suffering revealing and to some extent healing. Regardless of Eliot's detractors, that community now spans the globe. Prufrock continues to find his audience.

Notes

1 Michael Levenson, *Modernism* (Yale University Press, 2011), 3.
2 Levenson, *Modernism*, 5.
3 Levenson, *Modernism*, 8.
4 Levenson, *Modernism*, 8.
5 Jayme Stayer, *Becoming T. S. Eliot: The Rhetoric of Voice and Audience in Inventions of the March Hare* (Johns Hopkins University Press, 2021), 3.
6 Quoted in Stayer, *Becoming T. S. Eliot*, 3.
7 Stayer, *Becoming T. S. Eliot*, 3.
8 Stayer, *Becoming T. S. Eliot*, 5.
9 *Complete Prose* 1:362.

10 Stayer, *Becoming T. S. Eliot*, 53.
11 Stayer, *Becoming T. S. Eliot*, 74; David Chinitz, *T. S. Eliot and the Cultural Divide* (University of Chicago Press, 2003).
12 Stayer, *Becoming T. S. Eliot*, 74.
13 Stayer, *Becoming T. S. Eliot*, 78–79.
14 Stayer, *Becoming T. S. Eliot*, 217.
15 Stayer, *Becoming T. S. Eliot*, 223.
16 Stayer, *Becoming T. S. Eliot*, 229.
17 Stayer, *Becoming T. S. Eliot*, 236.
18 Stayer, *Becoming T. S. Eliot*, 231.
19 Stayer, *Becoming T. S. Eliot*, 238.
20 Stayer, *Becoming T. S. Eliot*, 288.
21 Stayer, *Becoming T. S. Eliot*, 289.
22 Stayer, *Becoming T. S. Eliot*, 236–37.

Giving Eliot a Seat at the Table
Review of Derek Gladwin's *Gastro-modernism*

Christina J. Lambert

Gastro-modernism: Food, Literature, Culture, edited by Derek Gladwin. Clemson, SC: Clemson University Press, 2019. 256 pages.

"The Love Song of J. Alfred Prufrock" is littered with food imagery. From the "sawdust restaurants with oyster-shells" he passes on the street to the "coffee spoons" that measure his life, the environment that leads us to the "overwhelming question" is notably gustatory.[1] Are these fragments of food incidental to the milieu of Prufrock's wanderings, or does Prufrock's food commentary play an important role in the poem? Selections from Derek Gladwin's edited collection, *Gastro-modernism: Food, Literature, Culture*, suggest that Eliot scholars would do well to consider the peach Prufrock frets to digest. Gladwin's introduction gives essential context for modernist food criticism; Jeremy Diaper's chapter establishes Eliot's place within the world of gastrocriticism; and Lee Jenkins's contribution reveals the significant analyses that can come from thinking about Eliot's work in terms of food.

The introductory chapter serves up an excellent outline of gastrocriticism in the style of a five-course French meal. The section headers take us from *les apéritifs* to *les desserts*, as Gladwin skillfully sets the table with the methods and purposes for this intellectual meal that scholars of food and Eliot alike will find nourishing. Gladwin records the growing interest in modernism and food, illustrating that "gastronomy suffuses the literary landscapes of global modernisms from the specific to the broad from the late nineteenth century to the mid-twentieth century."[2] For Gladwin, identifying this collection as a work of "gastrocriticism" denotes a more comprehensive and less-siloed lens for literary criticism than food studies, because it gives attention to the topic of food, its practices, and the cultures surrounding these practices. His term captures the broader goals of the project: to transform how food is approached in literary modernism, so that "food serves less as an object and more as a subjective lens for studying culture."[3]

Gastrocriticism is essential to new modernist studies because it speaks to the relationship between high and low art, the transformation of culture and class that spurred this artistic movement, and the swift shifts between celebratory excess and anxiety that permeate modernist texts. "From Plato to Woolf, meals mediate discourse," and within the texts of modernism, food imagery speaks to everything from aesthetics to politics.[4] The collection is divided into four sections: Culture and Consumption; Decadence and Absence; Taste and Disgust; and Appetites and Diets. The breadth of the collection is expansive, including a consideration of the aesthetic of the starving artist from Peter Childs, an examination of cocktails in Noel Coward's work by Gregory Mackie, and Clint Burnham's chapter on experimental food deprivation in Canadian colonialism. Eliot's work receives attention in two chapters, solidly establishing him within this critical conversation.

Jeremy Diaper's "From 'Squalid Food' to 'Proper Cuisine': Food and Fare in the Work of T. S. Eliot" serves as a veritable bibliography of food references within Eliot's canon. Diaper not only gives a survey of references within Eliot's poetry, including significant changes to early manuscripts of *The Waste Land*, but also the references that permeate his plays, correspondence, and prose. Eliot's extensive knowledge of soil health and interest in cuisine was informed by and illustrated in his various positions editing for the *New English Weekly* and the *Criterion*. In addition, during Eliot's time as an editorial director at Faber & Faber, the publishing house was "one of the most prolific publishers of organic texts" and also published a collection of "cookery books."[5] Although Eliot's letters are often as carefully crafted as his poetry, Diaper suggests that his honest views about cuisine and food memories often slip out within the pages of his correspondence.

And Diaper's diligent and comprehensive research collects these morsels for the Eliot scholar, providing countless avenues for further research. Diaper's account of Eliot's relationship with the preparation of food ranges from his praise of the "practised salad-maker" in a letter to Enid Faber, to an archived photo of Eliot baking bread to show his, albeit brief, participation in country life and food preparation of his own.[6]

These tidbits are delightful in their own right, but the sheer number of anecdotes and quotations also act as substantial evidence for Diaper's twofold purpose in this chapter. First, Diaper establishes that if Eliot's works have not yet been given attention within the realm of food studies, it is through no fault of the poet. Eliot's work teems with attention to food—of every quality—that permeates his poetry and prose, and Diaper's chapter shows that Eliot belongs with this critical conversation. And second, Diaper explains how Eliot's attention to food is intimately connected to his involvement with the new organicist movement and its attention to the health of the soil and, consequently, the physical and spiritual health of humans. It turns out that following the food imagery in Eliot's work reveals a far less gnostic poet than some readers expect. Eliot writes to Geoffrey Faber, "If we are rightly directed, a good dinner can lead us towards God, and God can help us to enjoy a good dinner."[7]

If Diaper's chapter successfully places Eliot within the critical conversation of food studies, Lee Jenkins's chapter, "'The Raw and the Cooked': Food and Modernist Poetry," shows the kind of fruitful work that can be done in this vein of Eliot and food studies. Using Claude Lévi-Strauss's division between "the raw" and "the cooked," Jenkins shows how Eliot, D. H. Lawrence, and Wallace Stevens use food imagery to navigate the pressing artistic question of the relationship of "art to ritual, and to the 'real.'"[8] She gives attention to the putrid food that litters *The Waste Land* and Eliot's conception of poetry, in his own words, as "the Word made Flesh, so to speak."[9] For Jenkins, this means that the fleshy food of *The Waste Land* signifies an "emblem of a gross and unredeemed humanity."[10] Eliot's early food imagery reveals no delight, showing that humanity cannot be redeemed from this disaster.

On the other hand, Lawrence's food imagery reverses this relationship, focusing on flesh over word, as his work "collapses the binary between art and life."[11] Within this sliding spectrum, Stevens falls more toward Lawrence, but dresses up his fruit with art, his primary interest resting in the artwork of the natural object, rather than the object itself. Jenkins's argument reveals something significant about the difference between Eliot's early and later work and how he depicts material reality. However, while inquiring into this topic, Jenkins also demonstrates the kind of critical work possible through the lens of gastrocriticism, work that allows scholars to recognize how food might speak to and illustrate the qualities of modernist poetics.

For Eliot scholars, Gladwin's collection suggests the significance of Prufrock's daring question of whether to eat a peach. His decision to do so is inextricably bound up in the fleshy, embarrassing, delicious act of eating that ripened stone-fruit. Eliot scholars are plagued with a question of posterity. How will Eliot's difficult work be read and understood by generations so disconnected from his language and milieu? One way to answer this question is to understand how Eliot continues to speak to the most pressing issues of our time. As Julia E. Daniel writes, "Eliot has emerged as a modernist with significant biological and environmental concerns that find expression across his work, whether his poetic pieces or cultural commentaries."[12] Jenkins's and Diaper's contributions to Gladwin's collection reveal another aspect of Eliot's ecological commentary—within the avenue of food studies and gastrocriticism—even as Gladwin's collection contributes to a rapidly expanding avenue within modernist studies at large.[13]

While this reader wonders if the term gastrocriticism will take off, or needs to, the space that Gladwin creates with his definition expands our imagination for the work that literary criticism examining food in texts can do, connecting it to the most essential questions in the field. And this is nowhere truer than in Eliot studies, as Eliot's body of work continues, even now, to surprise readers with its depth and breadth. Our work as scholars must be to recognize the many conversations he is a part of, so that we might write about and teach them, showing how Eliot from time past continues to speak to time present.

Notes

1 *Poems* 1:5–9.
2 Derek Gladwin, ed., *Gastro-modernism: Food, Literature, Culture* (Clemson University Press, 2019), 1.
3 Gladwin, *Gastro-modernism*, 11.
4 Gladwin, *Gastro-modernism*, 13.
5 Diaper, "From 'Squalid Food' to 'Proper Cuisine,'" in Gladwin, *Gastro-modernism*, 168, 172.
6 Diaper, "From 'Squalid Food' to 'Proper Cuisine,'" 168, 176.
7 September 18, 1927, *Letters* 3:713, quoted in Diaper, "From 'Squalid Food' to 'Proper Cuisine,'" 178.
8 Lee M. Jenkins, "'The Raw and the Cooked': Food and Modernist Poetry," in Gladwin, *Gastro-Modernism*, 192.
9 "The Varieties of Metaphysical Poetry," Lecture 1 (1926), *Complete Prose* 2:616, quoted in Jenkins, "'The Raw and the Cooked,'" 185.
10 Jenkins, "'The Raw and the Cooked,'" 185.
11 Jenkins, "'The Raw and the Cooked,'" 188.
12 Julia E. Daniel, "Wind, Rock, Flower, Glass: The Family Reunion as Ecodrama," *T. S. Eliot Studies Annual* 3: 73.
13 See Alys Moody, *The Art of Hunger: Aesthetic Autonomy and the Afterlives of Modernism* (Oxford University Press, 2018); Catherine Keyser, *Artificial Color: Modern Food and Racial Fictions* (Oxford University Press, 2019); Jessica Martell et al., *Modernism and Food Studies: Politics, Aesthetics, and the Avant-Garde* (University Press of Florida, 2019); *The Cambridge Companion to Food and Literature*, ed. Michelle J. Coghlan (Cambridge University Press, 2020).

Review of Rick de Villiers' *Eliot and Beckett's Low Modernism*

Peter Lang

Eliot and Beckett's Low Modernism: Humility and Humiliation, by Rick de Villiers. Edinburgh: Edinburgh University Press, 2021. 264 pages.

In the introduction to his book *Eliot and Beckett's Low Modernism: Humility and Humiliation* (2021), Rick de Villiers describes the telling error of Samuel Beckett's biographer, who asserts the influence of Eliot's "Little Gidding" on Beckett's early novel, *Dream of Fair to Middling Women.* Despite the fact that Beckett's novel was written ten years before Eliot's poem, this error signals a link between the two works—"a fundamental belief in fallenness." De Villiers writes: "For Eliot, it is mostly a question of one's relation to God; for Beckett, it is a matter of self-emptying. Though of a similar species, the way up and the way down are not the same."[1] Allowing for their contrasting approaches, De Villiers sees notions of fallenness at the heart of subjectivity for both Eliot and Beckett, most evident in their respective treatments of humility and humiliation. Beyond the etymological link between these terms, De Villiers traces a notion of humility as a response to humiliation. Turning away from an Aristotelian, humanist notion of humility that smacks of virtue ethics and an assured sense of self, De Villiers reads humility and humiliation in Eliot and Beckett in more theological terms. While Beckett grounds subjectivity in the acceptance of affliction, Eliot finds it in the shame of original sin.

In both cases, the often violent sense of dispossession that accompanies humiliation actualizes what De Villiers recognizes as humility's "mimetic potential." The individual response to humiliation is precisely what allows humility to become "legible in the work of art."[2]

Following a relatively chronological reading of each author, De Villiers categorizes the performance of humility in Beckett and Eliot across three registers: the affective, the ethical, and the aesthetic. Within this schema, De Villiers delivers a rich study that engages embodied representations of embarrassment, humiliation as informing comportment or being-in-the-world, and finally each author's reckoning with a past body of work in the assertion of artistic agency. Yet while these distinctions provide a neat way to organize the evolution of each author's body of work within the boundaries of this study, the emphasis on "low modernism" and the overcoming of our "critical squeamishness" toward "the assertion of corporeal humility's thematic significance"[3] reveals that Eliot's poetry realizes an ethical project, while Beckett's emphasis on affect renders any ethical or aesthetic impulses that emerge from his work secondary to embodied representations of humiliation and humility.

Chapters 1, 3, and 5 trace an arc from embarrassment to humility in Eliot's work, revealing an ethical imperative that courses through his writing. For Eliot, the self is constructed from the outside, as evidenced by the Christian impulse inherent in his work. The first chapter focuses on his early (and sole) work of fiction, "Eeldrop and Appleplex," in which treatments of embarrassment resulting from the violation of social conventions foreshadow Eliot's later critiques of *bovarysme*, or escapist self-dramatization. Such situations, according to De Villiers, obscure the moral realities at work in even the most pedestrian moments. For example, Bistwick's eating habits are counterbalanced by the deeper scandal of marrying his mother's housemaid. The discomfort that Eeldrop feels from Bistwick's public behavior overlays the shame of his private behavior. However, the conflation of social convention and moral upheaval has a dual effect. On the one hand, it universalizes individual suffering. On the other, establishing a binary between public embarrassment and private shame in the story reveals within shame an attendant and perpetual alienation beyond the temporary sting of embarrassment. After all, Bistwick's transgression, like his eating (and, as De Villiers notes, Eliot's marriage to Vivien

Haigh-Wood), is not so bad. Examining Eliot's intertextual relations with Nietzsche and Shakespeare, De Villiers brings to life the "tension that hinges on the choice between translating the burden of suffering into general terms or embracing a private truth, however awful."[4] Ultimately, articulating private shame in public terms "obscures authentic subjectivity from the subject itself" as it elides the very (Kierkegaardian) tension that conditions it.

Chapter 3 looks at *Murder in the Cathedral* in relation to Eliot's rejection of secular humanism. Eliot's religious turn and increasing dogmatism (along with its attendant antihumanism), according to De Villiers, shaped his view of humility, emphasizing Christian participation and connection to God's love over reliance on mere human good will. The chapter begins by quoting a letter from Henry Ware Eliot, Jr. to his brother addressing concerns over the personal, political, and religious "posturing" in the play.[5] Taking these incongruities between Eliot's personal and public personas as a starting point, De Villiers develops the link between (Thomas) Beckett's sermons in the play and related sermons from Lancelot Andrewes. Staging the initial performances in Canterbury Cathedral, the site of St. Thomas's martyrdom, collapsed the boundary between life and art, emphasizing participation. The transhistorical implications of staging the play at the very site of the initial event moreover stress the philosophical foundations of Eliot's theological convictions. Chipping away at the teleological suppositions of a humanist appraisal of individual human good—specifically the Kantian notion of humanity as an end in itself—as incompatible with any idea of an absolute, Eliot's sermonizing posits a humility based on self-sacrifice and belief in Divine Grace. Calling to mind the imperative to kneel in "Little Gidding," and as the film version of *Murder in the Cathedral* makes clear, true humility arises from "becom[ing] an instrument of God, *who has lost his will in the will of God* [...] *for he has found his freedom in submission to God*."[6]

The final chapter on Eliot turns from participation to performance. Confronting the poet with his own work, specifically "East Coker," Eliot's relation to Yeats provides a means for self-criticism. De Villiers focuses on *dedoublement*, "[the] poetic re-inscriptions that call into question the accomplishments of the earlier work while casting doubt over the late work's authority to do so."[7] Beginning with an examination of poetic irony as congruent to religious asceticism and by extension as form of *autocritique*, irony signals a self-searching in Eliot's work that tracks with notions of humility developed in earlier chapters. In fact, taking up Yeats's criticism of his work, as well as his debt to the elder poet under the guise of *bovarysme*, Eliot manages to turn the subject away from the outside world and inscribe self-effacement into his work by means of a self-rejection of the past. The perpetual rejection of early works coupled by a lessening of the self in the eyes of God reveals in Eliot not the wise old man (despite the allusive link to Yeats), but an artist and his work made vulnerable at the precise point where "Here and there does not matter."[8]

The alternating chapters on Samuel Beckett follow a similar, chronological trajectory, revealing the centrality of *affect* to any ethical or performative readings of his work. In Chapter 2, on Beckett's 1934 short story collection *More Pricks than Kicks*, De Villiers reads Beckett's proactive strategies against embarrassment as a form of self-mortification. Self-inflicted humiliation carries with it the recovery of agency and prohibits the possibility of further harm. Embodiment gives way to ethics in the second chapter on Beckett, which explores his belief in a human condition based upon a common humiliation. People may suffer differently, but they all suffer nonetheless. Thus, humiliation and suffering collapse any social or class differences. De Villiers focuses on the shared suffering of Molloy and Moran in *Molloy*, which realizes "an existence 'unresentful of its insuperable indigence.'"[9]

The final chapter takes up the novel *How It Is* and Beckett's "formal poverty" expressing a sense of "lessness." Deprived of style, *How It Is* relies on a rhythmic and syntactical "penury" more extreme than in *Molloy*, *Malone Dies*, and *The Unnameable*. Despite this impoverished style, De Villiers identifies an intertextual relation between the novel and Darwin's caterpillar studies. Refusing "to build upon Darwin's advanced construction, upon his extrapolation from the biological to the rational," Beckett's bodies are "eternally larval," indeterminate, suspended between animal and human life.[10] Noting Beckett's references in this novel to *Waiting for Godot*, De Villiers emphasizes the "self-emptying" nature of the prose. As a result, one's language and one's will are expressed in equivalent terms.

De Villiers concludes his book with a short meditation on Beckett's *Happy Days* and Eliot's *The Cocktail Party*. Considering the characters of Winnie and Celia respectively,

> The difference between the two plays and between the humiliation of their sufferers may effectively be distilled as chosen suffering and given suffering. For Eliot, humiliation is sometimes a necessary component in Christian humility; for Beckett, humiliation is a fact of being to which one can respond in humility.[11]

Humiliation as a "necessary component" conditions the ethical injunction in Eliot's work just as it provides an ontological ground for Beckett. Their performances of humility—the ways in which notions of fallenness and humiliation are embodied in their art—differ, but their projects converge at a common, "low" ground.

Notes

1. Rick de Villiers, *Eliot and Beckett's Low Modernism: Humility and Humiliation* (Edinburgh University Press, 2021), 19.
2. De Villiers, *Low Modernism*, 2.
3. De Villiers, *Low Modernism*, 3.
4. De Villiers, *Low Modernism*, 49.
5. De Villiers, *Low Modernism*, 93.
6. De Villiers, *Low Modernism*, 109.
7. De Villiers, *Low Modernism*, 152.
8. De Villiers, *Low Modernism*, 172.
9. De Villiers, *Low Modernism*, 145.
10. De Villiers, *Low Modernism*, 198, 199.
11. De Villiers, *Low Modernism*, 213.

T. S. Eliot Bibliography 2021

By Joshua Richards

Primary Texts

Eliot, T. S. *The Letters of T. S. Eliot*. Vol. 9, *1939–1941*, edited by Valerie Eliot and John Haffenden. Faber & Faber, 2021.

Scholarly Books

Stayer, Jayme. *Becoming T. S. Eliot: The Rhetoric of Voice and Audience in Inventions of the March Hare*. Johns Hopkins University Press, 2021.

Scholarly Articles

Aers, David, and Thomas Pfau. "Exploring Christian Literature in the Contemporary and Secular University." *Christianity and Literature* 70, no. 3 (Sept. 2021): 263–75.

Ahmed, Rizwan Saeed, and Akhtar Aziz. "Modernist Sense of the End and Postmodernist Illusion of the End." *Philosophy & Literature* 45, no. 1 (Apr. 2021): 121–37.

Albayrak, Gökhan. "Conflict and Contact: From John Donne's 'Dialogue of One' to T. S. Eliot's Monologue." *Celal Bayar University Journal of Social Sciences/Celal Bayar Üniversitesi Sosyal Bilimler Dergisi* 19, no. 3 (Sept. 2021): 1–12.

Alhusami, Mohammed Abdullah Abduldaim Hizabr. "Tradition Versus Modernity in Laila al-Juhani's *The Waste Paradise*: An Intertextual Approach." *Theory and Practice in Language Studies* 11, no. 10 (Oct. 2021): 1197ff.

Alpaslan, Nimet. "T. S. Eliot's Theory of the Objective Correlative as a Framework for the Poem 'Yağmur Kaçağı' by Attila İlhan." *International Journal of Turcologia* 16, no. 31 (Spring 2021): 49–57.

Araujo, Anderson. "After Many Gods: T. S. Eliot and the Nagging Question of Ezra Pound's Beliefs." *Renascence* 73, no. 1 (Winter 2021): 13–28.

Archambeau, Robert. "Wide-Angle Poetry." *Hudson Review* 73, no. 4 (Jan. 2021): 671–78.

Balavage, Elysia. "Illumination, Transformation, and Nihilism: T. S. Eliot's Empty Spaces." *Journal of Modern Literature* 44, no. 3 (2021): 35–48.

Bartczak, Kacper. "The Paradigm of the Void: Louise Glück's Post-Confessional Deadlock." *Polish Journal for American Studies* 15 (2021): 69–87, 205.

Bhatta, Damaru Chandra. "Water as a Symbol of 'Shantih' in T. S. Eliot's *The Waste Land*: An Upanishadic Reading." *Theory and Practice in Language Studies* 11, no. 7 (July 2021): 821ff.

Blevins, Jeffrey. "Setting *The Waste Land* in Order." *Twentieth Century Literature* 67, no. 4 (Dec. 2021): 1–24.

Botîlcă, Cristina-Mihaela. "Retranslation as a Necessity for the 21st Century Reader. *Old Possum's Book of Practical Cats* – T. S. Eliot." *Philologica Jassyensia* 17, no. 1 (Jan. 2021): 143–52.

Brooker, Jewel Spears. "Eliot's Ghost Story: Reflections on His Letters to Emily Hale." First Readings of the Eliot–Hale Archive, edited by John Whittier-Ferguson and Frances Dickey. *The T. S. Eliot Studies Annual*, vol. 3, 147–50. Clemson University Press, 2021.

———. "T. S. Eliot in Ecstasy: Feeling, Reason, Mysticism." *Christianity & Literature* 70, no. 1 (Mar. 2021): 22–27.

Brown, Alistair M. "The Accounting Meta-Metaphor of 'The Hollow Men' by T. S. Eliot." *Qualitative Research in Accounting and Management* 18, no. 1 (2021): 26–52.

Budziak, Anna. "On the Parenthesis in T. S. Eliot's 'The Cultivation of Christmas Trees.'" *Essays in Criticism: A Quarterly Journal of Literary Criticism* 71, no. 1 (Jan. 2021): 46–65.

Carbajosa Palmero, Natalia. "Mythical Fear and Redemption in T. S. Eliot's Verse Drama: *The Family Reunion*." *Epos*, no. 37 (2021): 35–47.

Chandran, K. Narayana. "Possible Allusion to Shakespeare's Sonnet 147 in *East Coker* IV." *Notes & Queries* 68, no. 3 (Sept. 2021): 356–57.

———. "Robert Frost and T. S. Eliot: A New Source for 'Directive.'" *Notes & Queries* 68, no. 3 (Sept. 2021): 357–58.

Christensen, Karen. "The Love of a Good Woman." First Readings of the Eliot–Hale Archive, edited by John Whittier-Ferguson and Frances Dickey. *The T. S. Eliot Studies Annual*, vol. 3, 143–47. Clemson University Press, 2021.

Clarke, Tim. "Morbid Vitalism: Death, Decadence, and Spinozism in Barnes's *Nightwood*." *Twentieth Century Literature* 67, no. 2 (June 2021): 163–90.

Crace, Benjamin D. "An Incarnational Poetic at Play in T. S. Eliot's *The Cocktail Party*." *South Atlantic Review* 86, no. 1 (Spring 2021): 18–38.
———. "T. S. Eliot as a Pentecostal Playwright: Towards a Pneumatic Poetic." *Christianity & Literature* 70, no. 2 (June 2021): 123–41.
Crane, Ryan. "Cormac McCarthy's American Waste Land: *The Golden Bough*, T. S. Eliot, and Mythic Violence in *Blood Meridian*." *Cormac McCarthy Journal* 19, no. 1 (2021): 85–99.
Crowley, Ronan, Frances Dickey, Joshua Kotin, and Robert Spoo. "T. S. Eliot's Enclosures to Emily Hale: Three Uncollected James Joyce Letters." *James Joyce Quarterly* 58, no. 3 (2021): 343–53.
Cuda, Anthony. "Reinventing Modernism: Randall Jarrell's Unwritten Essay on T. S. Eliot." *Modern Language Quarterly: A Journal of Literary History* 82, no. 1 (Mar. 2021): 81–117.
———. "Unbuttoned and Unimportant: Tidbits from the Archive." First Readings of the Eliot–Hale Archive, edited by John Whittier-Ferguson and Frances Dickey. *The T. S. Eliot Studies Annual*, vol. 3, 151–54. Clemson University Press, 2021.
Daniel, Julia. "Wind, Rock, Flower, Glass: *The Family Reunion* as Ecodrama." Special Forum: Eliot and the Biological, edited by Julia Daniel. *The T. S. Eliot Studies Annual*, vol. 3, 69–92. Clemson University Press, 2021.
Däumer, Elisabeth, and Dominic Meo. "T. S. Eliot Bibliography 2017." *The T. S. Eliot Studies Annual*, vol. 3, 241–50. Clemson University Press, 2021.
de Meric, Natasha. "'Humankind cannot bear very much reality' (T. S. Eliot): The Dilemma of Remembering Forgotten Time." *Psychodynamic Practice* 27, no. 4 (Nov. 2021): 417–29.
Diaper, Jeremy. "'Life of the Soil': T. S. Eliot and Organicism." Special Forum: Eliot and the Biological, edited by Julia Daniel. *The T. S. Eliot Studies Annual*, vol. 3, 47–68. Clemson University Press, 2021.
Dickey, Frances. "Eliot's Letters to Emily Hale and His Personal Theory of Poetry." First Readings of the Eliot–Hale Archive, edited by John Whittier-Ferguson and Frances Dickey. *The T. S. Eliot Studies Annual*, vol. 3, 123–29. Clemson University Press, 2020.
———. "'Hydraulic': The Company and Its Archive." *The T. S. Eliot Studies Annual*, vol. 3, 235–40. Clemson University Press, 2021.
———. "T. S. Eliot and the Color Line of St. Louis." *Modernism/modernity* Print Plus 5, no. 4 (Mar. 2021).
Dickey, Frances, and John Whittier-Ferguson. "Joint Property, Divided Correspondents: The T. S. Eliot–Emily Hale Letters." *Modernism/modernity* Print Plus 5, no. 4 (Jan. 2021).
Diepeveen, Leonard. "T. S. Eliot, Fraud." *The T. S. Eliot Studies Annual*, vol. 3, 23–46. Clemson University Press, 2021.

Dowson, Jane. "Postsecularity and the Poetry of T. S. Eliot, Stevie Smith, and Carol Ann Duffy." *Sophia* 60, no. 3 (2021): 735–45.

During, Simon. "Exciting Discipline." *Australian Humanities Review* 68 (2021): 1.

Eichholz, Patrick. "Dadaism and Classicism in *The Waste Land*." *Twentieth Century Literature* 67, no. 3 (Sept. 2021): 269–92.

Esposito, Thomas. "Echoes of Ecclesiastes in the Poetry and Plays of T. S. Eliot." *Logos: A Journal of Catholic Thought and Culture* 24, no. 2 (2021): 98–123.

Feldman, Alex. "'With His Own Generation in His Bones': Claude C. H. Williamson and the Plagiarism of T. S. Eliot's Shakespeare Criticism." *ANQ: A Quarterly Journal of Short Articles, Notes, and Reviews* 34, no. 4 (Oct. 2021): 297–307.

Fitzgerald, Sara. "Emily Hale: The Beginning of All Our Exploring." *The T. S. Eliot Studies Annual*, vol. 3, 161–70. Clemson University Press, 2021.

———. "Searching for Emily Hale." First Readings of the Eliot–Hale Archive, edited by John Whittier-Ferguson and Frances Dickey. *The T. S. Eliot Studies Annual*, vol. 3, 133–40. Clemson University Press, 2021.

Gillard, Barry. "Lancelot Andrewes and T. S. Eliot's 'Journey of the Magi.'" *Quadrant* 65, no. 12 (Dec. 2021): 99–101.

Goldman, David P. "T. S. Eliot and the Jews." *First Things: A Monthly Journal of Religion & Public Life* (Mar. 2021): 1–9.

Gordon, Lyndall. "Letters to a T. S. Eliot Fan." First Readings of the Eliot–Hale Archive, edited by John Whittier-Ferguson and Frances Dickey. *The T. S. Eliot Studies Annual*, vol. 3, 129–32. Clemson University Press, 2021.

Ha, Sha. "Plague and Literature in Western Europe, from Giovanni Boccaccio to Albert Camus." *International Journal of Comparative Literature & Translation Studies* 9, no. 3 (2021): 1–7.

Hale, Emily. "In Her Own Words: Emily Hale's Introduction to T. S. Eliot's Letters." Edited by Sara Fitzgerald and Frances Dickey. *The T. S. Eliot Studies Annual*, vol. 3, 161–69. Clemson University Press, 2021.

Hamiti, Muhamet, and Lindita Tahiri. "Anglo-American and French Literary Studies and Their Impact on Kosovo/Albanian Scholarship." *Forum for World Literature Studies* 13, no. 3 (Sept. 2021): 421ff.

Hargrove, Nancy D. "T. S. Eliot at Merton College, the University of Oxford: 1914–1915." *South Atlantic Review* 86, no. 3 (2021): 110–20.

Hawkes, David. "Modernism, Inflation and the Gold Standard in T. S. Eliot and Ezra Pound." *Modernist Cultures* 16, no. 3 (Aug. 2021): 316–39.

Henderson, Archie, and Christopher McVey. "Pound and Eliot." *American Literary Scholarship* 2020, no. 1 (Sept. 2022): 123–41.

Higgins, Sørina. "[Re]cycled Fragments: The End of *Sweeney Agonistes*." *The T. S. Eliot Studies Annual*, vol. 3, 181–214. Clemson University Press, 2021.

Keena, Justin. "The Reception of C. S. Lewis's 'A Preface to Paradise Lost' in Milton Scholarship, 1990–2015." *Milton Quarterly* 55, no. 1 (Mar. 2021): 1–38.

Kim, Seonghoon et al. "Implications of Vocabulary Density for Poetry: Reading T. S. Eliot's Poetry through Computational Methods." *Digital Scholarship in the Humanities* 36, no. 2 (June 2021): 371–82.

Kurlberg, Jonas. "Clashes Over Transcendence: T. S. Eliot and Karl Mannheim through the Lens of Programmatic Modernism." In *Historicizing Modernists: Approaches to "Archivalism,"* edited by Matthew Feldman, Anna Svendsen, and Erik Tonning, 117–34. Bloomsbury Academic, 2021.

Llorens-Cubedo, Dídac. "Man of the Theatre: Stage Performances of T. S. Eliot's Work in Spain (1949–2016)." *Neophilologus* 105, no. 4 (Dec. 2021): 555–71.

McGann, Jerome. "Suffering, Sacred, or Free: Romantic Revolutions of the Word, with Special Reference to Byron." *Studies in Romanticism* 60, no. 2 (Summer 2021): 175ff.

McIntire, Gabrielle. "Love's Errors and Effacements: T. S. Eliot and Emily Hale." First Readings of the Eliot–Hale Archive, edited by John Whittier-Ferguson and Frances Dickey. *The T. S. Eliot Studies Annual*, vol. 3, 155–60. Clemson University Press, 2021.

Majak, Aleksandra. "Eliot's (Im)personality and Voices of Polish Modernism." *The T. S. Eliot Studies Annual*, vol. 3, 215–34. Clemson University Press, 2021.

Matek, Ljubica. "Pjesme o Mačkama Za Djecu i Odrasle: T. S. Eliot i Pitanje Identiteta" [Poems about Cats for Children and Adults: T. S. Eliot and Identity]. *Libri & Liberi* 10, no. 1 (Jan. 2021): 7–24. Note: English title provided by the author.

Moitra, Samridhya. "Emerson's 'Quotation and Originality': A Reconciliation between Tradition and Individuality; and A Harbinger of Intertextuality." *Agathos* 12, no. 2 (2021): 131–41.

al Mubaddel, Arwa F. "'The typist home at teatime': Vivienne Haigh-Wood Eliot's Role in Shaping T. S. Eliot's *The Waste Land* (1922)." In *Thanks for Typing: Remembering Forgotten Women in History*, edited by Juliana Dresvina, 188–98. Bloomsbury Academic, 2021.

Query, Patrick. "Democracy, Punishment, Banality: Anti-Fascism 1940–2020." *The T. S. Eliot Studies Annual*, vol. 3, 171–80. Clemson University Press, 2021.

Richards, Joshua. "T. S. Eliot Bibliography 2019." *The T. S. Eliot Studies Annual*, vol. 3, 259–64. Clemson University Press, 2021.

Rizwan, Saeed A., and Aziz Akhtar. "Modernist Sense of the End and Postmodernist Illusion of the End." *Philosophy and Literature* 45, no. 1 (2021): 121–37.

Rudd, Anthony. "Joy as Presence: Reflections on Kierkegaard and Temporality." *Journal of Religious Ethics* 49, no. 2 (June 2021): 412–30.

Rulo, Kevin. "Eliot and Skin." Special Forum: Eliot and the Biological, edited by Julia Daniel. *The T. S. Eliot Studies Annual*, vol. 3, 93–112. Clemson University Press, 2021.

Palmer, William C. "'A strong brown god': T. S. Eliot's Mississippi River Exploration of the White Atlantic." *Comparative American Studies: An International Journal* 18, no. 1 (Mar. 2021): 24–37.

Patterson, Anita. "'Projections in the Haiku Manner': Richard Wright, T. S. Eliot, and Transpacific Modernism." *The T. S. Eliot Studies Annual*, vol. 3, 11–22. Clemson University Press, 2021.

Pérez Alonso, Leticia. "T. S. Eliot and the Question of the Will in *The Waste Land*." *Interdisciplinary Literary Studies: A Journal of Criticism and Theory* 23, no. 1 (2021): 149–67.

Phipps, Jake. "Antithetical Minds: Eliot's Byron and Byron's Burns." *Byron Journal* 49, no. 1 (June 2021): 15ff.

Semeiks, Jonna G. "Loss and Spring." *Confrontation* 125 (Spring 2021): 9ff.

Shahzad, Khurram, Muhammad Abdullah, and Naveed B. Mirza. "Analyzing Patriarchal Preoccupation and Instinctual Delectation in Waste Land: A Gender Perspective." *International Research Journal of Arts and Humanities* 49, no. 49 (2021): 101.

Smart, John. "Dreaming of Cheese." *Slightly Foxed* 71 (Sept. 2021): 54–59.

Stergiopoulou, Katerina. "'For Whom the Bell Tolls': Reading the *Quartets* after the Letters to Emily Hale." First Readings of the Eliot–Hale Archive, edited by John Whittier-Ferguson and Frances Dickey. *The T. S. Eliot Studies Annual*, vol. 3, 137–42. Clemson University Press, 2021.

Turner, Patrick. "Building an Unreal City: Reading the Construction of St. Louis in Eliot's *The Waste Land*." *Journal of American Studies* 55, no. 3 (July 2021): 576–95.

Whittier-Ferguson, John. "'After such knowledge…': Readings in the Eliot–Hale Archive.' Introduction to First Readings of the Eliot–Hale Archive, edited by John Whittier-Ferguson and Frances Dickey. *The T. S. Eliot Studies Annual*, vol. 3, 117–22. Clemson University Press, 2021.

Witonsky, Trudi. "'Something like Bringing the Entire Life': Muriel Rukeyser's Personal, Poetic and Social Development in the 1930s." *Women's Studies* 50, no. 4 (June 2021): 354–81.

Woelfel, Craig, and Jayme Stayer. "Introduction: Modernism and the Turn to Religion." *Renascence* 73, no. 1 (Winter 2021): 3–11.

Wood, Juliette. "I Cannot Find the Hanged Man: Tarot Cards in Fantastic Fiction." *Folklore* 132, no. 3 (Sept. 2021): 229–45.

Theses and Dissertations

Gordon, Parker. "Twentieth-Century Pageants: Word, Music, and Drama in Inter-War Britain." PhD diss., University of St. Andrews, 2021.
Izquierdo, Jose Antonio. "El mundo clásico en la obra ensayística de T. S. Eliot." Bachelor's diss., Universidad de Valladolid, 2021.
Pendry, Jane. "Music and Musical Culture in Ezra Pound and T. S. Eliot." PhD diss., University of Sussex, 2021.
Varela Horro, Jorge. "Death, Nature and Society in Cormac McCarthy's *The Road*, T. S. Eliot's *The Waste Land* and F. Scott Fitzgerald's *The Great Gatsby*." Bachelor's diss., Universidade da Coruña, 2021.
Wang, Ziyun. "Translating *The Waste Land*: History, Patronage, and Poetics." 王姿云 王姿云. "翻譯艾略特的<<荒原>>：歷史 贊助和詩學." 國立臺灣大學翻譯碩士學位學程. National Taiwan University, 2021.

Reviews

Barile, Laura. Review of *T. S. Eliot, Eugenio Montale e la modernità dantesca*, by Ernesto Livorni. *Italian Culture* 39, no. 2 (Sept. 2021): 240–42.
Burkett, Andrew. "Phonopoetics: The Making of Early Literary Recordings." Review of *Phonopoetics: The Making of Early Literary Recordings*, by Jason Camlot. *Victorian Studies* 63, no. 3 (2021): 440–42.
Epstein, Joseph. "Keeper of the Flame." Review of *The Complete Prose of T. S. Eliot: The Critical Edition*, gen. ed. Ronald Schuchard, 8 vols. *Wall Street Journal—Online Edition*, Nov. 26, 2021, http://www.wsj.com/articles/the-collected-prose-of-t-s-eliot-review-tradition-keeper-of-the-flame-joseph-epstein-11637943045.
Fraiman, Susan. Review of *Machines for Living: Modernism and Domestic Life*, by Victoria Rosner. *Modern Fiction Studies* 67, no. 3 (2021): 599–602.
James, Fitz G. Review of *Viral Modernism: The Influenza Pandemic and Interwar Literature*, by Elizabeth Outka. *Modern Fiction Studies* 67, no. 3 (2021): 593–95.
Linett, Maren. "Embodied Modernism." Review of *Modernism and Physical Illness: Sick Books*, by Peter Fifield, and *Invalid Modernism: Disability and the Missing Body of the Aesthetic*, by Michael Davidson. *Modernism/modernity* 28, no. 4 (2021): 791–95.
Lustig, T. J. Review of *The Medieval Presence in Modernist Literature: The Quest to Fail*, by Jonathan Ullyot. *Henry James Review* 42, no. 3 (2021): E-12–E-14.
Meyer, Kinereth. Review of *T. S. Eliot's Dialectical Imagination*, by Jewel Spears Brooker. *Partial Answers: Journal of Literature and the History of Ideas* 19, no. 1 (Jan. 2021): 189–92.
Robbins, Bruce. Review of *Land and Literature in a Cosmopolitan Age*, by Vincent P. Pecora. *Victorian Studies* 64, no. 1 (Oct. 2021): 142–44.

Journalism/Letters to the Editor

Anonymous. "Choicest Wits." *TLS. Times Literary Supplement*, no. 6163 (May 14, 2021): 27.

Anonymous. "Eclectic Shocks." *TLS. Times Literary Supplement*, no. 6164 (May 21, 2021): 28.

Anonymous. "First Mentions in the *Times*." *New York Times Book Review* (Oct. 2021): 44.

Anonymous. "Sweet Sins." *TLS. Times Literary Supplement*, no. 6157 (Apr. 2, 2021): 28.

Baddiel, David. "Left Out: On the Insidious, Pervasive, Exclusionary Nature of 'Progressive' Antisemitism: An Exclusive Extract from *Jews Don't Count*." *TLS. Times Literary Supplement*, no. 6148 (Jan. 29, 2021): 8ff.

Bird, Roger, and Anthony Julius. "Antisemitism, Eliot and the Left." *TLS. Times Literary Supplement*, no. 6151 (Feb. 19 2021): 6.

Goldman, David P. "T. S. Eliot." *First Things: A Monthly Journal of Religion & Public Life* (May 2021): 5–6.

Green, Abigail, and David Baddiel. "Jews, Tradition and Anti-Semitism." *TLS. Times Literary Supplement*, no. 6154 (Mar. 12 2021): 6.

Hux, Samuel. "T. S. Eliot." *First Things: A Monthly Journal of Religion & Public Life* (May 2021): 4–5.

Kitano, Christine. "Ars Poetica for the Next Decade." *American Poetry Review* 50, no. 3 (May-June 2021): 37ff.

Ross-Smith, Bruce. "Eliot, Montale, and Dante." *TLS. Times Literary Supplement*, no. 6153 (5 Mar. 2021): 6.

Wilson, James Matthew. "T. S. Eliot." *First Things: A Monthly Journal of Religion & Public Life* (May 2021): 3–4.

Notes on Contributors and Editors

Ria Banerjee is Associate Professor of English at Guttman Community College and consortial faculty in Film Studies at the Master's in Liberal Arts program of the Graduate Center, CUNY. She has published essays on writers including T. S. Eliot, Virginia Woolf, and D. H. Lawrence at venues such as *Modernism/modernity Print Plus*, *ELN*, and *South Atlantic Review*. She also works in media and film studies and has published on film noir and the intersections of literary modernism with the films of Alain Resnais. She is currently at work on a monograph on spatiality in interwar British fiction.

Caylin Capra-Thomas is a PhD student in English and creative writing at the University of Missouri, where she studies poetry and nonfiction through the lenses of place and ecocriticism. She is the author of a poetry collection, *Iguana Iguana* (2022), and her writing has received support from the Sewanee Writers' Conference, the Vermont Studio Center, the Studios of Key West, and Idyllwild Arts Academy, where she was the 2018–20 poet in residence.

K. Narayana Chandran has taught English for forty-odd years and published widely on Anglo-American literatures and English in India. His works on Eliot include an edited volume of essays, *DA/Datta: What Have We Given? Essays on Teaching* The Waste Land (2001). His essays and notes on Yeats, Stevens, Pound, Frost, Eliot, and others have appeared in *American Literature, Anglia, Archiv, Classical & Modern Literature: A Quarterly, English Language Notes, English Studies, Forum for Modern Language Studies, Journal of Modern Literature, The Midwest Quarterly, Modernism/modernity, Neophilologus, Notes & Queries, Orbis Litterarum, Paideuma, Papers on Language & Literature, Wallace Stevens Journal, Yeats Eliot Review*, and *Yeats Annual*, among others. He currently holds the Institution of Eminence Research Chair in Literary and Cultural Theory in the Department of English, School of Humanities, at the University of Hyderabad, India.

Anthony Cuda is Professor of English and Associate Head of the English Department at the University of North Carolina, Greensboro. He is the author of *The Passions of Modernism: Eliot, Yeats, Woolf, and Mann* (2010) and co-editor of *The Complete Prose of T. S. Eliot: The Critical Edition, Vol. 2: The Perfect Critic, 1919–1926* (2014). He is Executive Director of the T. S. Eliot International Summer School and Secretary of the International T. S. Eliot Society.

Julia E. Daniel is the co-editor of the *T. S. Eliot Studies Annual* and Associate Professor of English at Baylor University. She is the author of *Building Natures: Modern American Poetry, Landscape Architecture, and City Planning* (2017) and the co-editor of *Modernism in the Green: Public Greens in Modern Literature and Culture* (2020). Her work has appeared in *The Cambridge Companion to* The Waste Land, *Modernism in the Anthropocene, Ecomodernism, Modernist Cultures, Critical Quarterly*, and *Modern Drama*.

Frances Dickey is Associate Professor of English at the University of Missouri, Columbia, and has co-edited the *T. S. Eliot Studies Annual* with Julia Daniel since 2020. She also edited *The Complete Prose of T. S. Eliot, Vol. 3: Literature, Politics, Belief, 1927–1929* (2015) and *The Edinburgh Companion to T. S. Eliot and the Arts* (2016). She is author of *The Modern Portrait Poem from Dante Gabriel Rossetti to Ezra Pound* (2012) and articles on Eliot and other modern poets appearing in *Modernism/modernity, Twentieth-Century Literature, Contemporary Literature*, etc. She served a term as President of the International T. S. Eliot Society.

Leonard Diepeveen is the Emeritus George Munro Professor of Literature and Rhetoric at Dalhousie University. He is the author of *Modernist Fraud: Hoax, Parody, Deception* (2019); *The Difficulties of Modernism* (2003); and *Mock Modernism: An Anthology of Parodies, Travesties, Frauds, 1910–1935* (2014). As well, he is co-author, with Timothy van Laar, of *Artworld Prestige: Arguing Cultural Value* (2013) and, most recently, *Shiny Things: Reflective Surfaces and Their Mixed Meanings* (2021). He is a Fellow of the Royal Society of Canada.

Josh Epstein is Associate Professor of English at Portland State University, where he teaches courses in twentieth-century Anglophone modernism, film and media studies, and critical theory. He has authored one book, *Sublime Noise: Musical Culture and the Modernist Writer* (2014) and has published in *Textual Practice, James Joyce Quarterly, Modern Drama, Studies in the Novel, Victorian Literature and Culture, The New Ezra Pound Studies*, and *The Edinburgh Companion to Modernism and Technology*. His current research interests include the documentary filmmaker Humphrey Jennings, the 1951 Festival of Britain, the melodrama, sound studies, and cultural theories of failure. He gratefully acknowledges his canine research assistant Murphy, the dog that's friend to men.

Sara Fitzgerald is retired after a career that included fifteen years as an editor and new media developer for the *Washington Post*. She is the author of *The Poet's Girl: A Novel of Emily Hale and T. S. Eliot* and currently is working on a biography of Hale. She has shared her research on Hale in essays for earlier volumes of *The T. S. Eliot Studies Annual* and the *Journal of the T. S. Eliot Society* (UK). She is the author of *Conquering Heroines: How Women Fought Sex Bias at Michigan and Paved the Way for Title IX* (2020) and *Elly Peterson: "Mother" of the Moderates* (2011).

Manju Jain retired as Professor of English, University of Delhi, Delhi. She is the author of *T. S. Eliot and American Philosophy: The Harvard Years* (1992) and *A Critical Reading of the "Selected Poems" of T. S. Eliot* (1991). She has contributed a chapter on "Philosophy" to *T. S. Eliot in Context*, edited by Jason Harding (2011). Her article on "Eliot's Legacy to Cinema" was published in *Literature and Aesthetics* (2008). She has edited *Narratives of Indian Cinema* (2009) and translated Premchand's novel, *Rangbhoomi*, from Hindi into English, as *Playground* (2011).

Brian P. Kennedy is Professor of English at Pasadena City College in California. A Canadian, Kennedy teaches British literature as well as directing the college's Honors Program. He is the author or editor of ten books, including *Mixing Memory and Desire: Why Literature Can't Forget the Great War* (2017) and, most recently, *Voicing Bo Carpelan: Urwind's Dialogic Possibilities* (2020). He is also Senior Research Fellow with the Centre for the Study of Sport and Health, Saint Mary's University, Halifax, where he writes about sport and Canadian culture. He wrote the Canadian bestseller *Growing Up Hockey* (2007).

Sarah Kennedy is RJ Owen Fellow and College Associate Professor of English at Downing College, University of Cambridge. She has published on a variety of topics within modernism, modern and contemporary poetry and fiction, aesthetics, affect, feminism, and ecological criticism. She is the author of *T. S. Eliot and the Dynamic Imagination* (2018) and contributed a chapter on *Ash-Wednesday* to *The New Cambridge Companion to T. S. Eliot* (2016). Her essay on Eliot and Wallace Stevens won the John Serio Award in 2019. She has been a lecturer and seminar leader at the T. S. Eliot International Summer School.

Christina J. Lambert is a PhD candidate at Baylor University studying twentieth-century poetry and drama. She is writing on the intersection of food, bodies, and sacramental theology in the poetry and verse dramas of Wallace Stevens, T. S. Eliot, and Denise Levertov. Her scholarship has been published in *Tulsa Studies in Women's Literature* and *Christianity & Literature*, and she has a forthcoming article in *Modern Fiction Studies*.

Peter Lang is a visiting lecturer in English at the University of Central Arkansas. He received his PhD from the University of Missouri, Columbia. His recent scholarship on David Lynch will appear in the forthcoming *Critical Companion to David Lynch*.

Huiming Liu is a PhD student in English literature who currently researches on modernism, otherness, and cultural anxieties in the University of Edinburgh. Huiming's research interests cover twentieth- to twenty-first-century literatures, affect studies, world literature, postcolonial study, and queer theory. Huiming's article "T. S. Eliot in the 1918 Pandemic: Abjection and Immunity" was published in *Literature* in 2022. She has also contributed a book chapter titled "T. S. Eliot and the Avant-Garde: Sense, Energy and Gender" to *Cognition, Emotion and Consciousness in Modernist Storyworlds: The Feel of Experience* (2022).

Martin Lockerd is Associate Division Dean of Liberal Studies and a Core Fellow at the University of St. Thomas, Houston. He received his PhD in English from the University of Texas at Austin. His scholarship has appeared in the *Journal of Modern Literature*, *Modern Fiction Studies*, *Yeats Eliot Review*, and *Logos*. His monograph, *Decadent Catholicism and the Making of Modernism*, was published in 2020.

Douglas Mao is Russ Family Professor in the Humanities at Johns Hopkins University. He's the author of *Solid Objects: Modernism and the Test of Production* (1998), *Fateful Beauty: Aesthetic Environments, Juvenile Development, and Literature 1860–1960* (2008), and *Inventions of Nemesis: Utopia, Indignation, and Justice* (2020). He's also the co-editor (with Rebecca Walkowitz) of *Bad Modernisms* (2006) and the editor of *The New Modernist Studies* (2021). He has served as President of the Modernist Studies Association and as Senior Editor of *ELH*; he is currently editor of the book series Hopkins Studies in Modernism.

Timothy Materer is Emeritus Professor of English at the University of Missouri and the author of *James Merrill's Apocalypse* (2000), *Modernist Alchemy: Poetry and the Occult* (1995), *Vortex: Pound, Eliot, Lewis* (1979), and *Wyndham Lewis the Novelist* (1976); and he has edited two volumes of Ezra Pound's letters, *Pound/Lewis: The Letters of Ezra Pound and Wyndham Lewis* (1985) and *The Selected Letters of Ezra Pound to John Quinn* (1991). He has received fellowships from the NEH, ACLS, and the Guggenheim Foundation. His publications include articles on T. S. Eliot, Ezra Pound, Sylvia Plath, Elizabeth Bishop, and James Merrill. With the cooperation of

Washington University in St. Louis, he is constructing websites devoted to the poetry manuscripts of James Merrill. Currently he is teaching courses on modern authors for Osher Lifelong Learning.

Megan Quigley is Associate Professor of English at Villanova University, where she is also on the Irish Studies and Gender and Women's Studies faculties. She is the author of *Modernist Fiction and Vagueness: Philosophy, Form, and Language* (2015) and co-editor of the forthcoming volume *Eliot Now*. She has written essays on literary modernism, gender, #metoo, and philosophy, which are published (or forthcoming) in the *James Joyce Quarterly, Modernism/modernity, Philosophy and Literature, Poetics Today, LARB, nonsite,* and *The Cambridge Companion to European Modernism*. She is a three-time lecturer and seminar leader at the T. S. Eliot International Summer School.

Joshua Richards is Associate Professor of English at MidAmerica Nazarene University. His PhD was earned at the University of St. Andrews and he is the author of *T. S. Eliot's Ascetic Ideal* (2020). He serves as the bibliographer for the International T. S. Eliot Society and the T. S. Eliot editor for *The Year's Work in English Studies*.

Junichi Saito is Professor at the Department of Management at Kanagawa University, Japan. He has been a member of The T. S. Eliot Society of Japan since 1995. His articles, including "What Paris Meant to T. S. Eliot during 1910–1911," based on field research in Paris, can mainly be found at the *Kanagawa University International Management Review*.

Isabelle Stuart is a DPhil student at the University of Oxford. Her project seeks to recover the influence of verse speaking cultures on the development of modernist poetics from 1890 to 1945. She has work forthcoming in the *Edinburgh Companion to W. B. Yeats and the Arts* and in 2022 she was awarded the *T. S. Eliot Studies Annual* Prize for best peer seminar paper.

Edward Upton is Associate Professor of Humanities in Christ College, the Honors College of Valparaiso University, where he teaches courses in religion and literature, hermeneutics, and theology. He has published essays on T. S. Eliot in *Journal of Religion*, *Religion and Literature*, and *Journal of the American Academy of Religion*. His book, *Desire and the Ascetic Ideal: Buddhism and Hinduism in the Works of T. S. Eliot* is forthcoming.

Joshua Logan Wall is a lecturer in the English Department Writing Program at the University of Michigan. He is the author of *Situating Poetry: Covenant and Genre in American Modernism* (2022). His essays on modernist poetry and fiction can be found in *Modernism/modernity*, *MELUS*, and *Studies in American Jewish Literature*.

John Whittier-Ferguson is Professor of English at the University of Michigan, where he has been since 1990. His most recent book, *Mortality and Form in Late Modernist Literature*, was published in the fall of 2015. He is the author of *Framing Pieces: Designs of the Gloss in Joyce, Woolf, and Pound* (1996) and co-editor, with A. Walton Litz and Richard Ellmann, of *James Joyce: Poems and Shorter Writings* (1991). He has published articles on modernists in *Modernism/modernity*, *Modern Fiction Studies*, *James Joyce Quarterly*, *Journal of Modern Literature*, *War, Literature & the Arts*, and elsewhere. He is the current President of the International T. S. Eliot Society.

Johanna Winant is Assistant Professor of English at West Virginia University. She is completing a book titled *Lyric Logic: Modern American Poetry and Reasoning*. Her writing has appeared in *Journal of Modern Literature*, *Poetics Today*, *Paideuma*, *James Joyce Quarterly*, *Post45 Contemporaries*, *Slate*, *Boston Review*, and elsewhere.